Managing Wetlands for Private and Social Good

NEW HORIZONS IN ENVIRONMENTAL ECONOMICS

Series Editors: Wallace E. Oates, *Professor of Economics, University of Maryland, USA* and Henk Folmer, *Professor of General Economics, Wageningen University and Professor of Environmental Economics, Tilburg University, The Netherlands*

This important series is designed to make a significant contribution to the development of the principles and practices of environmental economics. It includes both theoretical and empirical work. International in scope, it addresses issues of current and future concern in both East and West and in developed and developing countries.

The main purpose of the series is to create a forum for the publication of high quality work and to show how economic analysis can make a contribution to understanding and resolving the environmental problems confronting the world in the twenty-first century.

Recent titles in the series include:

Managing Wetlands for Private and Social Good

Theory, Policy and Cases from Australia

Stuart M. Whitten

Institutional Economist, CSIRO Sustainable Ecosystems, Canberra, Australia and Visiting Fellow at University College, University of New South Wales, Canberra, Australia

Jeff Bennett

Professor of Environmental Management, Asia Pacific School of Economics and Government, Australian National University, Canberra, Australia

NEW HORIZONS IN ENVIRONMENTAL ECONOMICS

Edward Elgar
Cheltenham, UK • Northampton, MA, USA

Published by
Edward Elgar Publishing Limited
Glensanda House
Montpellier Parade
Cheltenham
Glos GL50 1UA
UK

Edward Elgar Publishing, Inc.
136 West Street
Suite 202
Northampton
Massachusetts 01060
USA

A catalogue record for this book
is available from the British Library

ISBN 1 84064 898 8

Printed and bound in Great Britain by MPG Books Ltd, Bodmin, Cornwall

Contents

Figures

Tables

Acknowledgements

We would like to thank those whose help has been instrumental in the writing of this book.

We are most grateful to Tim Croft and Jonathon Streat for their assistance and encouragement in relation to the biophysical modelling parts of the book. We also thank Dr Martin van Bueren, Associate Professor John Rolfe, Professor Peter Hall and the Staff and Associates at the Political Economy Research Center (PERC) in Bozeman for useful comments and suggestions.

We appreciate the assistance and helpful critiques of natural resource managers in the case study areas including local landholders, government staff and other stakeholders. We are also grateful to the various focus group participants and survey respondents who provided important feedback and much of the non-market valuation data analysed in this book.

The authors gratefully acknowledge research funds provided by Environment Australia and Land and Water Australia under the National Wetlands Research and Development Program, a Land and Water Australia Travel Fellowship, a PERC Graduate Fellowship and The University of New South Wales.

A special thank-you to Jill Kenna and Mandy Yialeloglou for providing – patiently and cheerfully – excellent expertise in the production of the manuscript.

Thanks further to the capable and efficient editorial and production staff at Edward Elgar Publishing.

Finally, but not least importantly, the book is dedicated to our families, in particular our respective partner and wife Carolyn and Ngaire.

SMW and JB

1.   Managing Wetlands for Private and Social Good

1.1   THE FOCUS

The management of natural resources located on private lands is a contentious and topical issue worldwide. Conflict is focused on aspects of resource management that are perceived to generate benefits and costs that extend beyond the current landowner and are seemingly not considered by the landowner within existing decision-making mechanisms. That is, landholders who focus on the private values generated by the natural resources that they own may not take into account the impacts their management decisions may have on public values. For instance, in Europe, the aesthetic value of farmland is enjoyed by the broader society but may not be considered important in a farmer's decision to remove hedgerows. In the United States of America (USA), profitable intensive livestock production may result in the contamination of ground water that imposes costs on urban dwellers who rely on wells as a source of water. In Japan, the heritage and cultural significance of rice production may be disregarded by landowners seeking to develop an industrial estate. Such external benefits and costs contribute to the 'multifunctionality' of agriculture.

Government responses to the conflict have often involved the use of legislation to change the private decision-making framework. Lobby groups representing landowners have argued that such legislative responses adversely impact on their own welfare and that of their local community. Their arguments are generally based on expectations of welfare reductions caused by restrictions to property right access, or anticipated additional transaction costs in accessing property rights. Conversely, environmental lobby groups have argued that the legislative response is inadequate to protect and enhance society's welfare. Hence, the debate has tended to centre on three interlinked areas:

1. the impact of private land management decisions on the welfare of the community as a whole;

2. the impact of government responses on landowner and local community welfare; and
3. the appropriateness of alternative policy frameworks to influence the management of privately owned natural resources.

These three aspects of the debate are addressed in this book in the context of the management of wetlands located on private lands. The welfare impacts of management decisions made by wetland owners on themselves and on the wider community are assessed in terms of the scale and distribution of the costs and benefits arising. This assessment is used as an input into the development of policies aimed at modifying the management of private wetlands where improvements to the well being of society as a whole are available. To ensure that the policies do create net social benefits, they are evaluated in terms of their potential to cost-effectively influence the management of privately owned wetlands.

1.2   WHY WETLANDS?

Wetlands have been chosen as the focus of this book because they are an ecosystem that provides a wide range of important benefits to society and they face pressures from a diverse array of alternative uses. While the case of wetlands is complex it is not unique and the lessons to be learnt from developing a better understanding of the management of privately owned wetlands can be readily applied to many other natural resources that provide both private and social benefits.

As a first step, it is instructive to formalise a definition of wetlands. There are at least four ways of defining wetlands:

- by their biophysical characteristics;
- by the combination of resources employed;
- by the processes they perform; or
- by the outputs (benefits and harms) they produce.

Biophysical characteristics define the appearance of wetlands and their physical location in the landscape. A sample of the biophysically based wetland definitions used by government and non-government based organisations is provided in Figure 1.1.

The definitions in Figure 1.1 indicate that several other resources are combined with land to create a wetland. The key resource in addition to land

The Ramsar Convention on Wetlands (Ramsar Convention Bureau 1998):
Wetlands are 'areas of marsh, fen, peatland or water, whether natural or artificial, permanent or temporary, with water that is static or flowing, fresh, brackish or salt, including areas of marine water the depth of which at low tide does not exceed six meters'. And 'may incorporate riparian and coastal zones adjacent to the wetlands, and islands or bodies of marine water deeper than six meters at low tide lying within the wetlands'.

Commonwealth Wetlands Policy (Commonwealth Government of Australia 1997):
'"Wetland" is the more general and more modern name for what we call swamps, billabongs, lakes, saltmarshes, mudflats and mangroves. Wetlands are simply areas that have acquired special characteristics from being wet on a semi-regular basis. The term also applies to depressions in the landscape of our more arid regions that only occasionally hold water but which, when they do, teem with life and become environmental focal points.'

United States (US) Army Corps of Engineers and US Environmental Protection Agency (Definition used since the 1970s for regulatory purposes (US Environment Protection Agency 2001)):
'Wetlands are areas that are inundated or saturated by surface or groundwater at a frequency and duration sufficient to support, and under normal circumstances do support, a prevalence of vegetation typically adapted for life in saturated soil conditions. Wetlands generally include swamps, marshes, bogs, and similar areas.'

Ducks Unlimited (Ducks Unlimited 2001):
'Wetlands are areas inundated, or saturated, by surface water or groundwater that support hydric, or water-loving, vegetation. Wetlands also are known as swamps, marshes, bogs, and many other localised names. Wetlands are the most productive ecosystems on earth, and they continue to be destroyed at an alarming rate. Wetlands provide us with benefits such as:
- cleaner water in lakes and rivers;
- groundwater recharge;
- moderation of flooding and soil erosion;
- commercial and recreational fishing; and
- boating, swimming and other outdoor activities.'

The Sierra Club (Sierra Club 2001):
'Lands that are transitional between terrestrial and aquatic ecosystems wherein the water table is usually at or near the surface and the land is covered periodically by shallow water; those lands must have one or more of the following attributes:
- at least periodically, it supports predominantly hydrophytes;
- its substrate is predominantly undrained by hydric soil; and/or
- its substrate is non-soil and is saturated with water or covered by shallow water at some time during the growing season of each year.'

Figure 1.1 A sample of wetland definitions used by government and non-governmental organisations in Australia and the United States[1]

is water. Water facilitates the processes that enable production of the flora and fauna resources in wetlands. The specific adaptations of flora to living in saturated and periodically dried conditions enable the identification of wetlands and the differentiation of wetlands from other parts of the landscape. None of the definitions mention the fauna resources associated with wetlands, however many fauna species also possess specific adaptations for living (and/or breeding) in wetlands. Fauna resources include fish, shellfish, water birds and other species. Hence wetlands can also be defined as a combination of land, water and wetland-adapted flora and fauna.

The action of combining these resources leads to a set of processes that are specific to wetlands. These processes can also be used to define wetlands. Some processes that are unique to wetlands are listed in Figure 1.2. For example, the combination of land, water and (dead) flora in a peat bog will trap runoff and release it gradually. In other wetlands the combination of land, water and flora will remove and store nutrients and pollutants from water.

- Habitat and production of a specific range of flora and fauna (food chain maintenance)
- Water storage from rainfall, run-off, snow-melt and other sources
- Gradual release of water to streams and rivers and/or groundwater
- Shoreline anchoring and dissipation of erosive forces
- Removal and storage of nutrients and other pollutants from water

---

Figure 1.2 Some wetland processes

The processes performed by wetlands are not, of and by themselves, the outputs of wetlands. The services that wetlands perform, or, alternatively, the benefits that they produce, are the outputs of wetlands. The outputs of the wetland processes are what individuals and the wider community value. The values placed on these benefits can be either positive or negative.

A generic list of wetland outputs is shown in Figure 1.3. Not all wetlands provide all outputs. Nor does the community value all outputs. For example, wetlands may or may not recharge aquifers. If aquifers are recharged they may not necessarily provide any benefits to the community.

1.3 WETLAND MANAGEMENT

Different wetland types and the same wetland type in different locations can produce differing mixes of outputs. The benefits and harms generated by estuarine wetlands differ significantly from those provided by freshwater wetlands, which differ from those provided by desert lakes and so forth. In addition, a benefit in one location may be a harm in another. For example, increased waterfowl populations could be beneficial (pest control) or harmful (consuming pasture) or even both – but to different individuals (pasture consuming waterfowl that are hunted for recreation).

- Fauna production
- Flora production
- Aesthetic impact on the landscape
- Mitigation of floods
- Mitigation of storms
- Aquifer discharge or recharge
- Improved water quality
- Impacts on neighbouring agricultural production
- Impacts relating to maintenance of natural ecosystems

Figure 1.3 Some outputs from wetlands

Furthermore, the outputs of wetlands vary depending on the ways in which they are managed. Wetland resources are valuable in many alternative uses, ranging from the provision of housing estates and marinas, through to water storages for agriculture and irrigated or dry land farming.

Of principal interest in this book are the conflicts arising in the management of wetlands that are potentially of value through agricultural production. Hence in this section, the trade-offs between wetland protection and agricultural production that are inherent in alternative wetland management strategies are considered. The types of wetlands considered are loosely restricted to floodplain wetlands and a dune-swale[2] wetland system. While the analysis is restricted, the techniques used are directly transferable to other industries that have major impacts on wetlands (for example, housing developments) and other wetland types (for example, estuarine wetlands).

Wetland benefits

Combining resources in a wetland leads to a number of processes. Wetland processes provide a range of outputs that may benefit different individuals and groups in the community and across time. It is these benefits generated by the combination of resources in wetlands that are valued by individuals. For example, water retention and release in wetlands may provide flood mitigation, aquifer recharge and improve stream base flow outputs. Some outputs generate benefits that may not be located within the same catchment as the producing wetland. For example, hunting, fishing and bird watching may be located away from wetlands that assist in generating these benefits. Other outputs are constrained to areas downstream of wetlands. In Table 1.1 a number of wetland outputs and the benefits they translate into are identified. Scodari (1990) further divides wetland benefits into intermediate, final and future benefits, based on the way in which they benefit society. Intermediate outputs are inputs into the production of other goods, final outputs are directly consumed and future outputs relate to future discoveries about the benefits of wetland outputs.

Table 1.1 Wetland outputs and wetland benefits

Wetland output	Wetland benefit
Waterfowl	Waterfowl hunted
Avifauna	Birds seen and identified
Avifauna	Pest control
Aquatic fauna	Fish and crustacean food sources
Flora – trees	Timber
Wetland ecosystem	Scenic vista
Wetland ecosystem	Recreation
Flood-storm mitigation	Erosion control
Flood-storm mitigation	Flood mitigation
Flora production	Grazing input
Non-combustible flora	Fire break
Aquifer recharge	Water supply
Water storage	Water supply
Pollution reduction	Improved water quality
Bio-diversity maintenance	Unknown future benefits
Wetland ecosystem	Existence of natural areas

Wetland harms

The combination of resources in wetlands can also generate outputs that harm individuals or groups in the community. These harms generate negative values from the combination of resources in wetlands. Joint production of benefits and harms reflects the fact that a decision to produce wetland benefits often also involves producing harms. Some harms that may be produced by wetland conservation are identified in Table 1.2. Like wetland benefits, wetland harms can be both geographically and time separated from wetlands.

Table 1.2 Wetland outputs and wetland harms

Wetland output	Wetland harm
Insects	Nuisance and disease vectors
Flora pest breeding	Weeds
Fauna pest breeding	Feral and pest animals
High water table	Reduced productivity
Combustible flora	Fire danger
Wet soils	Bogged livestock
Decomposing flora or fauna	Foul odours
Wet soil and water	Access difficulty
Wetland ecosystem	Impact of regulation on landowner

Notes Since the incentives to the owners of wetland resources are the focus of this paper both private and social harms are included.

Wetland protection opportunity costs

The resources that are combined in wetlands could be used in alternative production processes to produce alternative outputs. The decision to manage wetlands to provide a particular set of wetland outputs combines these resources in one way. This combination denies the opportunity to use the resources in different combinations to produce alternative sets of outputs. The highest valued set of alternative outputs that could be produced with the resources is the opportunity cost of producing the wetland outputs. A range of agricultural opportunity costs that arise from alternative resource combinations is indicated in Figure 1.4. The decision to reallocate the resources employed in wetlands to alternative production processes may impose social opportunity costs beyond the direct loss of outputs of wetlands, such as additional risk of species extinction or biodiversity loss and possible irreversibility of restoration (within a meaningful time or cost frame).

Some opportunity costs detailed in Figure 1.4 reflect absolute trade-offs between agricultural and conservation outputs while others are gradual. For example, clearing, draining and cropping a wetland will remove all conservation values (except possibly some landscape values). Alternatively, successful use of shallow wetlands for duck breeding may require that there is no grazing in wetlands while birds are nesting and fledging.

Estimating wetland values
Because alternative wetland management strategies generate different combinations and magnitudes of wetland benefits, harms and opportunity costs, the selection of strategies that are likely to make the society better off is facilitated by the estimation of their relative magnitudes and distribution. The possibility of estimating the values of wetlands in dollar terms has received much attention in recent years. This attention has led to the Ramsar Convention Bureau producing a guide to the economic valuation of wetlands (Barbier, Acreman and Knowler 1997) and a number of applications. The brief summary of a selection of those applications that follows makes no comment regarding the validity of the methodologies used or on the accuracy of the results. It is presented solely as an indication of the wetland values that have been estimated and their magnitude.[3]

- Foregone agricultural production (via crop production or grazing)
- Foregone timber production
- Foregone irrigation water storage
- Foregone irrigation drainage storage
- Foregone supply of irrigation water
- Foregone hunting benefits (where hunting is prohibited by the conservation decision)

Figure 1.4 Common agricultural opportunity costs of producing wetland outputs[4]

A range of US dollar values for wetlands is shown in Table 1.3 (sourced from Heimlich, Wiebe, Claassen, Gadsby and House 1998). All values are in 1992 US dollars and relate to estimates from the US, Canada, Europe and Africa. The range of values indicates that some wetland functions can be very highly valued by some communities.

Barbier, Acreman and Knowler (1997) also include a number of case studies of wetland valuation studies. They include agricultural, fishing and firewood benefits on the Hadejia-Hguru floodplain in Northern Nigeria

(1989/90 $US 34 to 51 per hectare), conserving areas of the Norfolk Broads in the United Kingdom (1989/90 $US 580 per hectare) and nitrogen removal in Swedish wetlands (1989/90 $US 34 per kg nitrogen reduction).

Woodward and Wui (2001) conducted a meta-analysis of the studies reviewed by Heimlich et al. (1998) as well as other studies. Despite finding that a need for site-specific studies remains, Woodward and Wui (2001) were able to predict a range of values for hypothetical wetlands yielding a single output or service. The most valuable services (1990 mean values $US per acre) were bird watching ($1 212), commercial fishing ($778) and wetland quality ($417).

Table 1.3 Economic values of wetland outputs

Wetland outputs valued	Number of studies	Median	Mean	Range of means
	Number	**Dollars per acre**		
Marketed goods:				
Fish and shellfish support	8	702	6,132	7–43,928
Fur-bearing animals	2	na	137	13–261
Non-marketed goods:				
General-nonusers	12	32,903	83,159	115–347,548
General users	6	623	2,512	105–9,859
Fishing users	7	362	6,571	95–28,845
Hunting users	11	1,031	1,019	18–3,101
Recreation users	8	244	1,139	91–4,287
Ecological functions	17	2,428	32,149	1–200,994
Amenity and cultural	4	448	2,722	83–9,910

Notes   All dollar amounts are in 1992 US dollars, standardised using a 6 per cent discount rate and a 50-year accounting period.
na = not available

Source Heimlich et al. (1998), Table 1, p. 15.

Comparative estimates of Australian recreation and non-use wetland values have also been significant. Two studies in Australia have sought to estimate the recreational value of wetlands.[5] Sappidean (1992) estimated the recreational values associated with game hunting, bird watching, bush walking and camping in the Ramsar listed Sale Wetlands in eastern Victoria using the Contingent Valuation method. Willingness to pay (as an entry fee to the wetlands to preserve water quality from increasing salinity) was estimated at $3.37 per visitor. Stone (1992) used the Contingent Valuation method to estimate the values associated with the Ramsar listed Barmah forest on the Murray River in Victoria. Respondents indicated a once-off willingness to pay $2.98 for their recreational use of the wetlands.

Other studies have concentrated on the 'non-use' values of wetlands or have estimated total values for wetlands. Australian studies include those by Gerrans (1994), Bennett, Blamey and Morrison (1997), Morrison, Bennett and Blamey (1999) and Bennett and Whitten (2000). Gerrans (1994) used the Contingent Valuation method to estimate the willingness to pay to preserve the Jandakot Wetlands south of Perth and to protect all Perth metropolitan wetlands. Respondents indicated an annual willingness to pay of $38.84–$40.81 for Jandakot wetlands and $37.71–$43.79 for all metropolitan wetlands. Bennett, Blamey and Morrison (1997) used the Contingent Valuation method to estimate the willingness to pay to avoid damage to Tilley Swamp and The Coorong in the Upper South East of South Australia. Respondents indicated a once-off willingness to pay of approximately $45 per household. Morrison, Bennett and Blamey (1999) used the Choice Modelling technique to estimate the willingness to pay of households to generate social and environmental improvements via rehabilitation of the Macquarie Marshes in central Western NSW. The once-off willingness to pay was dependent on the outcomes of the rehabilitation strategy pursued. Respondent households were willing to pay on average $24.49 per additional bird breeding event, $0.04 per additional square km of wetland, $4.53 per additional endangered species present and $0.14 per additional irrigation job in the region. Morrison et al. (1999) performed a similar analysis for the Gwydir Marshes in north-western NSW. Bennett and Whitten (2000) used the Contingent Valuation technique to estimate the willingness to pay to preserve Lake Gol Gol and Gol Gol Swamp in NSW near Mildura in north-western Victoria from damage from rising salinity. Respondents indicated a once-off willingness to pay of $9.33 per household.

A number of studies have been undertaken into marketed goods produced by wetlands including fish and crustacean production from wetlands in Australia and the United States. Only one such study relates to freshwater ecosystems. Amacher, Brazee, Bulkley and Moll (1989) estimated the value of additional marginal product from fish life support in Lake St. Clair, Michigan in the United States.

Other studies have focused on the services generated by wetlands including storm protection (Farber 1987), aquifer recharge (Farber 1996), riparian filtering (Lant and Roberts 1990), nutrient filtering and retention, and short term flood storage (Thibodeau and Ostro 1981; Folke 1991; Gren 1995).

1.4   CONFLICTING INCENTIVES

The size and distribution of the values generated by wetland protection relative to the values from reallocating the resources employed in wetlands (for example to agriculture) generates the incentives for private wetland owners to retain or reallocate resources in wetlands (wetland protection). Many of the outputs produced by wetland protection generate limited incentives to wetland owners to ensure their continued production. This is because many of the outputs of protected wetlands cannot be bought and sold within markets. They are 'public goods' because consumption by anyone cannot be prevented and consumption by one consumer leaves no less for others to consume.

Conversely, reallocating resources from wetland conservation to alternative uses such as grazing, cropping, forestry or water storage generates direct incentives to wetland owners via their contribution to the production of food and fibre outputs. These goods are 'private goods' because consumption can be prevented. Once consumed by one consumer, they are not available for consumption by others. These alternative resource allocations tend to, but do not always, significantly reduce the public good values that wetlands generate.

Hence, it is hypothesised that protected wetlands tend to deliver fewer direct incentives to wetland owners than do wetland resources when separated. Wetland owners receive skewed incentives towards separating the resources that are combined in wetlands. The skewed incentives may result in inefficient resource allocation outcomes whereby fewer resources are combined in wetlands than is desired by the community as a whole.

The conflicting incentives generated by the current decision-making framework fail to deliver the outcome desired by society. The decision-making framework (or social coordination system) selected by society must perform two key functions in allocating scarce resources amongst competing uses:

1. accurately signal information about individuals' desires and the availability of resources to meet these desires; and
2. generate incentives for individuals to act on the desires of others in the community.

Hayek (1945, p. 519) notes that the information required to allocate scarce resources 'never exists in concentrated or integrated form, but solely as dispersed bits of incomplete and frequently contradictory knowledge which all the separate individuals possess'. The decision-making framework selected by society must either bring together the scattered information to be assessed by a central planner or use an alternative framework such as the market to signal the relative importance of different information.

The coordination framework used by society shapes the incentives received by wetland owners. Wetland policy specifically seeks to influence this framework by altering the rules, the pay-off structure, or both, within which decisions about wetland management take place. Hence, wetland policy seeks to modify the coordination framework used by society to generate signals and incentives to facilitate production and consumption of wetland protection outputs (Wills 1997).

The skewed incentives to wetland owners imply a demand for policy. Policy is defined as government actions designed to influence the institutions and incentives that frame private agents' decision-making. Wetland policy is such government action as applied to decisions about wetland protection. The development of institutions and incentives to achieve a desired change to the biophysical outputs of wetlands, and escape the conflicting incentives, is the main focus of this book. Policy is intended to manage the problem of conflicting incentives by providing a coordination framework that generates a consistent set of incentives that reflect as closely as possible the desires of members of the community.

1.5   GOALS AND STRUCTURE

Choices between often conflicting alternative wetland management strategies are likely to be improved through the consideration of both the extent of the relative benefits and harms created and an analysis of who wins and who loses. Furthermore, the development of policy mechanisms that will generate the implementation of the management strategies is likely to be advanced through a more complete knowledge of the relative value of wetlands in various uses and the distribution of those values amongst members of society.

Hence, the goal in this book is to advance the design of policy relating to the production of environmental outputs, specifically those associated with wetlands. This goal is addressed via the estimation of values generated by alternative wetland management strategies and the explicit incorporation of these values into efficient policy design. The analysis of the values generated by current and alternative wetland management strategies requires the innovative application and refinement of established techniques. The policy analysis has two main innovative aspects. First, biophysical and economic information is combined to identify community preferences and to better assess the policy trade-offs involved in wetland management. Second, application of theories of new institutional economics, particularly relating to the interactions between alternative policies and transaction costs, provide the theoretical framework underlying the policy development and analysis.

The analysis presented is focused on wetlands in two Australian case study areas: the Upper South East (USE) region of the state of South Australia (SA); and the Murrumbidgee River Floodplain (MRF) between Wagga Wagga and Hay in the state of New South Wales. The management decisions made by private landholders and the impacts of outside management decisions differ significantly between the two areas. Hence, the policies appropriate to each area could also be expected to differ substantially. The diversity of conditions and policies presented by the case studies affords extrapolation to other wetlands and indeed other natural resources where conflict between public and private values is evident.

To address these goals, the book is set out in 10 chapters.

The key elements of the theory of alternative mechanisms for the provision of wetland protection outputs are elaborated in Chapter 2. The theoretical reasons why 'market failure' may occur with respect to wetland outputs are identified, followed by an analysis of a planned decision making framework. The theoretical scope for 'government failure' in a planned decision making framework with respect to wetlands is assessed. The approach of considering both market and planned allocation mechanisms explicitly incorporates the potential for 'government failure' to outweigh the impacts of 'market failure'. In that case the community benefits from avoiding market failure are exceeded by the costs of government action.

The theoretical framework established in Chapter 2 is used in Chapter 3 to consolidate the research methodology the results of which are reported in the following chapters of the book. A number of working hypotheses are set out. The hypotheses are designed to address whether wetland management in the Australian case studies constitutes a policy problem, and if so, how the development and assessment of an efficient policy approach should proceed – potentially incorporating elements of market and planned frameworks for production of wetland outputs.

The methodological processes used to test the hypotheses are also described in Chapter 3. They include bio-economic modelling, which is used to link wetland management and biophysical processes to societal welfare outcomes. It involves the incorporation of biophysical modelling and estimation of economic values into an integrated bio-economic model. A novel methodology for developing and evaluating the transaction costs associated with alternative policy options is then expounded. It involves the assessment of transaction costs under uncertainty and the use of threshold policy analysis to identify the best potential policy options. The relevant decision criteria to undertake hypothesis tests are defined as part of the explanation of these methods.

The two case study areas are defined and examined with respect to the research hypotheses identified in Chapter 4. For each case study area, current and potential resource allocations are defined. The specification of the resource allocations includes defining the case study area, the resource base, the potential values provided by the wetlands and how these interact with land management in the region. Finally, the biophysical consequences of wetland management in each case study are quantified for the current resource allocation ('business as usual') and a range of potential allocations ('alternative wetland management options').

Values generated by the current and potential resource allocations are estimated and reported in Chapters 5, 6 and 7. The private values generated to wetland owners are reported in Chapter 5. The analysis of private values employs a mix of qualitative and quantitative techniques to consider the benefits, costs and opportunity costs of wetland outputs under alternative management scenarios.

Recreation values of wetlands are estimated in Chapter 6. Two techniques are applied: the travel cost method, and benefit transfer from other suitable studies. The travel cost method is applied to estimate the values generated by duck hunting in the USE. Benefits are transferred from other studies to estimate the values of overnight tourism in the USE and the values of day visits to wetlands on the MRF.

Estimates of the non-monetary values generated to the wider community by wetlands in the two case study areas are reported in Chapter 7. The non-monetary values were estimated using the Choice Modelling method.

Chapter 8 addresses the issue of identifying the relative social welfare generated by alternative wetland management strategies. Three issues are considered:

- aggregation of the costs and benefits of potential wetland management changes to identify a first order optimum;
- distribution of the costs and benefits, and the implications for achieving the potential management changes that were assessed; and
- sensitivity of the costs and benefits estimated to the impacts of uncertainty and risk.

The theoretical framework developed in Chapter 2 and the conclusions regarding the relevance of policy development are then combined in Chapter 9. The goal of the chapter is to generate and evaluate potential policy outcomes for wetland management based on the case studies. Initially the concepts of identifying, developing and analysing policy options are revisited in more detail. A systematic identification of policy opportunities is carried out using the theoretical frameworks developed in Chapter 2 and the results of the bio-economic modelling exercise. The selection and adaptation of policy instruments to these opportunities is then outlined followed by an evaluation of alternatives using threshold policy analysis. This approach to policy development is then applied to the case study areas. Policy options are developed and appraised for multiple jurisdictional levels (local, state and commonwealth) using three primary mechanisms that are loosely analogous to market based, mixed and government based wetland management decision mechanisms (facilitate, induce or compel).

Conclusions are drawn in Chapter 10. They include an assessment of the implications of the findings for wetland management and policy beyond the case study areas. An assessment of the policy implications beyond natural resources policy and for broader approaches to policy development and assessment is then provided.

NOTES

1. The inter-governmental Convention on Wetlands was signed in Ramsar, Iran, in 1971. There are presently 125 Contracting Parties to the Convention, with 1078 wetland sites, totalling 81.9 million hectares, designated for inclusion in the Ramsar List of Wetlands of International Importance.
2. A dune swale system is composed of series of areas of flat land (the swales) between series of sand dunes as opposed to a continuous dune system. Wetlands in this system occur on the lower side of the flat land often leaving dry areas of flat lands.
3. Reference to a number of these studies can also be found in Envalue, a database maintained by the NSW Environment Protection Agency on its website: www.epa.nsw.au.
4. A more elaborate examination of opportunity costs requires consideration of the risk of legislative changes that impact on the options available to wetland owners. Specifically a risk-weighted premium is attached to the opportunity cost that is dependent on the probability of future legislative action that would change the opportunity cost structure.
5. All values reported in this section are Australian dollars indexed to 2001 using the all groups consumer price index (CPI).

2. Market Failure, Government Failure and Wetland Protection

2.1 POLICY OPTIONS

The pattern of wetland use that results from the skewed incentives referred to in Chapter 1 is inefficient from a society-wide perspective. This calls for the development of policy structures that realign the incentive structures towards the outcome which society desires. The policy frameworks that could be used to provide more appropriate incentives to wetland owners are:

A market framework   Government provides an institutional framework that encourages wetland owners to seek the highest valued use for their wetlands but does not provide any direct incentives to wetland owners (that is, no incentive payments or government coercion of wetland owners);

A planned or regulatory framework   Government purchases the wetlands or directly coerces or influences wetland owners to manage wetlands to produce the outputs it believes the community desires (influences could include direct payments to wetland owners for example); or,

A mixed framework   Government provides a market framework and supplements this framework with some regulatory measures that encourage wetland owners to increase their production of wetland protection services beyond the level that would be produced under the set of skewed incentives that are likely to result.

All policy frameworks require decision-makers to possess sufficient information to choose the appropriate mix of extractive and natural uses of wetlands and so avoid the current inefficient outcomes. The choice between the available policy frameworks depends heavily on the relative costs of gathering this information and the impact of distortions when this information is held asymmetrically. The costs of gathering information and the impact of asymmetric information are the primary sources of the failings in the market and planned frameworks. These failings are the focus in this chapter. The source and likely impact of market failure are dealt with in the first part of the chapter and failures in the planned/regulatory framework, called 'government failure', are considered in the second.

2.2 THE SOURCES AND CONSEQUENCES OF MARKET FAILURE

2.2.1 Market Underpinnings

Property rights and transaction costs

If one individual values wetland output more highly than another, there is the possibility that gains to both can be generated from trades between them. Markets are the mechanism by which these potential gains from trade can be accessed. Specifically, the potential gains arise from individuals trading property rights (see Figure 2.1) that define access to the benefit streams generated from resource ownership. Markets act by generating information for buyers and sellers about the costs and benefits of producing wetland outputs and price incentives to act on these signals. However, the information is not cost free and relies on the establishment of property rights for resources. For example, in the case of wetland resources, a market for access to waterfowl will not exist if duck hunting is banned. Not all wetland outputs have property rights defined, and therefore some signals are not generated.

The transfer of information within markets is not frictionless. Rather, there are costs involved in gathering and sending information in markets. These costs are referred to as 'transaction costs' (see Figure 2.2). Transaction costs are important because they consume resources that could be used for other purposes (Wills 1997). Where transaction costs lead to non-Pareto efficient outcomes market failure is said to occur.[1] Thus the size of the transaction costs can determine the relative efficiency of the market when compared with alternative decision-making structures and hence are an important policy consideration.

Transaction costs in contracting for wetland outputs

Wherever an exchange of property rights takes place a contract exists that defines the rights of the purchaser and the rights that pertain to the seller. Contracts may be either legally enforceable or supported by norms of behaviour. A legal contract[2] is the ability to call on the State to enforce an agreement. 'Because human actors will not reliably disclose true conditions upon request or self-fulfil all promises, contract as mere promise, unsupported by credible commitments, will not be self enforcing' (Williamson 1999, p.8), and so, the need for legally enforceable contracts arises. Legal contracts are not cost free to negotiate (where applicable) or enforce. Hence, norms or conventions of behaviour support many contracts as a way of reducing transaction costs.[3] For example, leaving remote campsites clean is not normally legally enforceable (due to the high costs of policing) but most people leave such campsites clean (Wills 1997).

Resource ownership is defined by a set of property rights. Property rights are 'a claim to a benefit (or income) stream that the state will agree to protect' (Bromley 1991, p. 2) or *'the individual's ability, in expected terms, to consume the good (or the services of the asset) directly or to consume it indirectly through exchange'* (Barzel 1997, p.3). Property rights must be excludable, divisible (in both space and scope) and transferable to be effective (Kasper and Streit 1998). These attributes are defined as follows:

1. Excludability allows the owner to prevent others from consuming wetland outputs and relies on the practicality of identifying and stopping potential consumers. Consumption of the benefits of some wetland outputs is essentially non-excludable. For example, enjoyment of scenic vistas and flood mitigation;
2. Divisibility is the ability to separate the bundle of property rights in space and scope. Divisibility allows property right owners to manage sub components of the resource separately or to divide off and sell excess resources (for example, a single wetland or trees from a wetland or the rights to fish and yabbies in the wetland); and
3. Transferability grants the ability to sell the property rights to others. It also requires that property rights can be functionally transferred.

Figure 2.1 Property rights

Kasper (1998) emphasises the importance of property rights and contracting institutions as follows: 'Institutions serve to reduce transaction costs by allowing members of society to depend on broad behavioural patterns, reducing the range of outcomes without making a particular outcome certain.' Hence, search costs are reduced as owners of benefit streams are identified, bargaining costs are reduced as the benefit stream is defined, and enforcement costs are reduced due to identified and defined benefit streams. Libecap (1989) reminds us that property right institutions are not perfect. In particular, modification of property rights is subject to similar policy transaction costs as other legislation – an issue expanded upon in Section 2.3.

Transaction costs can be defined as those costs that are attributable to:

- codifying property rights, and identifying and enforcing ownership over property rights;
- seeking out buyers or sellers of property rights;
- negotiating a sale;
- measuring the quality and quantity of goods; and,
- contracting specifications about the transfer of property rights. Contracting issues include when delivery will occur and the uncertainty about any intervening period and incomplete aspects of the contract.

Figure 2.2 Transaction costs

Well-defined property rights that are excludable, alienable and divisible satisfy the first factor in Figure 2.2. Elements of the remaining four factors are satisfied by well-defined contract rules (institutions). However, transaction costs will remain due to incomplete property right specification and the costs of contracting. Market failure occurs where these transaction costs lead to outcomes that are non-Pareto optimal.

There are three primary sources of transaction costs in contracting arrangements pertaining to wetlands (assuming complete property right specifications).[4] The first source is inadequate knowledge about the range of wetland outputs from wetland production systems. The second is asymmetric information about the production or consumption of wetland outputs. Transaction costs such as search and negotiation costs will remain prevalent even where there is adequate information which is known to all parties. These transaction costs exist for all marketed commodities, and are not expected to differ for wetland products, and are hence not further discussed.

Inadequate or asymmetric knowledge
Wetland protection goods and services (both benefits and harms) are relatively straightforward to identify. A generic list of wetland outputs is identified in numerous papers from policy documents (see for example the Wetlands Policy of the Commonwealth of Australia 1997 or through

academic papers (see for example Smith 1999). But not all wetlands produce all outputs in the same proportions. Hence, linking particular outputs to a specific wetland (or group of wetlands), and linking these outputs to specific consumers, is a much more difficult proposition that complicates the potential for market contracts.

Many wetland benefits cannot always be linked to production from a specific wetland. For example, the wetland benefits and harms shown in Table 1.1 and 1.2 are reproduced in Table 2.1 along with the nature of their link to the wetland from which they are produced. Some benefits and harms are difficult to relate to a specific wetland and are represented by a 'No' or a 'Sometimes' in the column headed 'Defined link to wetland' in Table 2.1. For example, the goods and services provided to birdwatchers are an 'end product' consumed at the wetland location, however the bird species that are observed may have been produced by a number of different wetlands and/or ecosystems. The linkages between the producing wetland and other wetland goods and services are poorly defined for many wetland areas. For example, Scodari (1990) states that current knowledge and information is inadequate to measure the effectiveness of individual wetlands in providing flood mitigation or water quality outputs. Identifying benefits such as biodiversity or option benefits are concealed by the difficulties of predicting the future. Hence, it can be complex and costly to estimate the quantity of these outputs produced by wetlands.[5] Furthermore, this information may be asymmetrically held by potential market participants with incentives to use the information strategically in contract negotiation and monitoring.

The reverse problem occurs where a wetland protection output can be identified and quantified but the specific consumer of the output cannot. That is, while a demand for wetland outputs may exist, it may not be individually identified. Identification is simplified if thought of in two parts: the location at which consumption takes place; and, whether individual consumers can be identified. In Table 2.1, the consumption location of the benefits and harms is identified. The immediate consumer or consumer group of the wetland good or service is also identified.

Consumers of goods and services that are consumed at the wetland site are readily identifiable with the exception of aesthetic benefits to passers-by. For example, waterfowl are hunted in or near a wetland by hunters and domesticated stock that graze in a wetland are owned by the farmer. Consumers of goods and services provided to surrounding areas are more difficult, but not impossible, to identify. For example, pest control by waterfowl is only possible within a certain range of the wetland and only applies where the pest exists (for example in pastures). Similarly, the distance that mosquitoes can travel from a wetland is limited. Likewise, potential consumers of downstream goods and services are identifiable by the boundaries of flooding downstream of the wetland. Consumers of 'fugitive resources'[6] are more difficult to identify. For example, it is technically possible but prohibitively expensive to mark and identify ducks from wetlands where they hatch, but it is not currently possible to identify all the wetlands they use during their lifetime and the relative importance of each. Again, information may also be asymmetrically held with incentives for strategic use in contract negotiations.

The advancement of scientific knowledge and technological innovation is likely to make the identification and measurement of the benefits and harms of wetland protection easier (and less costly). The advancement of scientific knowledge may also reduce the opportunity for wetland owners or consumers of wetland outputs to strategically reveal the information they hold. However, inadequate and asymmetrically held knowledge about wetland production and consumption systems demonstrates that the transaction costs associated with definition of actual or expected values can be high. This is in contrast to production and consumption processes for standard consumer goods that produce well identified outputs, for example a car factory produces cars and specific waste or by products. This does not automatically result in market failure and thus preclude conservation of wetlands on private land as will be shown later, but it does mean that a market for these outputs is less likely to exist.

2.2.2 Wetland Production and Output Attributes and Transaction Costs

A number of attributes of production or consumption of wetland outputs have the potential to increase significantly the transaction costs incurred in markets. These attributes can be divided between those that result from the nature of wetland outputs or inputs to wetland production and those that are generated by how wetland outputs are either produced or consumed. Attributes related to the nature of wetland outputs or inputs are the result of non-excludable or non-rival public good attributes. Attributes related to production or consumption processes are the result of aspects of the production or consumption functions of wetlands such as joint production or consumption, economies of scale or scope and threshold impacts.

Public goods
Goods and services produced by wetlands range from pure private goods (for example grazing for livestock) through to pure public goods (for example existence values). In Figure 2.3 a number of categories of goods that are

Table 2.1 Linking consumers to producers (wetland owners)

Benefit / harm	Location to which output supplied	Identifiable consumer	Defined link to wetland*	Type of good
Wetland benefits				
Waterfowl hunted	Wetland	Waterfowl hunter	End product	Open access
Trapping/hunting	Wetland	Trapper/hunter	Yes	Private
Birds seen and identified	Wetland	Birdwatcher	End product	Open access
Fish and crustaceans	Wetland	Fishers	End product	Open access
Fish and crustacean nursery	Water linked areas	Fishers	No	Open access
Timber	Wetland	Timber harvester	Yes	Private
Scenic vista	Wetland	Land owner and passers-by	No	Local public
Recreation	Wetland	Wetland visitors	Yes	Club good
Pest control	Surrounding areas	Neighbouring farmers	Sometimes	Local public
Erosion control	Downstream	People downstream	Sometimes	Downstream public
Flood mitigation	Downstream	People downstream	Sometimes	Downstream public
Grazing input	Wetland	Land owner	Yes	Private
Fire break	Wetland	Land owner and neighbours	Yes	Local public
Ground water supply	Aquifer	Land owners within aquifer	Sometimes	Common property
Water supply	Wetland	Land owner	Yes	Private
Improved water quality	Downstream	People downstream	Sometimes	Downstream public

22

Table 2.1 continued

Benefit / harm	Location to which output supplied	Identifiable consumer	Defined link to wetland*	Type of good
Unknown future benefits	Unlimited	The wider community	No	Public
Future alternative uses	Unknown	The wider community	No	Public
Existence of natural areas	Unlimited	The wider community	No	Public
Wetland harms				
Nuisance and disease vectors	Surrounding areas	Local community	Yes	Local public
Weeds	Downstream	Downstream farmers	Sometimes	Downstream public
Feral and pest animals	Surrounding areas	Land owner and neighbours	Yes	Local public
Reduced productivity	Surrounding areas	Land owner and neighbours	Yes	Local public
Fire danger	Surrounding areas	Land owner and neighbours	Yes	Local public
Bogged livestock	Wetland	Land owner	Yes	Private
Foul odours	Surrounding areas	Local community	Yes	Local public
Access difficulty	Wetland	Land owner	Yes	Private
Subject to regulation	Wetland	Land owner	Yes	Private

Notes

* Beneficiaries can and often do include the landowner.

* 'Yes', if the benefit can be linked; 'No', if the benefit cannot be linked; Sometimes' where some benefits can be linked and not in others; and, 'End product' where only the final output can be linked.

often generically referred to as public goods are described. These goods exhibit either non-rivalry or non-excludability in consumption.

Non-excludability is the inability of the producer to exclude potential consumers from actual consumption of the output and hence to access the gains from trade. In this context, Cornes and Sandler (1996, p. 4) define exclusion costs as 'the value of the resources expended to erect and man the barriers that force preference revelation.' For example, a wetland owner is (usually) unable to cost-effectively prevent passers-by from enjoying the aesthetic benefits their wetland generates. On this basis, local and downstream public goods are non-excludable within the range they are supplied.

Non-rivalry in consumption can be expressed in two equivalent ways:

1. one individual's consumption makes no less available for others to consume (Samuelson 1954; Layard and Walters 1978); and
2. the marginal costs of production or provision of the good to additional consumers are zero (Demsetz 1970; Schmid 1989).

Samuelson (1954) defines non-rivalry from the point of consumption while Demsetz (1970) defines it from the point of view of production.[7] In contrast to public goods, purely private goods are completely rival in consumption. That is, one individual's consumption completely removes the opportunity for another's. For example, when one individual consumes an apple there are no consumption possibilities for other individuals with respect to the apple.

Most public goods are not 'pure public goods' because they exhibit some degree of excludability or rivalry. These goods are termed impure public goods or mixed goods. The Organisation for Economic Development and Cooperation (OECD) (2001) divides pure and impure public goods into five classes that are adapted to wetland protection goods in Figure 2.3. In Table 2.1 the final column contains a classification of each good or service according to the definitions in Figure 2.3. For example, recreation is categorised as a 'club good' because, once supplied, it is non-rival until congestion occurs (of course congestion will occur at different levels for different consumers).

It has been inferred that non-excludability of consumption means public goods cannot be supplied by the private sector, and at a minimum, non-rivalry means that supply by the private sector will be inefficient. However, private production is possible outside the government sector for many impure public goods. The writings of Olson (1965), Buchanan (1965) and Cornes and Sandler (1996), although pessimistic, provide a theoretical framework within which the private production of club goods and local public goods can occur.[8] Ostrom (1990) provides a more optimistic framework for provision of common property resources, and to a lesser extent, local public goods. Many writers including Ostrom (1990), Anderson and Leal (1991) and Wills (1997) have suggested property rights solutions to open access resource management. Entrepreneurs also find ways of excluding consumers from goods that were non-excludable or other ways of reducing transaction costs within the existing production framework. In each case these researchers show ways in which the transaction costs can be reduced sufficiently for private sector producers to access the gains from trade.

Pure public goods (for example, biodiversity existence values): Fully non-excludable and non-rival over a large area.

Local public goods (for example, fire breaks): Fully non-excludable and non-rival over a relatively small area. The scale of the area can be any size within a State or regional area.

Downstream public goods (for example, flood control): As for local public goods but the benefit is restricted to areas downstream of the wetland.

Open access resources (for example, fugitive fish and waterfowl): Fully non-excludable but rival under the existing property right structure.

Common property resources (for example, groundwater recharge): Excludable and rival within a defined community - but not as part of current bundles of property rights. Because they are excludable and rival a local community can manage them so long as appropriate rules can be established.

Club goods (for example, recreation aspects of wetlands): Fully excludable and congestible. The OECD defines un-congested club goods as 'excludable and non-rival goods'. The difference is that there is no marginal cost attached to supplying these goods to an additional person until they become congested. Hence, a zero price is suggested until congestion occurs.

Source Adapted from OECD (2001)

Figure 2.3 Categories of public goods

Olson (1965) states that the benefits to at least one consumer may be large enough to ensure production of the good, which can then be enjoyed by other consumers. However, the formation of a group to purchase the desired public good (be it pure or impure) becomes less likely as individual benefits fall relative to the total costs of provision (Olson 1965). Olson draws a key distinction between inclusive clubs, with no membership size restrictions, and exclusive clubs, requiring size restrictions. Inclusive clubs supply benefits that are non-rival while exclusive clubs supply goods that are rival, at least beyond some level of use.[9] Hence, optimal club size is a trade-off between the costs and benefits of provision and the degree of rivalry in consumption. For example, use of wetlands for eco-tourism generates a consumers' surplus that is partly dependent on the number of other tourists (Cicchetti and Smith 1973). Olson recognises that the larger the optimal club size, the greater the opportunity to 'free ride' and the larger organisational costs will be. The transaction costs of organising large groups may be prohibitive (Olson 1965; Buchanan and Tullock 1965). The distinction between group size hinges on the degree of excludability in conjunction with the potential for congestion or rivalry in consumption. For example, a large body of literature (commencing with Charles Tiebout) refers to local or regional club goods (see for example Sandler and Tschirhart 1980). That is, individuals living outside a region are effectively excluded from consumption of local public goods by transport costs or service boundaries.

Open access resources are characterised by a lack of property rights to a rival resource. Wills (1997) and Anderson and Leal (1991) among others, propose that society allocates property rights such that the resource becomes excludable. Once the resource is made excludable the gains from trade can be accessed subject to transaction costs in markets.

Entrepreneurs also find ways to reduce the transaction costs sufficiently to access the gains from trade. New technologies are a key tool in reducing many transaction costs (for example, use of satellite technologies to monitor fishing vessel locations). Other entrepreneurial actions include the use of organisational status or creation/joining institutions that signal information to consumers that reduce the transaction costs. For example, certification schemes are often used to signal to potential consumers the accuracy of quantity measurements and quality control procedures. Similarly, non-profit status may be used to signal information about products that are difficult to monitor because the quality of the good may change after purchase (see for example Glaeser and Shleifer 2001 or Ricketts 1994).

Externalities and wetland inputs

Externalities are defined as the 'consequences (benefits or costs) of actions (consumption, production or exchange) that are not borne by the decision maker, and hence do not influence his or her actions' (Wills 1997 p. 63). The existence of externalities means that one or more aspect of property rights definition must be incomplete because either there is non-ownership or non-transferability of the property rights associated with the externality.

Wetland inputs may include externalities from other production activities. Likewise, some wetland protection outputs may impose externalities on other activities and possibly include the wetland harms listed in Table 2.1. In principle, externality impacts on wetland inputs may be costs or benefits, as may the outputs of wetlands; however the focus here is on the external impacts on wetland inputs. Wetland inputs comprise natural resources including water and debris carried by water and atmospheric inputs. External impacts on these can be imposed by other users of these natural resources that impact on either the quality or quantity of the resource inputs to wetlands. For example, quality impacts include the nutrient, sediment, weed and salt pollutants in rivers. Quantity impacts include unconsidered flood impacts as a result of irrigation extraction. Many of these externalities negatively impact on the productive capabilities of wetlands thus reducing their potential benefits. However, addressing externality impacts through market mechanisms imposes transaction costs on wetland owners that may be prohibitive.

Joint production and consumption
Many wetland outputs are either consumed or produced jointly. Joint consumption can arise from three aspects of consumption of wetland outputs (OECD 2001):

1. technical interdependencies in production or consumption of wetland outputs (for example, travel costs and recreation experiences);
2. non-divisible wetland input or output sets (for example, consumption of wetland vistas and consumption of mosquito harms); and
3. competition for an input or output fixed at the wetland or individual level (for example, ducks hunted and birds watched from a single wetland).

Technical interdependencies may be either complementary or competing. For example, technically complementary consumption arises where the utility of consuming one output is increased by joint consumption of another (for example, bread and jam). On the contrary technically competing consumption arises where the utility of consuming one output is reduced by joint consumption of another (for example, catching fish to eat, and scaling and gutting the fish).

Most wetland outputs are the result of joint production, commonly of private and public good outputs. Production of the private good will necessitate production of the public good where the relationship is technically complementary or due to non-divisible wetland inputs. Hence, production of public goods will occur, albeit at inefficient levels, where sufficient private goods are jointly produced. Joint production in this fashion can also be referred to as production of a single good with multiple attributes following Lancaster (1966).

The joint production of public and private goods does not ensure efficient production of environmental public goods. The price mechanism only reflects information and incentives about demands for private goods that are jointly produced. For example, the price mechanism may reveal information and generate incentives relating to demand for bird-watching facilities but not for biodiversity. This information will determine the production of jointly produced environmental public goods in relation to other private (or excludable) goods. That is, the production of the public good will depend on the ratio of demand types relative to the ratio of joint production.

Similarly, potential exists for market failure to be overcome, and production of wetland outputs to be ensured, where technical interdependencies (technically complementary) or non-divisibilities exist between consumption of private goods or impure public goods and pure public goods. While production is unlikely to occur at efficient levels it may occur at levels beyond the pure private level of efficiency.

Economies of scale and scope and production thresholds
Wetland production systems, like many others, exhibit a range of characteristics relating to the nature of the production function such as economies of scale and scope. As a result the range and quality of wetland outputs can be increased by coordination between multiple resource managers. Economies of scale or scope can generate natural monopolies under certain conditions. Like other natural resource systems wetlands also exhibit a range of thresholds related to their management. For example, varying hydrological regimes within a range will tend to produce a similar set of outputs, but beyond certain points outputs may cease such as when birds abandon nests due to rapidly falling water levels.

Capturing economies of scale and scope may require coordination between multiple wetland owners. Scale division occurs where a wetland crosses ownership boundaries within a relatively uniform resource, for example a contiguous wetland across different land titles. Two forms of scope division occur. The first occurs where different parties own differing constituent resources. For example, the State may own rights associated with water, vegetation or fauna in a wetland. The second form of scope division occurs where differing types of wetland are required to produce a single output and these are owned separately. For example, waterfowl may require different feeding and nesting habitats.

Decisions involving multiple resource owners will be necessary to produce wetland outputs where resource ownership is divided in scale or scope. Decisions may involve resource exchange, ceding of property rights, or sharing of the gains from trade. Where exchange takes place, part of the potential gains from trade are lost in the process through transaction costs (Barzel 1997). The range of possible exchanges includes those both within and between individuals, firms, governments, clubs, families and non-profit organisations (Barzel 1997). Each of these exchanges is potentially subject to market failure. The potential for market failure is reduced by the institutional structures within which the resources are exchanged or combined. Repeat negotiation and enforcement costs can be replaced by once-off transaction costs associated with purchase of the resource. Hence, Coase's seminal article on the nature of the firm (Coase 1937) and the subsequent body of literature (see for example Williamson and Winter 1991 or Williamson 1986).

Concentration of resource ownership can lead to substantial benefits resulting from horizontal or vertical integration. However, concentration of ownership through either markets or via government ownership of resources can result in a monopoly or similar concentration and exercise of market powers. Monopolies are divided between natural monopolies and extreme concentration of market powers (see for example Randall 1993). Natural monopolies are the most efficient form of production in an industry due to the cost structures of production, but remain a potential source of market failure due to their potential to exploit pricing. Extreme concentrations of market power arise when a single firm is able to influence prices due to market share rather than cost structure.

Ownership of wetland resources is often divided between the government and private sectors. For some resources the government has monopoly control over their use, for example water. In these cases there is potential for market failure to arise as a result of the monopoly framework. The diverse and disparate ownership of private land in Australia means that monopoly private ownership of wetland resources is unlikely to arise except in rare occurrences in relatively local areas and hence is not a significant issue.

Many wetlands exhibit a range of thresholds in production that can be termed 'lumpiness' in production. Lumpiness is non-divisibility in the total quantity of outputs. Lumpiness is a technical constraint to production of some environmental public goods. Wetland resources need to be a certain size before some outputs can be produced or the nature of the production function changes. Lumpiness is essentially an extreme case of economies of scale or scope. For example, maintenance of a particular wetland output may become more and more difficult (or at least more costly) below a certain threshold. Similarly, once animal and plant populations fall below a critical level they are no longer self-sustaining and eventually become locally extinct; hunting requires some minimum quantity of land; or, management costs per hectare may fall by orders of magnitude above a certain size. Market failures may also arise where insufficient economies of scale can be achieved to efficiently produce wetland outputs.

2.3 THE SOURCES AND CONSEQUENCES OF GOVERNMENT FAILURE

'It does not follow that whenever *laissez faire* falls short, government intervention is expedient; since the inevitable drawbacks of the latter may, in any particular case, be worse than the shortcomings of private enterprise' (Sidgwick 1887).

It has long been known that the transaction costs in markets may outweigh the potential gains from trade. In these situations the market has failed and appropriate signals and price incentives cannot be generated through a pure market mechanism. In these instances and in other cases[10] society may seek non-market institutions in preference to markets. Some of these institutions are:

- behavioural conventions and norms (tradition);
- organisational structures that encompass the externality (central planning within voluntary smaller groupings such as clubs and firms);
- non-voluntary exchanges of rights in courts; and
- government created signals and incentives (central planning by governments).

Some of these institutional structures co-exist within market frameworks and even help form a basis for market outcomes. For example, behavioural conventions and norms are important in reducing the transaction costs of contract negotiations. However, the potential drawbacks of the alternative planned decision-making structure should also be considered where market systems are rejected for ethical or distributional reasons. These potential drawbacks are the 'transaction costs' within a planned framework. The focus in this section is on government created signals and incentives because of their prevalence in modern democratic society and the potential for these to be reshaped within a relatively short period of time.

Decision makers within a planned or government environment require the same information about the relative costs and benefits of producing wetland outputs as is necessary within markets. The costs of gathering this information are significant and the information may not always be accurate (see for example the discussion in Wills 1997). Furthermore, an effective set of incentives to act on this information must also be provided. Therefore, transaction costs in a planned framework can arise from three sources:

1. difficulty and cost of obtaining information about wetland costs and benefits;
2. incentive structures at the political, bureaucratic and property right owner levels in planned frameworks; and
3. distortions to other activities in the economy that may result from government actions.

These government transaction costs must be compared against the similarly inevitable drawbacks of a market framework in order to assess which are the greater shortcomings. Wills (1997) indicates that even in fully planned frameworks a residual set of property rights falls to on-the-spot users of resources. Therefore, while the focus in this section is on the possibility of government failure in the supply of wetland outputs, some aspects of wetland production will always remain outside of a planned framework.

2.3.1 The Cost of Information in a Planned Framework

Politicians and planners must know at least as much about production as resource owners, and at least as much about consumption as consumers in order to achieve optimal production and consumption. Substantial costs are incurred in identifying this information that are similar to transaction costs in markets. The planner could simply ask producers and consumers to tell them the information they need. However, Wills (1997) identifies two major problems with such an approach:

1. it is very difficult and costly to gather such detailed information; and
2. producers and consumers may have an incentive to distort the information they provide.

Information gathering – detail and cost
Hayek (1945) states that it is physically impossible for a planner to obtain all of the information that might benefit the outcome. Hayek further notes that information can only be gained by an individual's 'active cooperation'. Full

information about individual preferences can only be gained by approaching each individual separately – an extremely costly means of information collection that virtually ensures that the costs will outweigh any potential benefits. Furthermore, concentration of the information required means that diffuse information must pass between more people en route to the planner and information must be recollected each time preferences are thought to have changed. Costs are incurred each time the information is transferred or recollected.

Wills (1997) notes that it is less costly to gather less detailed information via opinion polls, voting or lobbying. However, information gathered via these practices is likely to be unrepresentative or inaccurate (as opposed to biased). The crux of the problem is that information can only be obtained from individuals where their expected benefits outweigh the costs (including penalties for not providing information). Individuals who choose not to pass on their knowledge are said to 'free-ride' on the signalling efforts of others (Wills 1997). Other reasons why information delivered through voting mechanisms (especially multiple issue voting) may be unrepresentative or inaccurate include:

- the paradox of voting, which shows that any set of voting rules subject to a basic set of fairness conditions may produce illogical results (Arrow 1951);
- the relative intensity of preferences may deliver an outcome voted for by the majority but where the benefits are outweighed by the costs to the minority – sometimes termed as 'tyranny of the majority'. Such outcomes are also complicated by bundling decisions on several policies together and by the nature of electorates in representative democracies;
- the separation of responsibilities between different levels of government complicate use of voting mechanisms to deliver information; and
- the impact of time on voting cycles whereby decisions made now may have no impact until after the next round of decision making and hence there is insufficient information available to voters to monitor and vote.

The second aspect is the complexity of dealing with such a large quantity of detailed information if it could be gathered. Hayek (1945) argues that it is not possible for a central planner to take into account all of the information required and to set individual production levels and prices that take account of such information. For example, it is not possible (or it is prohibitively expensive) for the central authority to take into account the relative net benefits from hunting in differential regions and charge accordingly, hence a single uniform licence price is issued that does not contain such information.

Incentives to distort information

There are two potential scenarios for achieving wetland management change that place differential incentives on the planners and wetland owners. Where no compensation is offered wetland owners have an incentive to distort information in order either to seek compensation or to retain access to their current benefits by arguing the costs of change are too high. Where compensation is offered wetland owners have an incentive to distort information in order to access a greater share or quantity of compensation. The potential gains from distorting information supplied to planners are generically termed rents and the act of seeking access to these rents is termed 'rent seeking'.

Vining and Weimer (1990) note that the degree to which information can be distorted in order to gain access to rents is largely dependent on the nature of the project envisaged. If the project requires specific outputs from specific wetlands then supply of these outputs is effectively a monopoly controlled by the wetland owner and is said to be 'non-contestable'. In this case, the monopoly supplied (wetland owner) will be able to access excess rents if they are able to credibly inflate their costs. The act of seeking these rents is referred to as a 'directly unproductive activity' and the resources contributed to seeking the rents are termed a 'dead weight loss'. In such cases the planner will often seek ownership of the relevant property rights, which may lead to other incentive problems that are the focus of the next section. If numerous alternative sites could produce the wetland outputs, potentially also including restored wetlands, supply is said to be contestable. In such cases the planner could seek bids to supply the desired output. Competition to win the desired change would ensure that wetland owners reveal the information about the true cost of changing management.

2.3.2 Incentives within a Planned Framework

It is not enough for the planner to merely obtain sufficient information about the costs of production and benefits of consumption to determine the appropriate level of production and consumption, all the while avoiding the pitfalls of information distorted by rent seeking. The planner must then seek to create a set of incentives that leads to the selected outcome. However, planners rarely have the power to create a complete set of incentives, and where they do their own motivations rarely correspond directly with those of society and are subject to a range of additional influences beyond benevolence and professionalism. In most cases the resultant problems are variations on the 'principal-agent' problem.

The 'principal-agent' problem arises where one individual (the principal) employs another (the agent) to provide certain services (Gwartney 1985). The principal lacks full information about the agent, and is unable to judge how well the agent performs the services. Information is missing because it is prohibitively expensive or otherwise not possible to monitor the agent. The size of the principal-agent problem is dependent on the importance of the missing information. The key aspect of the missing information is the nature and relative strength of other incentives facing the agent.

In a planned framework at least three principal-agent issues are of importance, those between:

- voters (the principals) and politicians (the agents);
- politicians (the principals) and bureaucrats (the agents); and
- bureaucrats (the principals) and government suppliers or property right owners (the agents).

A similar relationship between differing levels of government is also of importance in understanding the potential for government failure and is also considered in this section.

Political incentives
Few politicians are believed or expected to be purely benevolent. Rather a range of other incentives influences their behaviour. Vining and Weimer (1990) mention five reasons for politicians not acting in the interests of society:

1. politicians' lack of information about the true preferences of society (discussed in Section 2.3.1);
2. personal advancement interests such as re-election or ministerial promotion;
3. conflicting and unstable political demands;
4. inability to capture the full social benefits of effective supervision; and
5. the skewed benefits from posturing.

Vining and Weimer (1990) indicate that politicians are more likely to approve projects that generate an immediate benefit (especially prior to the next election) and less likely to approve projects with immediate costs and future benefits. A similar impact may apply to actions that may lead to ministerial promotion or demotion.

Conflicting policy demands may generate conflicting incentives. For example, constituents might demand increased wetland biodiversity on the one hand and reduced disease risk from mosquito bites on the other. In addition, Westminster style governments often allocate oversight of departments to multiple politicians who may have conflicting priorities (for example, ministers assisting and parliamentary or senate secretaries/spokespeople). Finally, changing political priorities during terms of office may not be in line with society's preferences.[11]

Politicians do not own the public organisations that they oversee and are unable to capture the full benefits of the managerial effort that they input. Hence, they may shirk on their supervisory responsibilities relative to the expectations of their principal, the community.

Finally, politicians face skewed benefits resulting from the competition for electoral office, particularly through the media (Weimer and Vining 1992). Furthermore, information used by voters to monitor politicians is often gained from low cost media sources. Opportunities that publicly and beneficially reflect politicians' contribution or potential contribution to society are extremely highly valued while negative publicity is a high cost. Politicians may also devote more time to high impact actions that create significant attention rather than to *ex ante* appropriate rules of governance in organisations (Vining and Weimer 1990). These and other activities may also be influenced by political 'sunk costs' which politicians may be loathe to abandon because it could be seen as an admission of a mistake (and hence negative publicity) and precedents (firm X received a subsidy so it is only fair that firm Y does).

Bureaucratic incentives

The agents of politicians are the government departments and authorities. But within these organisations there are a range of additional internal influences and incentives. A number of aspects make these internal incentives inherently difficult to monitor, including (Wolf 1988; Weimer and Vining 1992):

1. lack of a profit test;
2. difficulty in measuring and monitoring outcomes; and
3. internalities and organisational goals.

Government organisations generally do not sell their output (with the exception of government business enterprises). Furthermore, government is often a monopoly supplier where output is not sold in part or full. Hence, there is a break in the linkage between the costs of production and the revenue from sales and no clear test of ongoing desirability (Wolf 1988). The lack of a profit test creates substantial difficulties in measuring the efficiency of public organisations. Mueller (1989, p. 261) reports 50 studies of provision of similar services by public and private firms showing that 40 found public firms significantly less efficient than private firms and only two found public services better than private. Borcherding (as quoted in Mueller 1989) indicates that government production of a good previously produced by the private sector will tend to double its costs of production. Leibenstein (1982) dubs this as 'X-inefficiency'.

X-inefficiency can arise from several sources. Some of these include:

- internalisation of the discretionary budget;
- lower incentives for innovation (Weimer and Vining 1992);
- barriers to innovation (Weimer and Vining 1992); and
- lack of flexibility.

The discretionary budget is the difference between the minimum cost of producing a specified output and the actual cost. In a firm the difference would accrue to the owners. In a bureaucracy the difference cannot normally be retained but must be returned to treasury, thus revealing information about the minimum costs of production. Executives may therefore seek to retain the discretionary budget by such measures as spending faster as the end of the financial year approaches, overstaffing to allow for shirking, and additional travel or supplies.

The private sector is driven to innovation by the profit motive. Other firms must adopt these innovations or they will eventually become bankrupt. Firms can also retain some of the benefits of innovation via patents. Executives in bureaucracies have no direct competitors to imitate in adopting innovations. They are unable to borrow funds against future earnings to adopt innovations and public service rules may make it difficult to change the current mix of inputs or to acquire specialised expertise. This disincentive to innovation extends to flexibility in staff management, general decision-making and supply management.

The break in the linkage between costs and revenues makes it more difficult to measure and monitor outcomes in order to efficiently allocate resources. Market failure makes resource allocation even more difficult because the market imperfections mean that outcomes are difficult to value (Wolf 1988). Therefore, monitoring is conducted via other, potentially costly, measures such as audits, client surveys and comparisons with other organisations (benchmarking). A second response is greater use of *ex-ante* versus *ex-post* measures of performance (Vining and Weimer 1990).

Faced with the paucity of information on the value of environmental outcomes, economists have developed a number of valuation techniques to assist in their measurement. These techniques include revealed preference methods such as the travel cost method and hedonic pricing and stated preference techniques such as contingent valuation and environmental choice modelling. These tools impose additional monitoring costs but are able to measure the value placed on the outcomes by society.

All organisations, firms, bureaucracies and non-profits, require a set of rules to deal with day-to-day management and operations. These rules include those for dealing with staff recruitment and management, allocation of budgets and office behaviour. Government departments often extend these rules as one way of dealing ex-ante with measurement and monitoring problems. Wolf (1988, p.66) terms these rules 'internalities' or organisational goals and defines them as 'the goals that apply within non-market organisations to guide, regulate, and evaluate agency performance and the performance of agency personnel'. Wolf labels these rules as internalities because without the pressure of competition, or a clear linkage to budget constraints, they affect the performance of bureaucracies in much the same way as externalities degrade market outcomes. Specifically, internalities raise the supply curve because they raise the costs of production. Typical internalities suggested by Wolf are:

- budget growth (more is better). Variations on the 'more is better' maxim include maximising revenue in private sector firms and maximising employment in bureaucracies;
- technological advance (new and complex is better, often referred to as 'gold-plating'). A similar bias against new technology and change may exist creating the opposite internality. That is, new technologies generating net benefits are not adopted; and
- information acquisition and control (knowing what others do not know is better).

Government suppliers

Where government interacts with markets a principal-agent arrangement arises between the bureaucracy and the market supplier. Some aspects of the principal-agent problem in this context are closely related to the rent-seeking behaviour discussed in Section 2.3.1. Where supply is contestable government should seek to supply the good via contracting (Vining and

Weimer 1990). This is analogous to supply of generic wetland outputs that can be obtained from many wetlands in many locations. A barrier to entry is created where suppliers are required to make specific investments to acquire appropriate skills, facilities or trust. Trust may be required where it is difficult to monitor the good or service being purchased. Hence, specific investments or trust may be required for wetland conservation, particularly where rehabilitation actions are required to supply the service or outputs are difficult to monitor (as is often the case).

Supply of goods is not likely to be contestable where a high level of specific investment or trust is required. In the extreme case the supplier is effectively a monopolist who may be selling to a monopsonist buyer. For example, an icon wetland with irreplaceable and high value biodiversity conservation attributes. In the absence of contestability the supplier is able to engage in opportunistic and rent-seeking behaviour while the specificity of investment or trust may lead to X-inefficiency. Other organisational structures, such as non-profit organisations, may reduce the risk of such behaviour because the organisational structure does not allow dispersal of such gains via profits to owners (Vining and Weimer 1990).

The split between *ex-ante* rules of supply and *ex-post* monitoring of outputs is also important. Low-cost and effective *ex-post* monitoring is more efficient than *ex-ante* rules. However, the less contestable supply is, the less information that is conveyed by prices and the more likely that *ex-ante* rules will be more efficient (Vining and Weimer 1990). Hence, *ex-ante* rules of supply are more likely to be efficient for difficult to monitor wetland outputs that require a significant element of trust.

Other levels of government

Where multiple levels of government are required to achieve outcomes desired by the community a principal-agent arrangement may arise between one or more levels. Three issues are apparent:

1. the impact of an additional layer of principal-agent relationships;
2. the impact of heterogeneity in applying government programs at higher levels; and
3. the opportunity for inefficiencies due to duplication or cost-shifting.

The costs imposed by an additional layer of principal-agent relationships comprise the transaction costs associated with negotiating and monitoring agreements including the potential for opportunistic or shirking behaviour by agent levels of government.

Heterogeneity of demands for environmental outcomes at lower levels of government poses a problem where programs are uniformly applied by higher levels of government. Weimer and Vining (1992) note that this problem can lead to displacement of local government expenditure (where the local government would have undertaken the expenditure anyway) and targeting problems where expenditure is not focused on valued outcomes. In some cases problems may be compounded by constitutional requirements that require equal opportunity to lower levels of government.

Duplication occurs where, not only would the lower level of government have undertaken the project anyway, but the project is undertaken in addition thus duplicating expenditure for similar goals. Cost shifting occurs where the resources are diverted from the intended use to support other priorities of the lower level of government.

2.3.3 Distortions Induced by Government Actions

The actions of government to address market failures can have a number of non-direct or unintended impacts that can induce transaction costs in other markets. These costs should also be included when considering whether the gains from government action outweigh the costs. These can be loosely grouped into three areas:

1. the costs of redistributing resources via the taxation system;
2. the impacts of known but unbudgeted impacts of government actions; and
3. the unintended consequences of government actions.

The second and third areas are closely related because it is often difficult to determine what the government knew or should have known, especially given the legal protection that government often enjoys.

The costs of redistributing resources
It is often assumed that a dollar contributed by government is equal to a dollar contributed by the private sector, but this ignores the welfare costs of tax collection in the economy (Alston and Hurd 1999). Some of these costs are due to the layers of bureaucracy required (including the potential for inefficiencies due to principal-agent problems as discussed in Section 2.3.2). Other costs are due to distortions induced in the economy as a result of the structure and collection of taxes. These costs raise the marginal cost of an additional dollar of government spending. The extent of these costs is an important element in whether the community is better off if government contributes money to achieving wetland management change.

Estimates of the scale of costs inherent in government collection and redistribution vary. In an Australian context the most recent estimates are by Campbell and Bond (1997), who suggest that the net present value of the benefits of any project to be funded through government must be at least 1.19 to 1.24 times the cost for a project to 'break-even'. Findlay and Jones (1982) and Freebairn (1995) have estimated broadly similar costs. Hence, the costs of market failure would have to exceed at least 20 per cent of total costs before government transfers should be considered. These studies were all conducted prior to the introduction of a broad-based consumption tax in Australia. No estimates are available of the likely impact of this significant tax change on the costs of government collection and redistribution.

Unbudgeted impacts of government actions

Unbudgeted impacts of government actions arise from the incentive structure facing politicians, bureaucrats and suppliers. They are defined as known externalities of government actions that are not explicitly taken into account in the decision making process. Unbudgeted impacts can be divided between government externalities and inter-jurisdictional spillovers respectively.

The legal powers of government mean that planners are often able to use resources without paying their full social costs (Weimer and Vining 1992). This is sometimes termed 'fiscal illusion' (Polasky, Doremus and Rettig 1997). Hence, these costs may not be explicitly or adequately taken into account. The failure to account for these costs (or the ability of government to access these resources without compensation) arises from poor property right definition and the extent of governments' coercive powers. The use of these powers by government can be seen as a special case of the principal-agent problem where a non-contracting third party is impacted.

Inter-jurisdictional spillovers are 'costs or benefits of local government goods and services to residents who live in other political jurisdictions' (Hyman 1990, p. 619). They are geographical externalities because they spill across the borders of government areas. The allocation of responsibilities between layers of government is usually intended to minimise the extent of such externalities (for example, defence is normally supplied at the national level). These externalities may be positive (for example the impact of large museums and libraries in cities or some forms of pollution control) or negative (for example, fiscal externalities caused by selective encouragement of high value residents in areas).

Unintended impacts of government actions

The unintended impacts of government actions result from unexpected consequences of specific taxation, subsidy or regulatory measures. These unintended consequences arise due to the information asymmetry between planners (politicians or bureaucrats) and the holders of private property rights. Wolf (1988) notes that unintended impacts are often the product of the political market that demands short-term action without sufficient information to consider long-term side effects, and that these side effects are generally more likely to occur later rather than sooner. They are also difficult to anticipate and measure because they are often remote from the original action.

Taxation or subsidy measures (both implicit and explicit) may generate rent-seeking activity. Similarly, creation of regulations designed to achieve 'public good' outcomes may create a range of perverse incentives to property right owners. Regulations have generally been premised on one or more of the following:

1. the 'public good' to the community as a whole outweighs the harm to individuals;
2. attempts to reduce the transaction costs associated with litigation in the courts by replacing it with a regulatory structure; or
3. shifting the cost, or burden of proof, from those harmed (as is the case under common law) to those who are potentially harming. This is otherwise known as the 'precautionary principle'.

'Public good' regulation is related to unbudgeted impacts of government actions and has two main impacts:

1. beneficiaries receive a 'free good', while imposing harms without compensation on others. This is generally referred to as a 'taking' (Brubaker 1995); and
2. this changes the incentive structure of both the beneficiary and those harmed.

The resulting incentive structure may be so severe that 'shoot, shovel and shut up' behaviour is induced whereby the resource is destroyed in order to avoid becoming subject to the regulation. Less severe behaviour may also arise. For example, Stroup (1997) reports one US landowner who changed his forest management to prevent it from becoming suitable habitat for an endangered species found in the region. Such behaviour is able to arise because landowners, who have the most control over land management, tend to have better information about habitats and species on their land than government does (Lueck 2000).

Regulations can also act as a direct impediment to production. Impediments may range from outright bans to actions through to complex and complicated regulatory arrangements, or place discretionary decision powers in the hands of government officials (Montgomery and Bean 1999). These measures serve to increase the transaction costs of potential suppliers. For example, Montgomery and Bean (1999) showed that the degree of regulatory control imposed significantly impacted on the private sector's willingness to provide climate-controlled walkways in US city centres.

The cost of accessing court structures remains high for most individuals. Additional disincentive is provided by the possibility of having to pay both parties' legal costs where the action is lost. Hence, government has often replaced common law rights with regulated outcomes but this effectively results in 'compulsory takings' at the arbitrator's price and may be subject to 'capture' by interest or industry groups leading to inefficient outcomes. Furthermore, because the regulators have a captive market, they have few incentives to keep transactions costs low, as there are no alternative mechanisms for complainants. In some cases, self-regulation arrangements, or devolved licensing arrangements can reduce the costs of compliance and policing.

The precautionary principle may be warranted in some cases (such as inherently dangerous activities), but where compensation is available, and damage is reversible, it is difficult to justify. For example, it may be warranted to impose the precautionary principle on marina developments that may cause acid sulphate soil discharges that are now known to damage potentially large parts of estuaries. But the imposition is not always warranted. For example, Anderson and Leal (1991) report the implications of the imposition of the precautionary principle on a wetland owner who actively encouraged an endangered species in his wetlands. As a result of encouraging the endangered species, the benefit streams he can access from his land resource have been restricted and he faces increased transaction costs to access some remaining benefit streams.

Fortunately both government and the private sector have found some approaches that incorporate some level of the precautionary principle' but do not include the transaction costs associated with full imposition. Licenses and permits are tools that have been used not only to grant rights but also to reduce the risk of harms, sometimes by non-government organisations. Licensing can be viewed as an enabling regulation that allows access to benefit streams, while reducing the likelihood of harm to others. For example, firearm licensing in Australia is designed to reduce the probability of firearm accidents and crimes while allowing beneficial firearm uses to continue (such as pest control).

2.4 CONCLUSIONS

Markets are mechanisms that transmit information from one individual to another about the relative costs and benefits of alternative options and, when compared against personal costs and benefits, also provide the incentives to act on that information. To do this they are reliant on a system of property rights and institutions for exchange of these property rights. These ensure that individuals bear the costs and are able to enjoy the benefits of their alternative courses of actions. That is, they facilitate access to any potential gains from trade.

A key to individuals bearing the costs and enjoying the benefits of their decisions is the use of the coercive powers of government to ensure compliance with both the system of property rights and the rules of exchange. Thus the extent of market failure and the opportunities for government failure are inextricably linked. Without a governmental structure to impose sanctions where property rights and rules of exchange are violated, markets may descend into anarchy where the costs and benefits to individuals equate to the probability of physical violence and intimidation. Conversely, overuse of the government's coercive powers by confiscation and holding of property rights or inhibiting market-place exchange may create a disjunction between the information held by individuals and the incentives to act on that information. Hence, overuse of government powers can reduce the net benefits (gains from trade) available to individuals and thus their incentives to act. In such cases, markets are less likely to transmit information about the relative values of alternative actions. This then is the dilemma in designing a mixed system. At what point do the transaction costs of markets or governments outweigh the potential gains from trade and government action respectively?

NOTES

1. The term 'market failure' is subjective because similar transaction costs may preclude trade in one market but not another as the gains from trade are larger in the latter. Furthermore, it could be argued that market failure does not exist because where it is said to occur the costs of achieving the potential gains from trade are simply too high – that is, an efficient outcome is no market transactions. However, this ignores the possibility that alternative institutions may reduce transaction costs. Hence, a more specific definition of market failures is where markets lead to non-Pareto efficient outcomes (Stiglitz, 2000).
2. The term legal contract is used in the sense that a legally enforceable relationship exists between the parties to the exchange, irrespective of whether the contract is set down in a written form.
3. 'A *convention* is a regularity in human behaviour by which everyone prefers to conform to a rule on the expectation that all others will also conform to that rule. A convention is a structured set of expectations about behaviour, and of actual behaviour, driven by shared

and dominant preferences for the ultimate outcome as opposed to the means by which that outcome is obtained' (Bromley 1989, p. 42).

4. Transaction costs directly generated by the attributes of wetland outputs under existing property right structures are considered in Section 2.2.2.

5. Where an unknown quantity of a defined product is produced an expected value can be quantified and traded (as in option and insurance markets).

6. Fugitive resources are those that can and do leave the wetland such as waterfowl and fish. An alternative way of viewing fugitive resources is as resources that require inputs from multiple locations including one or more wetlands.

7. Demsetz (1970) defines non-rival goods as public goods and considers goods with non-excludability characteristics as 'collective goods'.

8. Pigou (1920) and Knight (1924) had undertaken some early work relating to group size and optimal pricing for tolls on congested roads.

9. A similar analogy has been developed regarding the geographical scale of benefits in the local public good literature, in particular the 'Tiebout model'.

10. Other reasons for considering alternative coordination frameworks are the view that some assets (or property rights) should be shared (an ethical consideration), or an unacceptable distribution of property rights resulting through market mechanisms (a distributional or equity consideration). Both possibilities may be important in a democratic society such as Australia.

11. These are elements of adverse selection and moral hazard in the political contract between voter and politician according to Lane (1993).

3. Wetland Values and Policy Alternatives

3.1 HYPOTHESES AND METHODS

In the previous chapter, the conceptual issues that underpin our understanding of the management of wetlands in private ownership were outlined. These core concepts are used in this chapter to consolidate the methodology employed to generate the results that are reported in the following chapters. To achieve this 'translation' of concepts to results, two working hypotheses are developed. The hypotheses are designed to address whether the management of private wetlands constitutes a policy problem, and if so, how the development and assessment of an efficient policy approach should proceed – potentially incorporating elements of market and planned frameworks for production of wetland outputs.

Two main methods are used: bio-economic modelling and threshold policy analysis. Bio-economic modelling is a process designed to link wetland management and biophysical processes to societal welfare outcomes. It involves the incorporation of biophysical modelling and the estimation of economic values into an integrated model. A novel methodology for developing and evaluating the transaction costs associated with alternative policy options, termed threshold policy analysis, is then expounded. It involves the assessment of transaction costs under uncertainty and the use to identify preferred potential policy options. The relevant decision criteria to undertake hypothesis tests are defined as part of the explanation of these methods.

3.2 CONCEPTS AND QUESTIONS

The conclusion drawn from Chapter 2 is that the production of wetland protection outputs is unlikely to be at the level desired by the community. The incentive structures that are provided under both the market and the control paradigm are unlikely to generate wetland management outcomes that are desirable from a societal perspective. The potential inadequacy of wetland production is a likely consequence of a combination of market failures in signalling community demands to wetland owners and government failures in seeking to correct or remove these market failures. However, a number of potential avenues exist that would reduce the incidence of market or government failures. The goal of this book is to advance the design of policy that would allow society to move down these avenues.

The application of these theoretical concepts to the policy development goal suggests two hypotheses. First, it could be expected that the current level of wetland production is less than that which the community is willing to purchase. Second, opportunities exist to improve community welfare by reducing market and/or government failure in wetland policies. Hence, the hypotheses addressed in this book are based on two questions:

1. is there an under-supply of wetland protection outputs? If so,
2. what alternative policy approaches are available to secure the net benefits to society from changed wetland management?

The first hypothesis examines the justification of wetland policy by testing the practical implications of the theoretical framework. Specifically, it tests the conclusion from the theoretical framework in Chapter 2 that wetland protection outputs are likely to be under-supplied within the current wetland policy framework. However, the theoretical information presented in Chapter 2 was not sufficient to determine whether the costs of additional wetlands would be larger than the benefits. In order to determine whether there is under-supply of wetland protection outputs it is necessary to carry out an empirical assessment whether the valued outputs from wetlands outweigh the costs of inputs to wetland protection and the opportunity costs of foregone alternatives. This evaluation is posited via Hypothesis One as follows:

- Hypothesis One: an increase in the production of wetland protection outputs would generate a net benefit to the community.[1]

Evaluation of the first hypothesis involves an investigation of the relationship between the biophysical outcomes of wetland management and community welfare. The methodology appropriate to the testing of this hypothesis is based on the concept of bio-economic modelling. Bio-economic modelling compares the net social benefits of alternative courses of action, one of which is the level of wetland protection outputs generated by a continuation of current wetland management. The net social benefits are estimated by aggregating the total benefits less the total costs of alternative wetland management strategies. Benefits generated by wetlands that must be estimated include monetary and non-monetary values generated to the wetland owner and the wider community. They include the physical interaction of wetland management inputs and the outputs generated such as food and fibre products, as well as their value as recreation sites and in generating existence values. The major cost of wetland protection is foregone opportunities to use the land, water and other resources in alternative uses, mainly as agricultural inputs. Other potential costs such as negative impacts on other enterprises or activities also need to be evaluated. For example, using wetlands for duck hunting may generate a cost to individuals who oppose hunting on ethical or animal cruelty grounds.

If the bio-economic model shows that an increase in the production of wetland protection outputs would generate a net benefit – that is, Hypothesis One is accepted – the community would be better off if cost-effective policies were introduced that increase wetland production. The scope for policy development is the scale of the net benefits that would be generated by the additional areas of wetlands. Hypothesis One is explored and tested in Chapters 5, 6, 7 and 8.

The second hypothesis concentrates on the issue of policy development. The theoretical framework developed in Chapter 2 describes a number of potential sources of transaction costs leading to market or government failure. Determining whether these sources of government and market failure can be reduced or removed is the focus of the second hypothesis. Hence, whether alternative policies can be designed that would generate a net benefit to the community over the current policy framework is the focus of the second hypothesis:

- Hypothesis Two: policies alternative to those currently in place would reduce the extent of market or government failure in the production of wetland protection outputs.

The current set of wetland policies yields the base-line outcome examined in Hypothesis One. Acceptance of Hypothesis One confirms the existence of market or government failure within the current policy framework and thus the potential for development of alternative policies that would reduce the underlying transaction costs. Alternative policies can reduce the incidence of market or government failure where they reduce the sources of the transaction costs in the production of wetland protection outputs. However, all alternative policies will necessarily be subject to a degree of government failure in design and implementation at a minimum. Therefore, testing

Hypothesis Two involves evaluating whether policies can be developed that would generate cost-effective increases in the production of wetland protection outputs, thus reducing the extent of market or government failure.[2]

There are a number of challenges in testing Hypothesis Two. The true impacts of alternative policies on wetland production are subject to uncertainty, in part because it is not possible to conduct experiments to assess the impacts of policy on wetland production. Similarly, it is not possible to conduct policy experiments to measure the impact of alternative policies on the current extent of market and government failure. These constraints on wetland policy development have implications for the selection of methodology to test Hypothesis Two by explicitly confounding an experimental approach. Furthermore, the lack of policy variation across governments, the existence of untested policy options and the impact of different policy combinations, mean it is impossible to identify the impact of a sufficient range of alternative policies to assess relative market or government failure via comparative case studies of policy application.

The option selected in this study is to use a comparative, qualitative evaluation of the relative cost-effectiveness of current and alternative policies – termed threshold policy analysis. The goal of this evaluation is to assess the cost-effectiveness of alternative policy options when the impacts of transaction costs are included. A number of potential causes of transaction costs leading to market and government failure in the production of wetland protection outputs were identified in the theoretical framework. Each of these sources offers a potential avenue for potential policies that could lead to lower transaction costs in market or government solutions. For example, examining the implications of the current division of property rights for wetland owner incentives to manage their wetlands.

Potential wetland policies can be divided between those that facilitate, induce or coerce the production of wetland protection outputs. These categories can also be further subdivided between policies enacted at differing levels of government according to the division of responsibilities for property right enforcement and resource management. Development of alternative policies that pass the comparative test of reducing the potential for market or government failure can thus be subdivided as shown in Figure 3.1. In Table 3.1, numerals I to IX represent the potential categories of policy options that could be developed according to type and appropriate level of government (using a three level structure of government). Thus developing policy options that would logically reduce government or market failure within each sector of the array presented in Table 3.1 facilitates a test of Hypothesis Two.

Table 3.1 Array of policy option categories

		Type of policy		
		Facilitative	*Inducive*	*Coercive*
Level of	*Local*	I	II	III
government	*State*	IV	V	VI
applied at	*Federal*	VII	VIII	IX

Opportunities for the development of facilitative policies include examining options and resultant incentives from a range of property right ownership regimes at the local, state and federal levels along with opportunities to reduce transaction costs, for example by removing perverse incentives. At the inducive level, opportunities may include reducing market failure by influencing market outcomes and reducing government failure by using alternative preference revelation mechanisms and contracting arrangements. Such opportunities are likely to differ according to the level of government implementing the policy. Finally, coercive policy options will also be examined for opportunities to reduce the potential for government failure from principal-agent issues and government externalities in particular.

In many of these cases, information collected as part of the test of Hypothesis One will provide a guide to the likely scale of the costs and benefits of alternative options. Hypothesis Two will be accepted if there is clear evidence that a majority of the policy types nominated in Table 3.1 would reduce the extent of market or government failure.[3] It is recognised that policy effects may vary in magnitude as well as sign and the discussion in Chapter 9, where Hypothesis Two is tested, refines the consideration of the trade-offs that might be involved in reaching a balanced conclusion. Accepting Hypothesis Two indicates that the community would be better off if some or all of the alternative policies were adopted.

3.3 TESTING HYPOTHESIS ONE

The overarching methodology employed to test Hypothesis One is bio-economic modelling. The main components and tools used in the bio-economic modelling approach include the concepts of biophysical modelling, economic modelling and their integration into a bio-economic model.

In this section, the bio-economic modelling approach is defined and explained. The steps involved in bio-economic modelling and the major components of the bio-economic model are detailed.

3.3.1 What is Bio-economic Modelling?

The net social benefit to society of alternative courses of action can only be determined if the biophysical and consequential economic outcomes of these courses of action are known. The process of identifying and measuring the impact of alternative wetland management strategies is termed a *bio-economic model*. Bio-economic modelling is a three-stage process involving:

1. biophysical modelling – modelling of changes in the biophysical states of wetlands under alternative management scenarios;
2. economic modelling – modelling of community values associated with alternative bundles of wetland protection outputs and costs associated with alternative management actions; and
3. bio-economic integration – consolidation of the biophysical and economic modelling to estimate the changes in community welfare as a result of changes in the biophysical state of wetlands.

Bio-economic modelling builds on the concept of benefit-cost analysis and incorporates its key concepts. Benefit-cost analysis compares the net social benefits of alternative courses of action (Department of Finance 1991; Turner, Pearce and Bateman 1994). There are three key features of a benefit-cost analysis (Department of Finance 1991):

- benefits and costs are evaluated from a societal perspective rather than for particular individuals. Furthermore, the benefits and costs extend to non-market transactions;
- all costs and benefits are converted to monetary amounts; and
- benefits and costs occurring at different points in time are compared via discounting to a present value.

Bio-economic modelling extends benefit-cost analysis to incorporate explicitly biophysical modelling of altered environmental conditions that result from changes to environmental management. Benefit-cost analyses have traditionally been applied to large construction projects and to a lesser extent to proposed changes in government policies. The environmental impacts of such projects are generally small relative to other resource allocations that are proposed. Assessment of the environmental impacts is often undertaken externally to the benefit-cost analysis, for example via an environmental impact statement. This is in contrast with bio-economic modelling where modelling of the biophysical impacts of changing resource allocation is a key step in the process. The economic modelling and bio-economic integration phases of the project complement and extend the biophysical modelling of environmental changes to assess the impact on net social welfare.

Several models have been reported that can be termed bio-economic models, including Mallawaarachchi and Quiggin (2001), Heaney, Beare and Bell (2001) and Cacho, Greiner and Fullon (2001). Despite the integration of biophysical and economic modelling in these studies, only Mallawaarachchi and Quiggin (2001) explicitly seek to estimate and incorporate non-market environmental values within the bio-economic model. Furthermore, while all papers discuss the policy conclusions that may be drawn from their papers they do not translate the information within the bio-economic model into direct policy responses that are then evaluated in terms of cost-effectiveness (as is proposed in Hypothesis Two of this study). Finally, the major difference between the bio-economic model undertaken by Mallawaarachchi and Quiggin (2001) and that presented here is the difference in the focus of the analysis. Mallawaarachchi and Quiggin (2001) focus on an *ex ante* examination of an essentially irreversible, and therefore one-off, allocation of resources between a single consumptive use and conservation. Hence, Mallawaarachchi and Quiggin (2001) essentially focus on a dominant use strategy while the analysis presented here is directed towards multiple use strategies.

The test of Hypothesis One must explicitly assess whether an increase in the production of wetland protection outputs would generate a net benefit to the community compared to the current level of wetland production. The Kaldor-Hicks criterion from welfare economics is used to determine whether a net benefit is generated.[4] According to the Kaldor-Hicks criterion a net benefit remains if the gainers from the change to environmental management *could* compensate the losers (but compensation does not actually have to be paid) (Hanley and Spash 1993). The Kaldor-Hicks criterion is sometimes referred to as a potential Pareto improvement.

The Kaldor-Hicks criterion is applied by comparing the outcomes of the current wetland policy against the outcomes of alternative wetland management strategies. Continuing current wetland policy leads to wetland owners continuing 'business as usual' (BAU). Hence, continuation of existing policy is explicitly defined as the net present value of the BAU scenario. The BAU level of wetland protection outputs may not be constant into the future. Rather the future level of wetland protection is influenced by the wetland management impacts of current policy. Hence, definition of the BAU level of wetland production is a key aspect of an accurate bio-economic model and the test of Hypothesis One.

3.3.2 Steps Involved in Bio-economic Modelling

The practical development of a bio-economic model can be divided into a set of nine consistent steps.[5]

1. *Project definition:* this step is the selection and definition of the unit that is to be examined, including which resources could be reallocated in order to achieve additional wetland protection outputs. For example, resources could be reallocated from agriculture to wetlands by removing grazing in wetland areas or from irrigation to flooding wetlands on floodplains.

2. *Identification of the biophysical impacts:* in this step the biophysical impacts of reallocating resources are considered. This involves developing a conceptual model of what impacts a change to resource management will have on the biophysical conditions in wetlands and hence on the outputs they produce. For example, excluding stock from wetlands (thus reallocating grazing resources in wetlands away from domestic livestock) may improve the water quality in wetlands and downstream and in turn lead to increased fauna populations. The future biophysical impacts of continuing the current resource allocation (BAU biophysical conditions) must be considered in this step because any change as a result of altering resource allocation is only relevant relative to BAU conditions. Identification of the biophysical outputs is not explicitly anthropocentric as it considers all significant biophysical changes rather than only those changes that are likely to be valued by society.[6]

3. *Quantification of the biophysical impacts:* this step involves the physical quantification of the resource flows that are reallocated and their biophysical impacts on outcomes. For example, under each alternative reallocation proposal the amount of water reallocated from agricultural use to wetlands is estimated alongside the associated changes to fish populations. The level of detail for which biophysical modelling can be undertaken determines whether a continuous range of resource allocation options and associated biophysical outcomes can be considered, or whether outcomes must be predicted for a number of representative reallocation options. The outcomes of BAU are also quantified as part of this step. For example, any deterioration in the quality of wetlands through time under BAU should be included in this step. This is in essence the output of the biophysical modelling phase.

4. *Identification of economically relevant project impacts:* comprising a listing of the biophysical outcomes and resource allocations that have an

impact on one or more individuals, the nature of those impacts and the population of gainers and losers of relevance. For example, if the wetlands in the project area improve water quality, but there are no resulting benefits to individuals, either directly or indirectly, then the improvement is not economically relevant. The current and future economic impacts of the BAU resource allocation must also be defined in this step because any economic change is relative to the current allocation. This step in the bio-economic model is explicitly anthropocentric as only biophysical changes that impact on humans are considered in this and subsequent steps. Furthermore, only the outcomes of the reallocation are considered, the processes are not usually considered relevant. The analysis is therefore consequentialist.

5. *Monetary valuation of the relevant project impacts:* in order to compare differing physical impacts they need to be converted to a common comparative unit. Money is used as this unit because changes in marketed resource flows are already comparable in monetary terms. Other tasks involved in monetary valuation include: prediction of prices for changes in resource allocation that extend into the future (for example, the cost to landholders of a reduction in future wetland timber harvests); correction of market prices for any externalities; and estimation of non-market values.

6. *Discounting of cost and benefit flows:* reallocation of resource use will result in benefit and cost flows changing now and into the future. However, the time preferences of individuals mean that they prefer an identical gain now to one in several years time (that is, $10 now is preferred to $10 in several years time, even if inflation is zero). Hence, future cost and benefit flows need to be discounted back to present values to facilitate comparison against flows at different points in time.

7. *Aggregation:* the main goal of bio-economic modelling analysis is to determine whether implementation of a project would improve the well being of society according to the Kaldor-Hicks Criterion. Bio-economic modelling specifically recognises that there is no cost free outcome by comparing the (potentially reduced) future benefits of continuing BAU management against the costs of changing management and the benefits so generated. The test of improvement is via the net present value (NPV) criteria. The NPV criterion involves comparing the sum of discounted gains to the sum of discounted costs. A net social benefit remains if the sum of discounted gains exceeds the sum of discounted losses. That is, if those who gain could potentially compensate those who lose and still be better off.

8. *Distribution of gains and losses:* the population of gainers from adopting a project is likely to differ from the population of losers. Cost-benefit analyses are intended to identify resource allocations that improve the total welfare of society. Summing across gainers and losers implies that the marginal utility of income across all gainers and losers is equal. Utility differences are incorporated into some analyses (but not in this study) by applying differential weights to the costs and benefits of gainers and losers. Thus, the inclusion of weights can allow for differing marginal utilities across different groups within society. The inclusion of such weights is often contentious due to the subjective manner in which they are usually defined. Identifying who gains and who loses is important to facilitating equity goals in policy consideration.

9. *Sensitivity analysis:* the information included in a bio-economic model is often uncertain or subject to a known risk.[7] The risk and uncertainty arises due to the need to make predictions about changes to biophysical outcomes as a result of changing environmental management and the consequent changes to economic values. Further risk and uncertainty arise from the difficulty in predicting economic values at future points in time. These predictions can be changed and the NPV recalculated in order to conduct sensitivity analysis. Sensitivity analysis is normally conducted on factors including the discount rate, resource prices (including environmental values) and the life span of the project. Further sensitivity tests are conducted on the biophysical outcomes that are input to the bio-economic model.

The nine steps are combined into the three-stages of bio-economic modelling as shown in Table 3.2. The methodology used within each step is discussed in greater detail in the next three sections of this chapter.

3.3.3 Biophysical Modelling

The first step in constructing a biophysical model is the definition of the project in terms of the location and nature of the potential reallocation of resources. This includes defining the spatial and temporal context of potential resource reallocations. The spatial scale is chosen to encompass the area for which management changes are considered. At the same time, any impacts beyond the study area must also be included within the model. That is, the complete impacts of management changes must be incorporated in the scope of the model. The temporal context is determined by the time required to reallocate resources and for the resulting management changes in the biophysical outcomes to take place.

Table 3.2 Structure of bio-economic modelling process

Bio-economic modelling		
Biophysical modelling		
Step 1	*Step 2*	*Step 3*
Project definition	Identify biophysical impacts	Quantify biophysical impacts
Economic modelling		
Step 4	*Step 5*	*Step 6*
Identify relevant economic impacts	Monetary valuation of impacts	Discount values of future impacts
Bio-economic integration		
Step 7	*Step 8*	*Step 9*
Aggregate values of impacts	Analyse distribution of impacts	Sensitivity analysis of impacts

The next two steps are the key parts of the biophysical modelling. First, the biophysical factors in wetlands that will be impacted by changes to resource management need to be identified. Next, the proposed resource reallocations need to be defined for each of the potential representative reallocations. The impacts of resource reallocation on the biophysical factors impacts also need to be calculated for BAU resource allocation. That is, the impact of no changes to management but continued changes to outcomes must also be quantified. The time path of the quantified changes to the biophysical factors also needs to be forecast for each potential reallocation of resources and BAU. In practice, it is difficult to foresee aggregate outcomes and time paths. This is because wetlands, like all ecosystems, are in a continual state of change and flux. Hence, outcomes will continue to change over time with and without changes to management. Associated physical changes to wetland management practices (such as additional fencing) are also identified and quantified during the second and third steps of the biophysical modelling process. The basis for biophysical modelling and the underlying tools used to measure the predicted biophysical outcomes from changing resource allocation are briefly described in the remainder of this sub-section.

Basis for biophysical modelling
The biophysical and economic modelling elements of bio-economic modelling are based on the concept of the margin. Each alternative management strategy involves reallocation of a relatively small proportion of total resource use within the case study area. This relatively small proportion is referred to as 'the margin'.[8] Despite the relatively small reallocation of resources, the changes are posited to impact significantly on the biophysical outcomes within the system being modelled.

Adoption of any changes to wetland management in order to increase the production of wetland protection outputs would be undertaken over a relatively long-term period. For example, rehabilitation of degraded wetlands or purchase of sufficient water from irrigation to enable flooding of droughted wetlands is likely to be spread over a multi-year period. Similarly, the benefits generated by the rehabilitated and recreated wetlands will not be available until wetland vegetation returns or is sufficiently mature to generate such values. The time taken for wetlands to generate benefits associated with these attributes may be substantial. Thus an important aspect of biophysical modelling for inclusion in economic modelling is not only quantification of changes to the biophysical factors but also prediction of when these changes will occur.

Biophysical modelling concepts
A number of theoretical constructs in ecology underlie the biophysical modelling steps. The overarching science is restoration ecology, which is supported by a number of concepts including the theory of island biogeography, the theory of conservation reserve design and selection, the flood pulse concept and the serial discontinuity concept. These constructs provide the theoretical framework for considering the biophysical impacts of reallocating resources in wetlands and providing best estimates of the changes to biophysical factors. These concepts and their relevance to the biophysical modelling are briefly described in the remainder of this subsection.

Restoration ecology   Restoration ecology is the basis for management within areas from which production of wetland protection outputs is desired. Basic restoration concepts and their impact on ecosystems are shown in Figure 3.1. The main aim of restoration is to restore the lost natural values of wetlands through encouraging desirable species and discouraging or removing others (Cairns and Heckman 1996; New 2000).

A key theory within restoration ecology is facilitative succession (New 2000). Natural communities change through time because different species become dominant and the structure of constituent habitats changes. This process is termed ecological succession. Facilitative succession is designed to speed the process of habitat change towards a desired outcome, usually by actively managing the area in some way. For example, revegetation and pest and weed control in target areas may allow species to colonise and reach successional stages much faster than natural succession.

Restoration ecology also involves the application of a form of pressure-response model. For example, removing grazing pressures may facilitate natural succession and the values desired. Similarly, changing the timing or duration of flooding in wetlands may restrict or change the values generated. Engineered solutions are also applied in some aspects of restoration ecology.

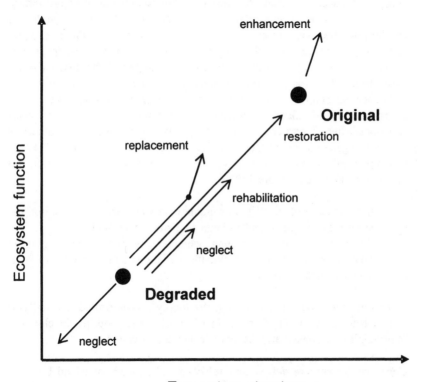

Source New (2000, p. 211).

Figure 3.1 Conceptual representation of ecosystem degradation, restoration and related processes

For example, if no mature trees are available to provide appropriate nesting hollows for a desired species, nesting boxes may be substituted. Similarly, mechanical or engineered solutions may be applied to facilitate flooding of wetlands during smaller floods. The most important ecological concepts for supporting restoration ecology in the context of wetland management are discussed in the remainder of this section.

Island biogeography MacArthur and Wilson (1967) developed the theory of island biogeography. The theory built on a well-known relationship between the size of the island and the resident number of species[9] by incorporating the impact of rates of colonisation and extinction on the total number of species present. According to the island biogeography theory, eventually the rates of colonisation and extinction will reach an ecological equilibrium because fewer new species colonise the island and the competitive pressures become too great for others and they disappear from the island (Cox and Moore 2000). In addition, the greater the distance of the island from other islands, the lower the rate at which colonisation will occur and hence the smaller the total number of species that will be present.

The theory of island biogeography has since been applied to many situations where a barrier to colonisation exists, for example, to patches of remnant vegetation. There have also been a number of criticisms of studies that supposedly supported the theory. These criticisms were based on factors that include (Cox and Moore 2000):

- the difficulty of identifying suitable case study areas that are not also subject to a range of human induced disturbances; and
- the difficulty in determining whether any site is in a state of equilibrium given historic climatic variations and longevity of some species (such as trees).

Despite the difficulty in proving the theory, it has provided a unifying approach to the analysis of and comparison of islands and the development of principles for conservation reserve design and selection.

Conservation reserve design and selection The theory of island biogeography is a core theory within the principles of conservation reserve design and selection. However, the influences of other factors on species survival, as well as the variability in prediction of the island biogeography models, mean that practical application is difficult. The six most important factors that should be considered in reserve design are (Diamond 1975, New 2000):

1. *Size:* the species area relationship that underpins the island biogeography theory indicates that, in general, a large reserve will support more species than a smaller one. A major contributor to this relationship is the ability of larger areas to support a mosaic of habitat types (also known as structural diversity in habitats) and thus allow species that rely on different habitats at different times of the year or stages of their lifecycle to survive (Forman 1995);

2. *Number:* in general a single large reserve will be better than an equivalent area of several small areas of the same habitat (commonly referred to by the acronym SLOSS – single large or several small areas). This conclusion is based on tradeoffs between the extinction possibilities of large and small populations, the number of populations, the correlation between reserves in the year-to-year fluctuation of environment and the probability of re-colonisation of a patch emptied by local extinction (Caughley and Gunn 1996);

3. *Spacing:* or the distance between reserves, is a key factor in the ability of species to recolonise areas after local extinction;

4. *Configuration:* like spacing, is important in the ability of species to recolonise an area or to use multiple ranges, thus a cluster of reserves is better than a line;

5. *Links:* or corridors, increase the ability of species to disperse, use multiple habitats and recolonise areas. They may be particularly important where open or ploughed fields, roads, railways or other altered landscapes act as barriers to migration of species; and

6. *Shape:* is the key determinant in the impact of edge effects. A reserve should in general be as circular as possible in order to minimise the perimeter to area ratio. Edges are important because they are the primary sites for invasion by exotic species or sources of disturbance. The structure of the habitat is also altered at the edge by climatic impacts such as wind, humidity and sunlight reaching through the canopy thus creating a different habitat structure at the edges when compared to the internal areas of a reserve.

Hence, in general the smaller the reserve and the greater the isolation and edge effects, the more likely the reserve will suffer from disturbance and breakdown of interactions and the finer the scale at which adverse impacts are likely to occur.

The principles of reserve design can also be applied to conservation on private lands. Where extractive uses are undertaken in combination with conservation activities their impacts on each of the principles of reserve design must be taken into account. The science of restoration ecology can also be helpful in assessing such impacts.

The flood-pulse concept Wetlands differ from purely terrestrial conservation reserves due to the key influence of water in the ecosystem. The flood-pulse concept developed by Junk, Bayley and Sparks (1989) recognised that the pattern of flooding and the lateral connections that flooding creates between floodplain wetlands and riverine systems are the main drivers of ecological processes in many Australian rivers and wetlands (Kingsford 2000). According to the flood-pulse concept, the periodic pulse delivered during a flood promotes exchange of nutrients and organisms amongst the multiple habitats that make up floodplains and floodplain wetlands (Sparks 1995). The interactions between the effects of the pulse and the adaptations of wetland and floodplain biota create the high abundance and diversity of biota on floodplain wetlands after flooding (Kingsford 2000). Thus, the flood-pulse concept is considered to be the primary driver of the hydrological conditions in floodplain wetlands and removal of the flood-pulse will lead to a reduction in the health and diversity of wetland biota. The application of the flood-pulse model was initially thought to require predictable and thus seasonal flood-pulses. However, non-seasonal flood pulses in Australia generate similar ecological responses suggesting the concept remains applicable (Walker, Sheldon and Puckridge 1995; Kingsford 2000).

The serial discontinuity concept The natural conditions that resulted in the flood pulse in many Australian rivers have been highly disturbed by alterations to rivers and their floodplains (Kingsford 2000). Alterations include those targeted towards water harvesting, storage and use, flood protection, and construction of transport and communications infrastructure. The largest and most significant impact on flows is the construction of large dams that can capture the flood-pulse and then release the water gradually thus reducing or eliminating flood events (Kingsford 2000). Ward and Stanford (1995) developed and then extended the serial discontinuity concept to address the nature of the changes to biota that result from the construction of dams. Dams and weirs are physical barriers to water movement and passage of aquatic migratory species. Hence, these structures impact rivers both upstream and downstream. The main downstream impacts include (Ward and Stanford 1995):

- changing channel structure and stability (which can include channel scouring and enlargement by a changed flow regime further reducing flows to the floodplain and wetlands);

- altering water temperatures downstream and thus the seasonal patterns in rivers and potentially also wetlands; and
- reducing or severing the connectivity of wetlands and floodplains to rivers by reducing or removing the flood-pulse.

These impacts can be significant as many species rely on different riverine and floodplain habitats at different stages in their lifecycle (Ward and Stanford 1995; Power, Dietrich and Finlay 1996; Ward 1998).

3.3.4 Economic Modelling Tools and Techniques

Whereas biophysical modelling is the compilation and analysis of the changes to biophysical conditions in wetlands caused by the reallocation of resources, economic modelling is the compilation and analysis of the changes to private and social values that result. The economic modelling component comprises the fourth, fifth and sixth steps of the bio-economic model. Economic modelling involves estimating the value of the cost or benefit of each of the marginal changes to resource allocation and the consequent biophysical impacts that were identified and quantified in the biophysical model.

Economic modelling requires the identification of economically relevant biophysical values and their relationships within welfare economics. An appropriate approach to comparing benefits and costs that arise at different points in time must be considered because resource reallocation and the consequent changes to biophysical outcomes and values will occur at different points in time. A suitable methodology for estimating and extrapolating the changes to economic values must also be determined. In the remainder of this section the approach taken to these aspects of economic modelling are briefly described.

Relevant economic values

The resources that are reallocated by changing wetland management along with the consequent biophysical changes to wetland protection outputs will generate values to wetland owners and others within the community. The concept of total economic value is applied to assess these changes. Total economic value encompasses all potential values (both positive and negative). The components of total economic value are well established in the environmental economics literature (see for example Hanley and Spash 1993 or Hodge 1995) and are illustrated in Figure 3.2. As shown in Figure 3.2, total economic value is comprised of use value and non-use values. In

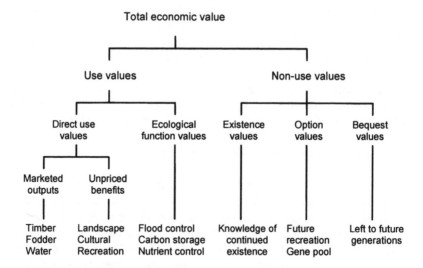

Source Adapted from Hodge (1995, p. 7).

Figure 3.2 The elements of total economic value

turn, use values comprise direct-use values and ecological values while non-use values consist of existence, option and bequest values.

A structure for identifying the relevant economic values is provided by combining the concept of total economic value with the nature of the wetland conservation values. The potential reallocation of resources and consequent changes to biophysical outputs is defined by the biophysical model. These changes may impact on wetland owners and the wider population. In each case, there may also be opportunity costs associated with resource reallocation along with costs and benefits of the consequent changes to wetland protection outputs. A change to economic values will only occur where one or more of the changes to resource allocations or biophysical outcomes will affect one or more individuals. For example, reallocating water from a drain direct to the ocean to wetlands would not impose any opportunity costs (assuming zero infrastructure costs and no ocean impacts) because the resource is not valued in the current use. Alternatively, reallocating water from irrigation to wetlands would impose an opportunity cost on irrigators. Hence, identifying the relevant economic impacts initially consists of merging the biophysical changes and resource reallocations from the biophysical model with the wetland values to identify the potential values that are impacted. The potential population that is impacted by a change to these values must then be identified. If no population benefits or loses from the change then there will be no change to values despite a change to resource allocations or biophysical conditions.

3.3.5 Welfare Economics and Economic Modelling

The goal in the economic modelling component is to quantify the changes to individual welfare. These changes may be quantified by estimating the change to the economic surpluses from reallocating resources and the consequent changes to individuals' values. These changes are then aggregated in the bio-economic integration phase of bio-economic modelling.

Estimation of the relevant economic surpluses is complicated by the possibility that reallocating resources may change the relative level of income of consumers by altering the relative market prices of goods. Thus, the consumer's surplus estimated from the Marshallian demand curve is not necessarily an accurate estimate of the change to consumer welfare (Hanley and Spash 1993).[10] Changes to consumer welfare are instead measured by Hick's income adjusted concepts of compensated and equivalent variations and surpluses (Hanley and Spash 1993; Johansson 1993). Compensating and equivalent variations allow individuals to adjust consumption in response to changes in prices while compensating and equivalent surpluses do not.[11] Reallocation of resources to wetland protection outputs is likely to lead to a significant increase in the non-market wetland protection outputs, many of which are public goods. Hence, compensating or equivalent surplus measures are appropriate where the change in welfare from a discrete change in the quantity of a public good is considered for which no adjustment to consumption can be made (Hanley and Spash 1993).

Estimation of changes to producer welfare is relatively uncomplicated because they can be derived from market data.[12] Hanley and Spash (1993) divide measures of producer's welfare between input and output market measures. Output measures are derived where the producer sells their production and are termed quasi-rent, of which one measure is producer's surplus. Producer's surplus is the equivalent of Marshallian consumer's surplus and is defined as the area above the short-run supply curve and below the price line (Hanley and Spash 1993).[13] This implies that the costs of fixed factors (such as land and output specific capital improvements) are assumed to be 'sunk costs' during the period of analysis. Input measures are reliant on assessing the economic rent attributable to specific factors of production such as land or managerial ability and are rarely used in empirical studies (Hanley and Spash 1993).

The focus in much of the remainder of this section is on a description of the tools used to estimate the changes to consumer and producer welfare from the reallocation of resources to produce wetland protection outputs.

Monetary values to private wetland owners

The wetland owner faces a number of costs and benefits if they wish to change the resource allocations in their wetlands. Marketed costs and benefits can be measured via the actions of people in the marketplace while estimation of non-marketed costs and benefits is more difficult. The monetary costs and benefits can be divided into three groups:

1. the change to producer's surpluses from a discontinuation of current wetland uses;
2. the direct costs of facilitating a change to wetland management; and
3. the change to producer's surpluses from new wetland uses into the future.

The change to the wetland owner's producer's surplus as a result of changing management includes the loss to producer's surplus from discontinued wetland uses, and savings on avoided cost inputs to these uses (where such costs are not included in producers' surplus estimates). Direct costs of changing wetland management include any costs to facilitate a change to wetland management. Future wetland uses may generate both monetary and non-monetary benefits to wetland owners but may also incur additional costs from managing wetlands to generate these benefits. The non-monetary benefits generated to wetland owners, as consumers of wetland outputs, are included with the non-monetary benefits generated by wetlands discussed below.

Monetary values to others in the community

Changes to wetland management may alter a range of marketed costs and benefits to others in the community. These can be divided between monetary benefits or costs directly resulting from changes to the management of publicly owned wetlands and those arising from resource allocation changes in wetlands that extend beyond wetland owners.

Changes to the management of publicly owned wetlands may change the monetary net benefits derived from sale of food or fibre products or from recreation entry fees in these areas. Such changes also need to be taken into account in order to ensure all costs and benefits of changing wetland management are considered.

Marketed value changes that extend beyond wetlands are of two types. Where resources are reallocated to wetlands that generate benefits outside the control of the wetland owner, the benefits of the resource allocation need to be considered. A second form of costs may occur where the changes to the resource allocation are large enough to change the price of the resource to other users.

Non-monetary values

The existence of both marketed and non-marketed values for wetland protection outputs complicates the economic modelling. While marketed values are relatively easily estimated using data generated from market transactions, non-marketed values are more difficult to estimate. Techniques to evaluate non-market values can be divided between those that do and do not involve estimating demand curves for non-market values. Methods that do not allow estimation of the demand curve do not facilitate calculation of changes to welfare and hence cannot be directly included within the economic modelling framework considered in this study. Therefore, methods such as the dose-response, replacement value, mitigation cost and opportunity cost methods are not considered. Methods involving estimation of a demand curve for the non-market outputs can be divided between those that rely on revealed preferences and those that rely on expressed preferences.

Revealed preference methods commonly employed include the travel cost and hedonic price methods while stated preference methods include contingent valuation and choice modelling.[14] For changes in wetland protection outcomes to be estimated by revealed preferences, they need to be directly related to actions in the market place. A second issue is that markets normally cover actions that have already occurred. It would not be possible to estimate and extrapolate the value of wetland protection outputs via revealed preference methods if they did not already occur. Hence, the impacts of a management change that leads to production of new wetland protection outputs could not be estimated using this methodology. Each of the methods available is briefly described in this subsection.

Travel cost method The Travel Cost Method (TCM) is a well-established technique that has yielded relatively consistent and reliable results (Bennett 1995). The TCM involves the estimation of the relationship between the recreational services provided and the purchase and use of goods and services by visitors who travel to the site (Turner, Pearce and Bateman 1994). By estimating this relationship, the value of the wetlands as a site for a recreational activity (for example hunting) can be estimated. Hence, the TCM method is suitable for the estimation of consumers' surplus from recreational activities.

The TCM assumes *weak complementarity* between the expenditure on goods and services and the recreational service (Hanley and Spash 1993). The implication of this assumption is that when consumption expenditure is zero, the marginal utility (and hence consumers' surplus) of the good is also zero. In other words, the consumers' surplus of the furthest distant wetland visitor approaches zero because the costs of the visit almost equal the benefits enjoyed from the trip. People living further away, with higher costs, do not visit because they would not enjoy any surplus. A second assumption made under the methodology is that the utility function of visitors is separable (Hanley and Spash 1993). That is, the demand for visits can be estimated independently of the demand for other activities (both recreational and non-recreational). Finally, the TCM method makes no distinction between a 'good' visit and a 'bad' visit. That is, there is no difference in the value estimated if the object of the visit is achieved or not. This is because the TCM methodology is based on visitors' expectations of trip quality.

Hedonic price method   The Hedonic Price Method (HPM) is used to estimate the value of environmental services (or disservices) that are not traded in markets but which directly affect prices in markets. The HPM involves the estimation of the contribution the environmental service provides to the aggregate price of the marketed good or service (Turner, Pearce and Bateman 1994). By estimating this relationship, the value of the environmental service (for example a viewshed) can be estimated. Hence, the HPM method is suitable for the estimation of consumers' surplus generated by some environmental services and disservices.

As was the case with the TCM, the HPM assumes that the utility function of visitors is weakly separable, and assumes *weak complementarity* between the expenditure on goods and services and the environmental service (Hanley and Spash 1993). For example, the values of individuals who enjoy a viewshed by walking through a scenic neighbourhood are not included by the HPM.

Contingent valuation and choice modelling   Many of the environmental outcomes for which monetary estimates are required in this book do not rely on marketed goods in any way. Hence, demand for these outcomes is not revealed in the market place and cannot be estimated via revealed preference methods. Stated preference techniques involve individuals being asked, in a questionnaire, to place a value on the change in environmental outcomes (Turner, Pearce and Bateman 1994). The use of surveys allows alternative environmental outcomes that are not related to markets in any way to be compared (Morrison, Blamey, Bennett and Louviere 1996). There are five main stated preference techniques. They can be divided between contingent valuation (CV) and conjoint based methods.

'The contingent valuation method (CV) involves asking a sample of respondents whether (or how much) they are willing to pay to prevent or obtain a particular environmental outcome' (Morrison *et al.* 1996 p. 2). The response of the sample is used to estimate the compensating surplus for an improvement in the environmental good and the equivalent surplus for a decline in the environmental good (Hanley and Spash 1993).[15] The advantage of CV methodology is that it is well known internationally with a relatively extensive listing of applications. However, the CV approach can only assess the outcomes of one proposed alternative management strategy compared to BAU within each application. Hence, the use of CV to value multiple potential changes would require a separate survey for each option – a potentially prohibitively expensive exercise. Assessment of multiple strategies is required in order to assess the scope for policy development that would generate net benefits to the community.

There are four potential conjoint based methods that can be used: contingent ranking, contingent rating, paired comparison, and choice modelling (CM). Each method involves respondents evaluating a number of alternative management strategies but only CM directly generates theoretically unbiased estimates of the willingness to pay (WTP) for each option (providing a BAU option is included) (Morrison et al. 1996). CM involves a sample of people being asked to choose their preferred option from a sequence of sets of alternatives. The alternatives are described in terms of a common vector of Lancastrian outcome 'attributes' that take on different levels in each alternative. So long as one attribute is monetary, it is possible to generate estimates of value via analysis of the tradeoffs respondents are willing to make in their choices. The unbiased WTP estimates generated by CM are thus suited for use in the bio-economic modelling framework. CM also provides additional information about preferences for the components (attributes) that make up the outcome. This information can be used in two ways:

1. to develop new management strategies leading to outcomes preferred to those initially examined; and
2. to compare other management options that may arise against those initially tested (so long as the outcomes of these new options can be measured and described using the same attributes as the existing options).

Benefit transfer

The term 'benefit transfer', also referred to as 'environmental value transfer', refers to 'the transposition of monetary environmental values estimated at one site (study site) through market-based or non-market-based economic valuation techniques to another site (policy site)' (Brouwer 2000, p. 138). The cost-effectiveness of benefit transfer makes it an attractive way of including non-use values and non-marketed use values within a bio-economic model. However, benefit transfer is subject to a number of criticisms based on specificity and contextual influences on the original estimates and their impacts on the accuracy or possibility of employing benefit transfer (see for example Brouwer 2000). These concerns, along with the results of tests of benefit transfer, indicate that caution should be exercised in using benefit transfer as a method of including non-marketed values within a bio-economic model (see for example Brouwer 2000, Ruijgrok 2001 or Morrison 2001).

Protocols have been developed that seek to minimise the concerns where benefit transfer is considered. These protocols serve to limit the potential for benefit transfer and emphasise the trade-offs between cost-effectiveness and accuracy in undertaking a bio-economic modelling exercise. A widely applied set of protocols were developed by Desvousges, Naughton and Parsons (1992). Their criteria seek to limit benefit transfer to situations where:

1. the valuation study from which benefit estimates are transferred is carried out properly;
2. the type and quantity of the environmental goods produced is similar; and
3. the populations and market characteristics are similar for both locations.

Brouwer (2000) refines these criteria and also suggests that stakeholder consultation is important in ensuring that transferred values and methodology are acceptable methods for decision making in the case study areas. Hence, benefit transfers are considered in this study where suitable valuation studies that meet Desvousges, Naughton and Parsons' (1992) criteria are available. Benefit transfers can be pursued where the values of these environmental outputs are anticipated to comprise a relatively small component of total economic values estimated and taking into consideration the costs of undertaking a valuation study. The potential for error that is introduced by the use of benefit transfers can be assessed in part by sensitivity analysis of the estimated values.

3.3.6 Bio-economic Integration

Bio-economic integration comprises steps 7 to 9 of the bio-economic modelling process. Specifically, bio-economic integration consists of aggregation of the costs and benefits of changing wetland management, analysis of the distribution of the population of gainers and losers, and, sensitivity analysis of the underlying assumptions. The bio-economic integration phase combines the biophysical and economic models to complete the bio-economic model and facilitate a test of Hypothesis One against the Kaldor-Hicks criterion.

Integration and aggregation

Bio-economic integration is the nuts and bolts of the bio-economic model and facilitates comparison of alternative biological states in terms of the net benefits they generate to society. The main object of constructing the bio-economic model is to facilitate a test of Hypothesis One. The underlying procedure used to test Hypothesis One is the 'Net Present Value Test' (NPVT). The NPVT asks whether the sum of the discounted benefits from additional production of wetland protection outputs exceeds the sum of the discounted costs to achieve the additional production. That is, the positive and negative values estimated as part of the economic modelling phase are summed to estimate the NPV of each strategy.

Aggregation across individuals for different types of values and across groups of individuals to estimate the net present value of changes to total economic value is reliant on several assumptions. First, at a minimum, it requires an assumption that income elasticities are similar for all individuals and that any changes in income distribution are small (Hanley and Spash 1993). Without such an assumption the aggregate measure of demand that is estimated is not unique. Valid aggregation also requires that the income distribution on which estimates are based be regarded as a sufficiently fair base for making comparisons. If the current distribution is regarded as unfair then the aggregate is meaningless because redistribution of income to meet equity criteria would alter the aggregate demand measures and thus the NPVs that are estimated.

Despite the reliance on an assumption that the current income distribution is fair, the outcomes of the bio-economic model can be used to help assess distributional concerns. Specifically, the nature of costs and benefits, and the population that they accrue to, can be identified within the model. Hence, the distributional impact of specific proposals that would facilitate actual compensation, rather than the hypothetical compensation within the Kaldor-

Hicks criterion, can be assessed within the bio-economic modelling framework.

Treatment of risk and uncertainty
Risk and uncertainty arise from incomplete information about the information within the biophysical and economic modelling components. For example, incomplete knowledge may range from the scale and scope effects of changing environmental management within the biophysical model to the impacts of external changes on relative prices and welfare estimates within the economic model. Risk and uncertainty within the components of the bio-economic model translates into uncertainty about the output of bio-economic integration – the aggregate NPV that is calculated from these estimates.

Risk is usually incorporated via estimation of either expected values according to the probability of alternative outcomes occurring, or via estimation of expected utilities that attempt to include elements of risk aversion for adverse outcomes via weightings on the probabilities. However, where the probabilities of different outcomes are too costly to estimate these approaches are not appropriate. There is also significant evidence that individuals do not view risk and uncertainty consistently with the expected value or utility models. Actual behaviour appears instead to be influenced by the conjunction fallacy (confusing probability with plausibility), the fallacy of optimism (it can't happen to me), incorrect perception of low probabilities, anchoring, and the context of the risk (Turner, Pearce and Bateman 1994). One means of reducing the specific uncertainty about the consequences to the aggregate NPV is to conduct sensitivity tests on the sources of uncertainty within the biophysical and bio-economic models. To conduct the sensitivity tests the assumptions about the sources of uncertainty are varied within their likely range. Hence, the likely limits of the impacts of uncertainty on the NPVs and resulting hypothesis test can be assessed.

Test criteria for Hypothesis One
The theoretical basis for testing Hypothesis One is the Kaldor-Hicks criterion. The Kaldor-Hicks criterion is met if the gainers from a change to wetland management could compensate the losers and still retain a net benefit. That is, if the sum of all the gains from changing wetland management exceeds the sum of all the costs of changing management. A test of the Kaldor-Hicks criterion is made operational by the concept of the NPVT. As indicated previously, the NPVT is used to assess whether the aggregated gains exceed the aggregated costs. That is, whether a positive NPV would be generated by the proposed change to wetland management. If the NPV is positive then the gainers from changing wetland management

could compensate the losers while retaining a net benefit and a *prima facie* case for acceptance of Hypothesis One exists.

The outcome of the bio-economic model is subject to risk and uncertainty as noted above. Sensitivity tests reduce the uncertainty resulting from the impact of incomplete knowledge about the components of the biophysical and bio-economic models. A stronger test of Hypothesis One would require all sensitivity tests to generate a positive aggregate NPV, while a weak test would only require the 'best estimate' aggregate total to be positive. The results of both the stronger and weak tests of Hypothesis One are reported in Chapter 8. Hypothesis One will be accepted if at least a *prima facie* case for acceptance exists (that is, a weak test is passed). This conclusion is strengthened if the stronger test of Hypothesis One is also passed.

3.3.7 Conclusions

The elements of the bio-economic model are the focus of Chapters 4, 5, 6, 7 and 8 of this book. In Chapter 4, the biophysical modelling process that entails the first three steps of the bio-economic model is detailed for two case study areas. These steps are the selection and definition of the case study, quantification of alternative changes to resource allocation and the corresponding changes to the biophysical mix of outputs generated from wetlands in the case study areas. Monetary valuation, including discounting future values to present values, is the focus in the following three chapters. In Chapter 5, the estimates of the monetary values generated by wetlands are compiled, the estimates of recreational values are presented in Chapter 6, and details of other non-monetary values including existence, option and bequest values are the focus in Chapter 7. The economic and biophysical modelling is integrated in Chapter 8. The gainers and losers from increasing wetland protection outputs along with the impacts on the aggregate NPV of the likely range of uncertainty about the biophysical and economic modelling assumptions are also provided in Chapter 8. The bio-economic integration in Chapter 8 facilitates the test of Hypothesis One according to the weak and strong decision criteria identified above.

3.4   HYPOTHESIS TWO TEST METHODOLOGY

Hypothesis One asserts that there is an under supply of wetland protection outputs.[16] Accepting Hypothesis One indicates the presence of market or government failure in the supply of wetland protection outputs. If market and government failures are identified, the next stage in the analysis involves the development of alternative policies to increase production of wetland protection outputs. Hypothesis Two asserts that such alternative policies can be developed that would cost-effectively enhance the production of wetland protection outputs. The costs of introducing any new policy, including market or government inefficiencies created by the new policy, must be less than the benefits of the wetland protection it creates plus any existing transaction costs (TC) that are avoided.[17] The transaction costs specific to the new policy option can be termed policy transaction costs (PTC). Thus a policy that would be accepted under Hypothesis Two can be expressed as:

$$PTC_{new} - \text{avoided TC} < \text{WP net benefits} \qquad (3.1)$$

Where: WP = wetland protection, and
WP net benefits includes only those benefits and costs included within the bio-economic modelling process, that is, the direct production costs and the market and non-market benefits.

Development of alternative policies will also draw heavily on the information about the distribution and nature of the costs and benefits generated by wetlands that was identified in the bio-economic integration in Chapter 8.

The most appropriate methodology to test Hypothesis Two is a benefit-cost analysis involving the policy transaction costs, avoided transaction costs and wetland protection net benefits of each alternative policy option compared to those of the array of wetland policies that are currently in place. Under this approach, collection and analysis of detailed information about the relative policy transaction costs for alternative policy options would proceed in a similar fashion to the steps in the bio-economic modelling process. These steps are to identify the policy transaction costs, determine appropriate economic tools and techniques to estimate these costs, and to integrate these costs within the alternative policy packages.

However, appropriate tools and techniques to estimate the scale of market or government inefficiencies are poorly developed and difficult to apply in many cases. Indeed the complexity and advances required to refine and apply appropriate tools and techniques to estimate these costs warrant a separate study. Therefore, insufficient information is available to facilitate an explicit test of the net benefits of adopting alternative policies once policy transaction costs are included.

Due to the impracticality of employing a formal benefit-cost analysis of relative policy transaction costs, the methodology employed to assess Hypothesis Two is a comparative evaluation of the cost-effectiveness of current and alternative policies. As a precursor to evaluating Hypothesis Two, the BAU policy framework supporting the production of wetland protection outputs is defined according to the key attributes of market and government frameworks identified in Chapter 2. The policy transaction costs associated with the BAU policy regimes are also identified. The BAU policy framework is then examined using the market and government failure theory discussed in Chapter 2 to identify opportunities for policy development that would reduce the transaction costs associated with BAU. The identification of policy opportunities is assisted by inputs from the distributional analysis of the bio-economic model and information about farmer perceptions. The policy transaction costs induced by the policy options developed to address these opportunities are then evaluated against the scale of the benefits from the increased wetland protection so generated. The evaluation provides a weak test of Hypothesis Two. Given the range of alternative policy options available, the value of this weak test of Hypothesis Two is in its ability to reduce the number of policies from which policy makers should choose.

The methodology employed to test Hypothesis Two is described in more detail in the remainder of this section. The context of policy development and its relationship to the theory described in Chapter 2 is briefly described, the applied policy transaction cost literature is reviewed in order to develop an appropriate methodological base and the process of identifying the elements of policy transaction costs in the BAU policy framework is detailed. A discussion of how alternative wetland protection policies will be developed along with the process of formally testing Hypothesis Two concludes the section.

3.4.1 What is Policy Development?

Policy development is the generic term for the design and implementation of institutions (by government) to achieve a desired change to outcomes, in this case, the outputs from wetland protection. Policy development:

1. is underpinned by the coordination framework used by society (market based, government based or mixed). Hence, policy development is grounded in the theoretical constructs of the relevant coordination framework as discussed in Chapter 2;
2. must consider the nature of the current and potential incentives faced by each of the participants that result from the decision-making framework adopted by society;[18]

3. proceeds by manipulating some or all of the incentives faced by participants. Policy manipulations facilitate, induce or compel changes to wetland management; and

4. is not a single step process, but involves review and readjustment over time to evaluate how well decision processes are meeting the objectives of society. The review and readjustment process results from the incomplete knowledge of the policy maker. Hence, outcomes cannot be predicted with certainty. Adjustment may also be required due to changes in tastes and changing relative scarcity of alternative outputs.

Wetland policy is directed towards influencing the institutions or rules within which decisions about wetland management to produce wetland protection outputs are made. These rules constitute the framework used by society to coordinate the actions of individuals to produce and consume wetland protection outputs and were discussed in Chapter 2. Hence, wetland policy seeks to modify this coordination framework by facilitating, inducing or coercing changes to wetland owner behaviour

3.4.2 Applied Policy Transaction Cost Literature

A number of researchers have noted a deficiency in traditional benefit-cost analysis in that it generally fails to consider policy transaction costs (see for example Colby 1990; McCann and Easter 1999; Thompson 1999; Krutilla 1999; Falconer, Dupraz and Whitby 2001). However, all wetland policy options will be subject to and impact on the transaction costs of wetland owners and impose at least some costs on government. Indeed, some policy options may directly target existing market or government transaction costs in order to improve the efficiency of outcomes. While the focus in this dissertation is explicitly on economic efficiency, it should be noted that policy considerations are also likely to incorporate equity, ethical and fairness concerns (Russell and Powell 1999). Finally, Thompson (1999) notes that it is the net change to policy transaction costs or other existing transaction costs that are induced by policy change that is important for assessing the relative cost-effectiveness of alternative policies.

The policy transaction costs incurred by government are defined to include (McCann and Easter 1999; Thompson 1999):

1. information costs: comprising research to define the scale and scope of the problem to be addressed and gathering and analysing information about potential policy solutions to the problem;

2. enactment costs: comprising the costs of legislating policy together with the deadweight loss costs of lobbying that may be associated with enactment;
3. implementation costs: comprising the costs of designing regulations and other necessary frameworks to implement policy such as promotion of the policy or scheme. These costs will in part be determined by the degree of organisational and participant capital (experience with the instrument in government and target private sector) (Russell and Powell 1999);
4. administration costs: comprising the ongoing costs associated with the policy such as negotiation and contracting costs. McCann and Easter (1999) and Thompson (1999) do not include administrative costs associated with collecting tax revenues to finance policy development – however, these also form part of the policy transaction costs;
5. detection costs: the costs of monitoring compliance with the policy and may also include scheme evaluation costs; and
6. prosecution costs: costs associated with enforcing compliance through legal systems.

These costs are an alternative specification of the sources of government failure together with the potential for unintended consequences as a result of policy action. Other aspects of economic efficiency that should also be considered include dynamic attributes (flexibility in the face of exogenous change or incentive for innovation to generate environmental benefits) and perceived risks (agency failure and to target parties) (Russell and Powell 1999).

The development and implementation of policies may impose or reduce several policy transaction costs incurred by market participants (Colby 1990):[19]

1. direct costs: fees or charges are additional to compliance costs and may be levied as part of some policy prescriptions. In these cases they comprise part of the market transaction costs associated with the policy but should be netted off from the policy transaction costs to ensure double counting does not occur;
2. information costs: the costs of collecting and supplying additional information beyond that required for direct compliance with the policy;
3. contracting costs: the costs of negotiating and completing contracts (including the costs of search and measurement and specification of who bears what risks); and

Table 3.3 Some applied research into the scale and scope of market and government inefficiencies

Authors	Cost incidence	Costs estimated	Summary of research	Methodology
Whitby and Saunders (1996)	Government	Implementation Administration	Includes the policy transaction costs of agreements under the Environmentally Sensitive Areas and Sites of Special Scientific Interest programs in a comparison of their financial costs.	Transaction costs are crudely derived from the operating cost categories for the two programs.
Thompson (1999)	Government	Information Enactment Implementation Administration Detection Prosecution	Compares the policy transaction costs of a tradable effluent permit policy against an effluent charges (tax) policy for equivalent outcomes.	Benefit transfer, interview and best estimate based on knowledge of industry.
McCann and Easter (1999)	Government	Information Enactment Implementation Administration Detection Prosecution	Compares the policy transaction costs of achieving a 40% reduction in biochemical oxygen demand in the Minnesota River through extension/education, conservation tillage regulations, purchase of conservation covenants and a fertilizer tax.	In-depth interviews with a range of government agencies.
Gangadharan (2000)	Market	Contracting Detection and protection	Estimates the impact of transaction costs on trading probabilities in the Regional Clean Air Incentives Market (RECLAIM) in Los Angeles.	An econometric examination of the attributes of trades and traders in RECLAIM.

Table 3.3 continued

Authors	Cost incidence	Costs estimated	Summary of research	Methodology
McCann (1999)	Government	Unclear – includes: Implementation Administration Detection	Derived a ranking of agency costs and perceived farmer costs (not specifically transaction costs) of 17 alternative salinity policies in WA.	A survey of people working on WA salinity issues in (government agencies, environmental groups and individuals).
McCann and Easter (2000)	Government	Implementation Administration Detection Prosecution	Assesses the policy transaction costs of the National Resource Conservation Service (NRCS) per acre. The components and causes of these transaction costs are also assessed.	An econometric examination of a nationwide NRCS survey.
Falconer, Dupraz and Whitby (2001)	Government	Implementation Administration Detection Prosecution	Compared the market and policy transaction costs of farmer payments within the 22 English Environmentally Sensitive Areas.	An econometric examination of site panel data including: participant numbers; and area enrolled.
Colby (1990)	Market	Direct Information Detection and protection	Compares the market transaction costs induced by policy (termed policy induced transaction costs) of current water transfer policies in several Western US States.	A sample of professionals (government and private) involved in the target policy.

4. detection and protection costs: monitoring and enforcement costs
   associated with claiming (or codifying) and protecting property rights
   under the policy option selected.

These costs comprise part of the market transaction costs discussed in
Chapter 2.

A number of researchers have attempted to derive information about the
scale and scope of some or all policy transaction costs. Several of these
studies are summarised in Table 3.3 including the methodology employed
and the nature of the costs so estimated. A general conclusion can be drawn
that measurement of transaction costs is complex and difficult, particularly
where a large number of policies are compared, several of which have not
previously been implemented. Furthermore, no study considers market and
government transaction costs simultaneously, and comparative studies (with
the exception of McCann 1999) limit comparison to either policies with
equivalent outcomes or the same policy under heterogeneous targets.

A wide range of methodologies is used in the studies reported in Table
3.3 including surveys of perceived costs, best estimates and econometric
examination of existing data. Where information about the policy transaction
costs of alternative policies is available it is often subject to uncertainty. The
uncertainty in policy development arises due to incomplete knowledge about
the scale and scope of market or government inefficiencies inherent in
alternative policies. In the case of wetland policy, only survey-based
mechanisms and 'best estimates' are appropriate for comparison of new
policy options because appropriate data will not exist for benefit transfer for
new policies.[20] Use of survey-based mechanisms is complicated by the
potential application of policy at multiple levels of government and a lack of
experience with some policy mechanisms (and hence difficulty in deriving
estimates). Similarly, the lack of pre-existing data on the range of policies
anticipated complicates a best estimate method and essentially relegates
estimation to relatively coarse measures of the likely scale and scope of
policy transaction cost impacts (such as small, medium or large).

Falconer, Dupraz and Whitby (2001) and Gangadharan (2000) found
policy transaction costs to be a combination of fixed and variable costs.
Hence, some economies of scale can be anticipated from a single policy over
a mix of policies, however a single policy option may not be appropriate with
a heterogeneous target population. Economies of scale will also be
counterbalanced by higher marginal costs of achieving outcomes using a
single instrument.

3.4.3 The Business as Usual Policy Framework

The review of the *status quo* or 'business as usual' (BAU) policy framework is a necessary step in identifying the base for comparison of alternative policy proposals and thus any test of Hypothesis Two. It is also a useful step in policy development by identifying market or government failures that alternative policies may target.

The BAU policy framework can be defined with reference to the resources that are combined in wetlands as discussed in Chapter 1 and BAU policies that impact on wetland management decisions. Specifically, BAU policies will result in the BAU distribution of property rights between wetland owners, other individuals or groups in the community and government. These distributions define the potential benefit streams available to each property right owner from engaging in wetland protection and cause the existing scale and scope of market and government failures. Identifying elements of market or government failure and their likely scale provides the basis for the development of cost-effective policy alternatives and is thus a necessary condition for the comparative hypothesis evaluation. The scale and scope of market and government failures for the existing policy framework will be identified in Chapter 9.

3.4.4 Developing and Testing Policy Alternatives

Bio-economic modelling and policy development

The elements of government or market failure that are identified in the review of the BAU policy framework provide a starting point for the development of policies. They also provide a base for comparing the net impact of the policy transaction costs imposed by alternative policies. Policy alternatives may be developed to address the elements of government or market failure directly or indirectly using the potential solutions to government and market failure that were discussed in Chapter 2. The outputs from the bio-economic model are an important input to developing policy options. The distributional analysis undertaken in the bio-economic integration phase of the bio-economic model (in Chapter 8) identifies the beneficiaries and those who have costs imposed on them as a result of resource reallocations. The relative scale of the costs and benefits can be identified from the output of the economic model. Information about the identity of gainers and losers and the scale of their gains or losses indicates the degree of influence wetland policies would need to employ to achieve a change in the production of wetland protection outputs and hence the potential scale and scope of policy transaction costs that may exist.

The information from the bio-economic model can be used to target policy development towards options that are likely to influence significantly the decisions of environmental managers by impacting on the costs and benefits that result from management change, and particularly those aspects that are related to government or market failure. The likely relative effectiveness of policy options in achieving wetland protection can also be judged, in part, through the significance of the costs and benefits it addresses. The use of the bio-economic model to facilitate policy generation rather than simply to evaluate pre-determined policy options (that may or may not target key costs and benefits) is an important strength of the approach and differentiates this study from other bio-economic models. Finally, information about the wetland owner perceptions is used to ensure that all policy opportunities are identified and relevant policy options developed.

Cost-effectiveness of policy options
Evaluation of the relative cost-effectiveness of alternative options requires an assessment of the net policy transaction costs of each policy option compared to the wetland protection benefits so generated. That is, an alternative policy will not be cost effective if the costs of changing management outweigh the net benefits of the change. A bio-economic model of the type discussed in this dissertation normally does not include the policy transaction costs because there are a number of policies that may achieve the management change, each of which has a different impact on a range of market and government inefficiencies. For example, the transaction costs within a tax rebate will differ from those of a materials grant program or a subsidy payment program. The implications of policy transaction costs means that accepting Hypothesis One does not necessarily signify that cost-effective policies can be developed such that Hypothesis Two will be accepted. That is, acceptance of Hypothesis One and rejection of Hypothesis Two implies that the BAU policy mix is more efficient than the alternatives considered once policy transaction costs are taken into account.

The difficulty in measuring the scale and scope of policy transaction costs means that a test of quantitative evidence as was undertaken for Hypothesis One is not possible in this dissertation for Hypothesis Two. Uncertain net changes to policy transaction costs can be included in policy assessment (albeit less accurately) where sufficient information is available to make a judgement about the likely scale of the cost or benefit and its range of variation. The technique developed to assemble and assess the net estimates of cost-effectiveness of the policy options developed is termed *policy threshold analysis*. Policy threshold analysis involves a comparison of the likely range of the uncertain net policy transaction costs (as assessed for each of the policy transaction costs) against the (also uncertain) additional environmental outputs so produced. A threshold policy analysis is conducted in a similar fashion to a threshold value analysis in benefit-cost analysis. A threshold value analysis compares how large a benefit or cost would need to be to alter the conclusions of the analysis and assesses the likelihood of the threshold value being achieved. Threshold policy analysis asks how large the net policy transaction costs would need to be in order for a policy option to be either not cost-effective, or less cost-effective than an alternative policy option.

The threshold cost is defined by the net benefit to society of achieving the desired environmental management change when all costs of policy adoption including net policy transaction costs are included. The likelihood that the net policy transaction costs exceed the threshold is then judged and the conclusions about the cost-effectiveness of the policy options or packages altered accordingly. Judgement is primarily based on qualitative information about the costs. Hence, a cost effective policy will generate a net benefit to the community via increased wetland production or reduced market or government failure costs according to the threshold policy analysis. Thus, threshold policy analysis provides a consistent, qualitative, judgement-based methodology for assessing the relative cost-effectiveness of alternative policies.

Hypothesis Two evaluation criteria
The policy options that are developed may facilitate, induce or compel change to wetland management. The adoption of policy options will also often be specific to the level of government that has legislative powers over a particular aspect of property rights. Hence, the policy options that are developed can be subdivided into categories based on both their type and the jurisdiction of relevance as was illustrated in Table 3.1.

An evaluation of Hypothesis Two proceeds by assessing whether the policy options that were developed from the review of the BAU policy framework and the distributional analysis in the bio-economic model satisfy the cost-effectiveness criteria (using threshold policy analysis).[21] The threshold policy analysis is based on evaluating qualitative information in order to compare the change to policy transaction costs and wetland protection benefits so obtained against the BAU outcomes where the BAU outcomes will be defined using the methodology in Section 3.4.3. The criteria used in threshold policy analysis were identified in Section 3.4.2. They are the impact of changes to information, enactment, implementation, administration, detection and prosecution costs on government policy transaction costs and the impact of changes to direct, information, contracting, detection and prosecution costs on market policy transaction costs. Changes to the dynamic incentives of government and market participants and changes to perceived risks will also be considered within the policy threshold analysis framework. If threshold policy analysis suggests cost-effective policy options for at least one policy type/jurisdiction mix in Table 3.1 this will support Hypothesis Two. Support is strengthened by identification of additional cost-effective policy types and in alternative jurisdictions.

The criterion for accepting Hypothesis Two is the evaluation of cost effective policy options (according to the policy threshold analysis criteria) for a majority of the cells in the array in Figure 3.1. That is, Hypothesis Two will be accepted if cost-effective policy options as assessed by the policy threshold analysis process exist for a majority of policy types and jurisdictions. This is a weak test of Hypothesis Two because it is based on the qualitative information included in the threshold policy analysis, and is dependent on the judgement by the author of the net policy transaction costs of alternative policies. However, a strong test is not possible given the paucity of estimates of the transaction costs of alternative policy options as discussed previously.

3.4.5 Conclusions

The presentation of evidence relating to Hypothesis Two is the focus in Chapter 9. In that chapter, the methodology developed to identify policy opportunities and design policy options is extended along with definition of the BAU institutional and policy framework. The chapter progresses with the identification of policy opportunities and development of cost-effective policy options. The cost-effectiveness of the alternative policy options is then assessed using policy threshold analysis. The evaluation of Hypothesis Two that is carried out is based on whether cost-effective policy options to increase the production of wetland protection outputs, according to policy threshold analysis, can be developed for a majority of jurisdictions and incentive types.

3.5   NEXT STEPS

A case study approach is used as the research design for testing the hypotheses developed in this chapter. It is desirable that a multiple case study research design is used incorporating replication to enhance the generalisation of results. It is recognised that the case study approach has a number of advantages and disadvantages and, like all research, involves a trade-off between the quantity of resources available and the certainty of the research outcomes. The research design used in this study takes into account the strengths and weaknesses of the approach where possible.

In the remainder of this book, the methods described in this chapter are applied. In the next five chapters, a bio-economic model is developed for each of two case study areas in order to test Hypothesis One. In Chapter 9, a range of policy opportunities are identified and corresponding policy options developed. These policy options are evaluated using threshold value analysis to facilitate an assessment of Hypothesis Two.

NOTES

1. Logic dictates that accepting Hypothesis One necessarily rejects the hypotheses that constant or reduced supply of wetland protection outputs would increase community welfare.
2. This is distinct from testing whether policies could be developed that would exactly achieve the level of wetland protection outputs desired by the community as identified by the methodology used to test Hypothesis One. Achieving this level is both impractical and impossible because:
    - the limits of accuracy in estimation mean that the optimal quantity of wetland protection outputs desired can only be estimated and therefore aimed for with a degree of confidence;
    - the quantity of wetlands desired by the community will change over time rendering development of policies directed towards achieving a specific level of wetland production inappropriate; and,
    - the true impacts of policy on production of wetland protection outputs are also subject to uncertainty. Hence, policy development and implementation always requires an iterative approach, but an iterative approach introduces the element of shifting preferences over time.
3. The test criterion of a majority is applied in order to strengthen the conclusion because of the uncertainties inherent in the evaluation process.
4. The Kaldor-Hicks criterion was developed separately but simultaneously by Kaldor (1939) and Hicks (1940).
5. In this section the cost-benefit methodology as defined by Hanley and Spash (1993), and Sinden and Thampapillai (1995) is adapted to the requirements of bio-economic modelling.
6. Biophysical modelling is however implicitly anthropocentric as only those changes considered significant by humans are included.
7. A situation involving risk is defined as one in which the probability of different outcomes is known. Uncertainty is characterised by unknown probabilities.
8. The biophysical modelling approach used is akin to a partial equilibrium analysis and it is acknowledged that this will inevitably omit some potential broader impacts that would be included in a general equilibrium approach. A partial equilibrium approach is undertaken because there is insufficient biophysical knowledge to support a general equilibrium approach and the additional impacts that would be captured by a general equilibrium approach are believed to be small. Within the partial equilibrium approach definable impacts may occur beyond the area that has changed landuse, that is, beyond boundaries of changed landuse. These are 'externalities' of changes in land management and are also included in the analysis. For example, were wetland management changes to significantly

affect fish stocks outside the study area, then these impacts would need to be included. The difficulty of defining appropriate limits to the analysis of changes is a potential weakness of the research design.

9. A tenfold increase in area is associated with a doubling of the species present.

10. Hanley and Spash (1993) describe the potential problems in some detail, as does Johansson (1993). Sinden and Thampapillai (1995) provide a more general introduction to consumer's surplus theory.

11. Specifically, compensating variation and surplus is the amount of tax or payment required such that the individual receives the same utility at the new price level and new level of production. Equivalent variation and surplus is the amount of tax or payment required such that the individual has the same level of utility as at the new level of production but at the old price level. Compensated and equivalent surpluses are estimated with consumption constrained. In all cases the Hicksian surplus measures are measures of changes to consumer welfare adjusted for changes to income. Johansson (1993) refers to compensating and equivalent surpluses as compensating and equivalent variation. Furthermore, the equivalent surplus will be larger than the compensating surplus (for normal goods) (Johansson 1993).

12. Complications arise where the producer is also a consumer and the act of producing also generates benefits as a consumer. These benefits can be considered and estimated as part of the consumer's welfare rather than producer's welfare.

13. Hanley and Spash (1993) note that producer's surplus as a welfare measure is also based on an assumption that the firm operates in perfectly competitive input and output markets, implying fixed input and output prices, and is an explicit profit maximiser. Relaxing these assumptions leads to the producer's surplus being unrelated to producer welfare. For example, relaxing the profit maximising goal implies other sources of welfare that are not included in the producer's surplus measure.

14. *Revealed preferences:* Demand for the wetland protection outcome is *revealed* via behaviour in a market necessary to enjoy the wetland product (Turner, Pearce and Bateman 1994). For example, the value of a wetland view can be estimated by comparing the price of houses with a view to similarly located houses with no view of the wetland (using the hedonic price method). Another example of revealed preferences is the costs incurred by visitors to a wetland (estimated using the travel cost method).

    Stated preferences: Demand for the wetland protection outcome is estimated via a survey of the community in which respondents *state* their preference about wetland protection outcomes. For example, the value of a change in a wetland outcome is estimated by asking a sample of the community about their willingness to pay to achieve, say, a specified increase in waterbird breeding events, or to prevent a specified reduction in waterbird breeding events.

15. Compensating and equivalent variations are estimated by asking individuals their willingness to pay for a welfare enhancing or declining change respectively. Equivalent and compensating variations are estimated by asking individuals their willingness to accept compensation for a welfare enhancing or declining change respectively. If the environmental change is a discrete amount of a public good then the appropriate theoretical measure is compensating or equivalent surplus.

16. A one-way test of under supply of wetland protection outputs is based on the conclusions drawn from the theory in Chapters 3 and 4 that market or government failures are unlikely to result in oversupply.

17. This approach is equivalent to recognising that any wetland management strategies identified as generating net benefits to the community in Chapter 8 will be subject to implementation costs and then asking whether the least cost implementation outweighs the benefits so generated. The approach taken is to evaluate individual policies in order to develop a mechanism that can be used to assess the generalisation of alternative wetland

protection policies to other locations and for assessing policy mixes (assuming no synergistic effects of combining policies).

18. Including the cultural and other norms within the community.

19. Policy will also impose direct compliance costs. These costs are the direct costs of complying with the policy by changing the mix of resources input and environmental outputs. They are included in the bio-economic modelling process used to test Hypothesis One and hence they are not part of the policy transaction costs that are the focus of Hypothesis Two. Similarly, the equivalent direct costs of wetland provision to government are also incorporated in the bio-economic modelling process and should not be included in this process.

20. 'Benefit transfer' of policy transaction costs should satisfy the criteria discussed in Section 3.1.4 but as applied to policy.

21. The development of alternative policy options does not necessarily imply their adoption either immediately or in the future. Adoption requires the policy to proceed through a political process that takes time and may be influenced by participant perceptions, other unrelated policy trade-offs, the relative importance of the policy change that is being considered, among other factors, and is beyond the scope of this dissertation.

4.   Case Study Wetlands

The analysis presented is focused on wetlands in two Australian case study areas: the Upper South East (USE) region of the state of South Australia (SA); and the Murrumbidgee River Floodplain (MRF) between Wagga Wagga and Hay in the state of New South Wales. The wetlands in these regions are primarily located on private land and are likely to generate significant values to their owners and the wider community. They are, therefore, potentially important in policy terms. The case studies were selected to be sufficiently different to give useful insights into the conditions across a range of circumstances.

The management decisions made by private landholders and the impacts of outside management decisions differ significantly between the two areas. Hence, the policies appropriate to each area could also be expected to vary. In order to provide the necessary background on the two case study regions, the current and potential resource allocations are defined in each case. The specification of the resource allocations includes defining the case study area, the resource base, the potential values provided by the wetlands and how these interact with land management in the region. The biophysical consequences of wetland management in each case study are quantified for the current resource allocation ('business as usual' or BAU) and a range of potential allocations ('alternative wetland management options'). A BAU case is necessary as a basis to test Hypothesis One. The alternative biophysical resource allocations generate the increased wetland outputs that are compared against the BAU case in order to test Hypothesis One.

4.1   CASE STUDY 1: THE UPPER SOUTH EAST OF SOUTH AUSTRALIA

4.1.1 Location and Potential Values of Wetlands in the USE Region

The USE case study is located in southern Australia as shown in Figure 4.1. The USE region of SA is located between 150 and 250 kilometres south east of Adelaide. Over 630 square kilometres of wetlands remain in the region or nearly one tenth of the total study area of 6,922 square kilometres (km^2). Approximately 380 km^2 (or 70 per cent) of wetlands are located on private land.

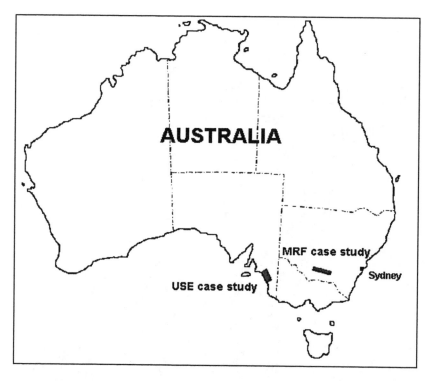

Figure 4.1 Location of case study areas

The catchment and hydrological boundaries of the region are not well defined as the region is characterised by extremely low relief and highly porous underlying sediments. The major contributory streams are ephemeral and some only contribute during excessively wet seasons. Historically the catchment extended into larger areas but several streams have been diverted directly to the ocean to facilitate draining and clearing for agriculture. Figure 4.2 shows the wetlands in the case study area in more detail and the main lines of water movement within the case study area.

The USE wetlands lie within four local government areas and a number of different planning regions for different South Australian State Government resource planning. However, there are few policy differences that impact on wetland management. Furthermore, the USE wetlands lie completely within the USE Regional Dryland Salinity and Flood Management Plan (USEDSFMP) area, which is the most critical policy instrument impacting on wetland management in the region at present.

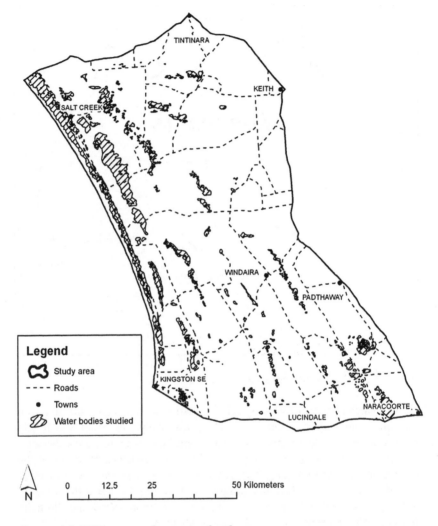

Figure 4.2 USE case study area wetlands

In the USE of SA, large areas of wetlands have been cleared and/or drained and converted to pasture for agricultural production. The reduction in wetland area is further threatened by the impacts of dryland salinity. Dryland salinity has resulted from landscape scale replacement of native vegetation with annual pasture species. Of the wetlands located on private land, 220 km^2 are regarded as degraded and the remainder (160 km^2) as healthy.

The conversion of the landscape to pastoral production was motivated by the private values so obtained. However, the private and social values generated by natural wetlands in the region have been significantly reduced by the subsequent resource degradation. These values include drought refuges for water birds from southeastern Australia, bird-breeding events, landscape appearance, recreation, fodder production and hunting. The management of many degraded and converted wetlands in the region could be changed to rehabilitate or re-create healthy wetlands in the region thus changing the mix of values generated.

The USE region contains a wide range of wetland types. The most important influences on wetland type are hydrology, landuse practices (such as whether the land has been cleared and grazing intensity) and soil type. Wetlands range from relatively permanent wetlands to highly ephemeral wetlands that may only be filled once in ten or more years. Other wetlands may be filled in most years but dry relatively quickly. Vegetation ranges from open-water wetlands that dry back to saltpans to river red gums. Despite the high degree of biophysical variation, the management influences of importance are relatively consistent (water and vegetation management including pest and weed control). Similarly, the private values (mainly conversion to grazing or management for personal recreation and enjoyment) and public values (native animal and bird habitat, biodiversity, native flora, aesthetic values and potential recreation values) are relatively consistent across USE wetlands. The values generated by wetlands in the USE are interrelated with the area of healthy remnant vegetation in the region.

4.1.2 USE Resource Base

Wetland resources comprise land, water and wetland-adapted flora and fauna. The impacts of wetland management may also influence the level of socio-economic, infrastructure and cultural resources in the region, hence these should also be defined. The nature and current condition of each of these resources in the USE is briefly described in this section. The information in this section is largely based on information prepared for and contained in the 'Upper South East Dryland Salinity and Flood Management Plan Environmental Impact Statement' (USEDSFMPEIS) and background reports (USEDSFMPSC 1993).1 The current USE resource base is summarised in Table 4.1.

Managing Wetlands for Private and Social Good

Table 4.1 Current USE resource base

Resource	Unit	Current base
Agricultural landuses	km^2	5,435
Healthy wetland	km^2	379
Degraded wetland	km^2	253
Healthy remnants	km^2	513
Degraded remnants	km^2	342
Grazing productivity *	dse	2,684,000
Waterbirds hunted	No.	8,300
Waterbird hunting trips	No.	1,500
Total tourist numbers	No.	6,350

Notes   *A dry sheep equivalent (dse) is a measure of the carrying capacity of pastures or land. One dry sheep equivalent is defined as a sheep eating sufficient feed to maintain 50 kilograms live-weight. Other animals are rated in dse according to the relative amount they eat (USEDSFMPSC 1993).

USE land resources

USE wetlands are located at the eastern base of dunes within a series of roughly parallel, north-south aligned, stranded dune and swale (interlying flats) systems that interrupt the natural flow path of water from east to west. The dune systems are generally less than 50 metres in height and the interlying flats up to ten kilometres wide. The agricultural system in the region has evolved around the constraints imposed by wetlands or by removing the wetlands through drainage. Thus, use of the 6 922 km^2 land resource is divided between agricultural and non-agricultural uses with much of the non-agricultural use land being publicly owned.[2]

Past decisions to drain or otherwise use wetlands on private land is the key factor in the total area of wetlands in the USE region but not in future wetland health. Many of the wetland and remnant vegetation areas are degraded due to a combination of grazing by domestic livestock, alteration of hydrology and impacts of dryland salinity. Approximately 1 500 km^2 of wetland and remnant vegetation are located on private land, or 15 per cent of all private land.

The productivity of agricultural resources is being impacted by soil salinity.[3] The existence and potential for soil salinity in the region is well known (see for example Taylor 1933). Management techniques to reduce the incidence of soil salinity are also well known (see for example Jackson and Litchfield 1954). Soil salinity is impacting on both agricultural land and wetlands in the region as soil and surface water salt content rises. As a result a major dryland salinity and flood management scheme is currently under construction in the USE region. The goal is to maintain a winter water table in the order of one to two metres across much of the case study area. The scheme is also aimed at maintaining wetlands in the region by directing relatively freshwater flows into wetlands and redirecting more saline flows around wetland areas.

USE water resources

The USE region exhibits a typical Mediterranean climate with a pronounced winter rainfall maximum and hot dry summers. The pronounced winter rainfall peak, when precipitation greatly exceeds evaporation, is the critical factor in creating a flood pulse in the surface run-off and in groundwater recharge (USEDSFMPSC 1993). Watercourses generally only run following winter rains and wetlands are often ephemeral and do not always fill every year. The winter flood pulse historically ponded in wetlands and slowly evaporated over summer. Significant water flows have been diverted directly to the ocean and no longer fill wetlands in the USE. In addition, stop-banks, levees and cuttings have vastly reduced the area of natural wetland areas. Further drainage of wetlands in the region is illegal thus protecting the existing hydrological relationship.

Several major wetland basins are being restored by Wetlands and Wildlife4 in the Watervalley Wetlands, and as part of the Wetlands Waterlink scheme.5 There is some concern that existing drains and diversions will limit the supply of water available to improve wetland management in the region.

USE flora resources

Wetlands and buffer strips contain a large variety of vegetation types and habitats that are important for flora and fauna diversity. Typical USE wetland vegetation includes red gums, tea-tree (melaleuca species), sedges, native halophyte/aquatic herbs, reeds and rushes. Some wetlands are also naturally non-vegetated. The variety of wetland habitats in the USE creates a mosaic of aesthetic appearances and increases the range of habitats available to fauna species.

A gradation of native flora resource condition can be identified in the region. Initial grazing usage of land displaces native fauna with domesticated stock. As stocking intensity increases the mix of flora species in wetlands changes and is gradually degraded. Forty per cent of existing remnants and wetlands are assessed as degraded.6 Management of native flora in wetlands and remnant vegetation is a key factor in maintaining biodiversity. There are currently 33 flora species that are regarded as rare, vulnerable or endangered within the USE region (collectively termed threatened) and ten wetland vegetation classes regarded as threatened.7 Most areas that are managed for conservation require some degree of ongoing weed control across the case study area. A north-south linkage is considered particularly important for allowing fauna movement between parks and conservation reserves and sustaining viable fauna populations (USEDSFMPSC 1993).

An unimproved mixture of native and introduced species, usually dominated by annual grasses, dominates agricultural pastures in the USE region. Nearly 20 per cent of pastures in the region have been 'improved' (by the addition of pasture species, fertilizer and weed control) to feed a greater number of livestock. Pasture condition is the key attribute determining grazing productivity in the region. Little agro-forestry has been undertaken in the USE due to low rainfall and inadequate soil fertility.

USE fauna resources

Wetlands in the USE provide habitat for a wide range of waterbirds, other bird species, mammals, reptiles, and to a lesser extent, fish and crustaceans. The region is also rich in terrestrial and aquatic invertebrate species. Wetlands in the region provide habitat for both local and migratory waterbirds as well as being an important drought refuge in southeast Australia. Eighteen bird species in the region are listed as rare, vulnerable or threatened (Atkins 1988; Environment Australia 2001). Wetlands in the region meet the criteria for Ramsar listing due to their importance for waterbird species (White 1997). The total population of waterbirds has declined dramatically as a result of wetland drainage in the region (Fordham 1998). Several waterfowl species are hunted in wetlands in the USE during open seasons declared between mid February and June each year depending on waterfowl populations and seasonal conditions. Approximately 8 300 ducks are hunted each year on about 155 km^2 of wetlands although the number and area hunted varies widely according to seasonal conditions.8

Few native fish species have been recorded in the study area and redfin and mosquito fish have been introduced into wetlands in the region (National Parks and Wildlife Service South Australia and Department of Environment and Planning South Australia 1992). Water quality and management constraints mean that commercial aquaculture and significant recreational fishing are unlikely in the region.

Many mammal, reptile and amphibian species in the region exploit a variety of habitats including wetland areas during parts of their lifecycle. Eighteen native mammal species are present in the region, of which six are regarded as rare, vulnerable or threatened (USEDSFMPSC 1993). Reptile and amphibian knowledge in the area is regarded as inadequate and no species are designated as rare, threatened or vulnerable (Thompson and Tyler 1983; Croft and Carpenter 1996).

Maintenance of appropriate habitat for these species is a key factor in their regional survival. Conservation of remnant vegetation in association with wetlands significantly increases the range of fauna species that benefit, as do improved linkages between the existing islands of vegetation.

Domestic and feral species are also important agents in many of the biophysical relationships in wetlands. Feral species such as rabbits, foxes and cats are a particular threat to waterbird populations via either predation or competition for food. There is also concern about the impact of the increasing population of feral deer on USE wetlands. Domestic stock numbers in the region peaked in 1976 at 3.25 million dse but had fallen to an estimated 2.6 million dse in 1993 due to the loss of lucerne pastures and exacerbated dryland salinity. Domestic livestock production in the region is split between Merino Wethers (12%), Merino ewes (40%) and Beef cattle (48%), or approximately a 50% sheep/cattle split based on dry sheep equivalents (USEDSFMPSC 1993).

USE socio-economic, infrastructure and cultural resources

Five small towns (population 250 to 5 000) lie on the edge of the study area but none are contained within it. Relatively few aboriginal cultural resources have been identified despite evidence of a long history of aboriginal occupation near many USE wetlands. A network of sealed roads borders the study area but roads within the region are mainly unsealed and may become impassable during wet periods. The highways bordering the region allow rapid transport to and from the region and access to markets in Adelaide and Melbourne.

Property sizes increase and population density falls from south to north in the study area. Farm numbers across the South East Region have fallen by 1.4 per cent between 1985/86 and 1994/95 (Lindsay and Gleeson 1998). In 1993, 410 – 450 farm establishments existed in the area (USEDSFMPSC 1993).

Tourism infrastructure within the region is very limited and it is estimated that approximately 6 350 visitor days are spent in the region (excluding the Coorong). Accommodation, restaurants and retail facilities are limited to the small towns fringing the study area. A few properties currently offer farm-stay accommodation and more are under consideration. Wetland visit infrastructure is limited to a few walking tracks and picnic areas. These characteristics do not allow the supply of a consistent tourism product across time. Other nearby tourist attractions include the Coorong Ramsar listed wetlands, the world heritage listed Naracoorte Caves and the Coonawarra premium wine district. In addition to standard tourism visits approximately 1 500 duck hunting trips are made to the USE region each year.

Currently only 204 km^2 out of a total area of 1 487 km^2 of wetlands and remnant vegetation on private land are fenced to facilitate grazing management in wetlands.9

4.1.3 USE resource allocation scenario development

In order to assess the impacts of alternative management strategies (including continuing the current allocation) their biophysical impacts must be identified and quantified. Physical quantification is also a key step towards facilitating the economic modelling component because specification is an important prerequisite of estimating values for outcomes in both actual and hypothetical markets. These impacts can either be identified as a production function under differing management inputs or as a set of alternative management scenarios and biophysical outcomes. The latter strategy has been used in these case studies because the relationships underlying the biophysical modelling are not sufficiently well understood to facilitate the estimation of a continuous relationship.10

Only those biophysical impacts of resource reallocations that lead to a change in the values generated to individuals (within or outside the case study area) need to be quantified. The likelihood that a change in the biophysical impact or resource allocation needs to be assessed can be determined by asking:

1. whether a population exists that could be positively or negatively impacted; and
2. whether the scale and scope of the change is likely to generate a significant change to values.

For example, the flood mitigation benefits of USE wetland protection do not need to be considered because the reduction in flooding is likely to be small and the population that would be impacted is extremely small. Conversely, the biodiversity impacts of wetland management need to be specified in some form because they are likely to generate values to both local residents and those living further from the wetlands.

The selection of an appropriate future point of comparison of biophysical outcomes is an important decision in the quantification process. Changes to USE resource allocations will take time to influence biophysical conditions in the USE. Hence, the comparison point must allow time for biophysical changes to be relatively complete. The ephemeral nature of many of the wetlands in the USE case study area complicates the selection process by introducing significant annual and El Nino driven variations in wetland biophysical conditions. Despite these complications, most significant wetland and remnant restoration impacts in the region are likely to occur within 30 years time and continue for so long as the resource allocation in wetlands is maintained. Hence, the biophysical outcomes of the alternative resource allocations are forecast in 2028, which is 30 years from the initial baseline conditions described in Section 4.1.2.

USE biophysical outcomes from continuing current management

The BAU biophysical outcome is the expected set of outcomes resulting from completion of the dryland salinity and flood management scheme. A major reallocation of landuse from wetlands to agricultural uses has occurred in the USE over the last fifty years. The consequence of this reallocation has been a separation of the land and water resources in wetlands followed by an immediate or more gradual separation of the native flora and fauna resources in wetlands from the land resource. The remaining wetlands and remnant vegetation in the landscape are essentially islands within an agricultural landscape. Hydrological influences have been removed from many wetlands that have then been converted to pasture. In some cases, 'island' wetlands remain but are subject to fewer and shorter flood pulses. Engineering structures such as roads and levees have changed wetland hydrology on a local scale in other parts of the study area.

Many wetlands that remain are subject to continuing pressures and threats posing barriers to natural ecological succession. The most important of the pressures and threats on wetlands are pest and weed invasion and domestic livestock grazing. These threats also impact on species dependent on multiple habitats, particularly if these habitats are separate 'islands'. Other pressures result from the reduced connectivity of both water and habitat between these wetland and remnant vegetation islands. Finally, the historical reallocation of resources from wetlands to agricultural uses has unintentionally increased the influence of salt on the landscape due to increased allocation of water to groundwater systems. This influence extends to the remaining wetlands in the region.

The current allocation of resources in the USE region will not remain constant into the future because of the adoption of a dryland salinity and flood management scheme. The 'Wetlands Waterlink' is aimed at reducing the impact of salt on wetlands and integrating the management of some wetland and vegetation islands in a chain of wetlands, linked by wildlife corridors, from Bool Lagoon to the Coorong. The Wetlands Waterlink strategy includes rehabilitation of wetlands and remnant vegetation links along the corridor.

The reallocation of resources to wetland and remnant vegetation management by the Wetlands Waterlink scheme is insufficient to halt the long-term impacts to wetland flora and fauna. Hence, while the health of some wetlands in the region will improve, other wetlands will continue to degrade. The overall impact is a continued decline in wetland biodiversity and the fauna and flora species present, albeit at a lower rate than without the Wetlands Waterlink. Continued degradation of wetland flora and fauna will cause a reduction in some wetland outputs such as biodiversity (leading to regional extinction of some species) and availability of game species for hunting. Degradation will also reduce the contribution of direct and indirect wetland inputs to agricultural production.

The decline in wetland production is likely to be offset by an increase in non-wetland production due to improved agronomic practices. Degradation may also increase production of other wetland outputs such as weeds, nuisance insects and foul odours. Socio-economic interactions with wetlands are also likely to be adversely affected by a decline in the visual appearance of the wetlands and their amenity as recreation sites. This decline is likely to be offset by an increased demand for recreation. The impact on wetland biophysical relationships such as aquifer recharge/discharge in the region will be mixed due to the location of groundwater drains and their impacts on groundwater hydrology. Some wetlands previously subject to increasing salinity will benefit from being located near drains while other wetlands may dry faster, thus reducing natural wetland benefits. The projected impacts of these changes are documented in Table 4.2.

Potential resource reallocation in the USE

Consideration of potential resource reallocation can be considered as a two-step process. First, resources can be reallocated to reduce threats or pressures to current production of wetland protection outputs thus increasing production in existing wetland areas. Second, resources can be reallocated to re-create or restore additional wetland areas. In practice resource reallocations may contribute to both goals simultaneously (by reducing a threat through re-creating a linking wetland thus increasing production).11

Remaining wetlands in the USE area represent a chain of isolated vegetation islands in a sea of land used for agriculture. The specific management goals of any resource reallocation in this context are:

- facilitating a more natural flood pulse in wetlands;

- alleviating pressures on native vegetation from grazing and weed competition and to enhance natural succession towards the desired state and output mix;
- alleviating pressures on native fauna from feral animals and competition by domestic livestock; and
- facilitating increased resilience of flora and fauna communities to natural shocks such as disease and fire.

Conservation reserve planning and design concepts can be used to maximise the impact of management changes through increased connectivity or reduced edge effects.

Three management options are developed from these goals:

1. rehabilitation of remaining degraded wetland areas – termed '*wetland retention*';
2. re-create additional wetlands and linkages between wetlands to increase connectivity for wetland specific flora and fauna – termed '*pro-wetlands*'; and
3. rehabilitate additional remnant vegetation and re-create linkages between remnants and wetlands – termed '*wetlands and remnants*'.

These three options are considered in an additive framework when compared to continuing current management (termed '*business as usual*') as shown in Figure 4.3. This structure was pursued because it makes little sense in the context of increasing wetland protection outputs to consider re-creating wetlands or rehabilitating and linking remnants without first rehabilitating degraded wetland areas.

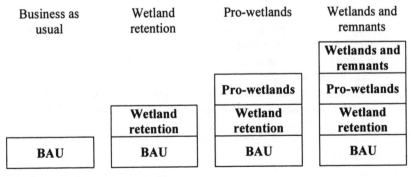

Figure 4.3 *USE modelling options*

The three potential options considered for increasing wetland protection require a reallocation of resources from agriculture to wetland or remnant vegetation protection and the input of additional resources. Specific resource allocations that must be quantified are:

- changes to landuse in the region (from grazing to conservation);
- resources saved in the future as a result of changed landuse (such as planned pasture improvements);
- capital works required to achieve changes in landuse (such as fencing);
- capital works required to re-institute the natural flood pulse (such as construction/removal of earthworks and drain interconnections);
- capital works required to facilitate ecological restoration (such as revegetation); and
- up-front and ongoing pest and weed control in wetlands.

4.1.4 USE Resource Reallocation Descriptions

Wetland retention
The wetland retention option involves the rehabilitation of two thirds of the degraded wetland area in the USE (20 per cent of total wetland area). Ten per cent of the total wetland area remains degraded following rehabilitation.12 Rehabilitation of degraded wetlands requires reinstatement of an appropriate mix of land, water, flora and fauna to facilitate production of wetland protection outputs. An unquantified amount of water may be diverted to the USE wetlands from outfall drains but this diversion is not anticipated to have any significant biophysical impacts at the drain outfall. Rehabilitation of wetland flora resources requires reallocation of flora resources from grazing production to conservation. The additional resources required to rehabilitate wetland hydrology and facilitate livestock management are:13

- engineering works in approximately half of rehabilitated wetlands or nearby surface water drains;
- construction of fences to manage livestock in approximately 70 per cent of wetlands; and
- ongoing management to maintain fencing, earthworks and to facilitate the desired ecological succession path via management of pests and weeds in all rehabilitated wetlands.

Pro-wetlands
The total area of wetlands in the USE is increased by 20 per cent under the

pro-wetlands option by re-creating wetlands in areas that were previously drained. The biophysical impacts of the strategy are maximised by focusing on linking existing wetlands. The additional area of wetlands requires reallocation of 126 km² of land from agricultural pasture use to wetland conservation use. Wetland re-creation requires further diversion of water into USE wetlands from outfall drains. Additional resources required to achieve the pro-wetlands option are:14

- engineering works in recreated wetlands and nearby surface water drains;
- construction of fences to manage livestock in approximately 80 per cent of re-created wetlands;
- revegetation works in approximately 75 per cent of re-created wetlands; and,
- ongoing management to maintain fencing, earthworks and to facilitate the desired ecological succession path via management of pests and weeds in all re-created wetlands.

Wetlands and remnants

The wetlands and remnants option extends the pro-wetlands strategy to rehabilitation and re-creation of remnant vegetation. Under this strategy the total area of remnant vegetation in the USE is increased by 20 per cent and all degraded areas are rehabilitated. The biophysical impacts of the strategy are maximised by focusing on linking remnants to wetlands, creating buffer strips around wetlands and linkages to other remnants. The additional area of remnants requires reallocation of 171 km² of land from agricultural pasture use to remnant vegetation use and facilitates rehabilitation of a further five per cent of total wetlands. Re-creation of remnant vegetation will require the replacement of introduced pasture and domestic livestock with native flora and fauna. The additional resources required for this strategy are:15

- construction of fences to manage livestock in approximately 60 per cent of rehabilitated and recreated remnant vegetation;
- engineering works in wetlands and nearby surface water drains for approximately half of the additional 5 per cent of wetlands rehabilitated;
- revegetation in all re-created revegetation areas; and
- ongoing management to maintain fencing, earthworks and to facilitate the desired ecological succession path via management of pests and weeds in all wetlands and remnants.

4.1.5 USE Resource Reallocation Biophysical Outcomes

Reallocation of resources in the USE will impact on the BAU biophysical factors. The reallocation of resources is intended to achieve an increase in the biophysical outputs from wetlands relative to BAU. The overall impact is an increase in wetland biodiversity and the fauna and flora species present compared to BAU. Reallocation of landuse reduces the consumptive values from wetlands to livestock production but increases the number of ducks hunted. The socio-economic interactions with wetlands are also likely to be increased because wetlands will be relatively more attractive visually and as recreation sites. These changes to the biophysical attributes in wetlands are shown in Table 4.2 along with the resource reallocations.

4.2 CASE STUDY 2: THE MURRUMBIDGEE RIVER FLOODPLAIN BETWEEN WAGGA WAGGA AND HAY

4.2.1 Location and Potential Values of Wetlands in the MRF Region

The second case study area, the Murrumbidgee River floodplain (MRF) in NSW, is the focus in this section. Figure 4.1 shows the location of the MRF case study. Figure 4.4 shows the Murrumbidgee catchment boundaries and the location of the study area.16 The study area focuses on the Murrumbidgee floodplain between Wagga Wagga and Hay Weir. Approximately 486 km^2 of wetlands remain in the region. Seventy three per cent (357 km^2) of wetlands are located on private land. State Forests NSW is the primary public land manager of forestry, grazing and recreation in wetlands in the MRF.

The MRF wetlands lie within a single State jurisdiction but are spread across seven local government areas. The wetlands are also divided between several inconsistent administrative regions for relevant State government departments and split between the lower and mid Murrumbidgee catchment planning regions. There is relatively little variation in wetland policies across the region despite the number of jurisdictions subdividing the region.

The Murrumbidgee River dominates the topography of the study area. The river falls just 100 metres over a linear distance of 240 kilometres between Wagga Wagga and Hay, or one metre over a linear distance of 24 kilometres. Due to the numerous meanders the true rate of fall is even lower. Prior streams, ancestral rivers and current watercourses dissect the Murrumbidgee River floodplain (Murrumbidgee Catchment Management

Table 4.2 *USE BAU and alternative resource allocation biophysical
outcomes*

Descriptive attributes	Unit	BAU	Wetland retention	Pro-Wetlands	Wetlands and remnants
Aggregate totals for USE					
Agricultural pasture	km²	5,435	5,435	5,309	5,138
Healthy wetland	km²	442	569	695	726
Degraded wetland	km²	190	63	63	32
Healthy remnants	km²	513	513	513	1,026
Degraded remnants	km²	342	342	342	0
Grazing productivity	'000 dse	3,333	3,316	3,253	3,075
Waterbirds hunted	No.	6,300	9,300	11,100	11,600
Hunting trips	No.	1,100	1,700	2,000	2,100
Total tourists	No.	6,350	18,250	41,500	41,500
Marginal change from BAU					
Agricultural pasture	km²	n.a.	0	−126	−297
Healthy wetland	km²	n.a.	127	253	284
Degraded wetland	km²	n.a.	−127	−127	−158
Healthy remnants	km²	n.a.	0	0	513
Degraded remnants	km²	n.a.	0	0	−342
Grazing productivity	'000 dse	n.a.	−16	-80	-257
Waterbirds hunted	No.	n.a.	3,000	4,800	5,300
Additional hunting trips	No.	n.a.	600	900	1,000
Additional tourists	No.	n.a.	11,900	26,150	35,150
Improved conservation status of species	No.	n.a.	15	24	35
Hydrological management works	km²	n.a.	63	190	205
Revegetation management works	km²	n.a.	0	98	269
Fencing required	km	n.a.	442	947	2,289
Ongoing management – wetlands	km²	n.a.	126	253	284
Ongoing management – remnant vegetation	km²	n.a.	0	0	513

Notes Conservation status of species is flora and vertebrate fauna species only.

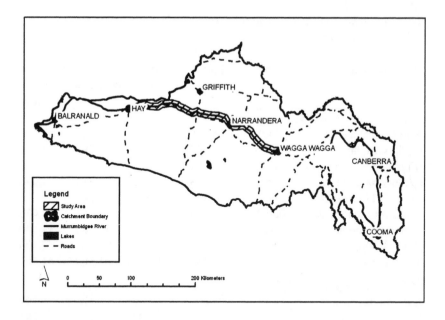

Figure 4.4 Murrumbidgee River Catchment and MRF case study area

Committee (MCMC) 1998). Wetlands in the MRF are formed within minor riverine depressions, prior streams and in some instances lakebeds. Wetlands may be filled following either prolonged local rain or when the watercourses are in flood.

Many wetlands on the MRF between Wagga Wagga and Hay have been subject to degradation as a result of land and water management practices. In the MRF, few wetlands have been drained relative to the USE. However, large-scale water storages for irrigation have caused most wetlands on the floodplain to be droughted while those closely linked with the river have become too wet. Wetlands in the MRF have also been degraded by logging, grazing and to a lesser extent, irrigation drainage management practices.

Current land and water management practices are largely motivated by the private values generated from irrigation, grazing and timber production. However, unlike the USE region where the private values are confined to wetland owners, private values in the MRF are divided between wetland owners (benefits resulting from grazing, logging and some irrigation) and irrigators downstream. The social values of wetlands have fallen over time due to reduced bird and fish breeding and deteriorating water quality and wetland health. Wetland management and the timing of water harvesting and release could be changed to increase the area of healthy wetlands in the region thus changing the mix of private and social values thus generated.

The biophysical characteristics of the MRF are broadly similar across the region. Upstream of Wagga Wagga the Murrumbidgee River floodplain is relatively narrow and confined. The floodplain becomes more extensive near Wagga Wagga thus allowing for much larger areas of wetlands. Downstream of Hay the characteristics of the floodplain change again with large shallow lignum depressions and floodplain lakes becoming more common. Despite the biophysical similarities across the region, the nature of farming enterprises on the floodplain changes and becomes more extensive or dependent on irrigation as rainfall decreases from Wagga Wagga to Hay. The direct impacts of farming systems on wetlands tend to remain grazing dominant resulting in similar farm management oriented threats to wetlands across the region.

4.2.2 MRF Resource Base

The MRF resource base is defined in terms of the land, water, flora and fauna resources in the region. Socio-economic and infrastructure resources of importance to the biophysical model are also identified in this section. The definitions in this section are based on a variety of sources including a survey of wetland owners undertaken in autumn 1999 (Whitten and Bennett 1999), a survey of wetlands in the region (Thornton and Briggs 1994)17 and 'State of the Rivers' reports for the Murrumbidgee (Buchan 1995a, b). The scope and nature of the resource base provides the context for the potential resource reallocations discussed in Section 4.2.3. The current resource base is summarised in Table 4.3.

MRF land resources
The MRF encompasses 1747 km^2 between Wagga Wagga and Hay Weir (Thornton 1994). The 486 km^2 of wetlands located on the floodplain are divided between freehold and crown lands (357 km^2 and 129 km^2 respectively). Floodplain soils are highly fertile due to the historic nutrient deposition. Irrigation development on the floodplain has increased in recent times despite the risk of flood to irrigated crops.

Table 4.3 MRF current resource base

Descriptive attributes	Unit	Current base
Grazing productivity (wetlands and buffer areas)	dse	55,000
Timber – saw logs	m³	20,600
Timber – residue	m³	41,200
Timber – firewood	m³	2,000
Area currently fenced	km²	175
Recreation trips	No.	500,000
Wetlands that are too wet	km²	15
Droughted wetlands	km²	469
Unknown hydrology	km²	2
Recreation trips	No.	250,000

MRF water resources

Rainfall in the region is winter/spring dominant and decreases from Wagga Wagga to Hay. Wetlands in the region may be filled following prolonged local rain or by over-bank flows when the Murrumbidgee River is in flood. Historically, small to medium floods in the Murrumbidgee River occurred in late winter/spring in most years due to a combination of seasonal rainfall and snowmelt (MCMC 1998). Once in ten to twelve years a major flood would cover the entire floodplain. Flows in the Murrumbidgee River are highly variable: flows at Wagga Wagga range from four to 637 per cent of median annual flows and at Balranald from 29 to 359 per cent (Department of Land and Water Conservation NSW (DLWC) 1996).

Irrigation, flood mitigation and hydro-electricity developments have substantially altered the flood pattern on the MRF. The major storages are Burrinjuck and Blowering Dams (completed in 1913 and 1968 respectively). The Snowy Mountains hydroelectricity scheme has also diverted 550 Gl from the upper Snowy River into the system. Close (1990) indicates storages affect flows in three main ways:

1. redistribution of flows within the year;
2. reduction in floods and increase in drought flows; and
3. by redistributing flows they facilitate larger total diversions from rivers.

When dams are used to mitigate floods the flood peak is delayed and the flood duration shortened (Close 1990). 'The impact of the dams on the flow regime is most marked in the mid-catchment of the Murrumbidgee where the degree of stream flow variations has been substantially reduced' compared to natural flow conditions (DLWC 1996 p. 12). Minor to moderate floods (one in a half to three years) that previously filled wetlands on the Murrumbidgee flood plain in the study area are now diverted or mitigated by Burrinjuck and Blowering dams (Buchan 1995a). Large floods (one in five or more years) are not mitigated to the same extent as small floods. The impact on the Murrumbidgee River at Wagga Wagga is shown in Figures 4.5 and 4.6.18 These figures show that the number of wetland filling flood events per year has fallen, with the reduction concentrated in May and the winter months. The seasonality of flows in these reaches has also been changed significantly. Within the region summer flows have increased and winter/spring flows have decreased. Irrigation weirs (such as Yanco and Hay Weirs) raise the water level and permanently flood some wetlands immediately upstream.

On average 2 506 Gl of water is diverted from the Murrumbidgee River per year for irrigation, town water and other purposes (Buchan 1995a; Murray-Darling Basin Ministerial Council 1995). The extent of the extraction of water for irrigation in the mid and lower Murrumbidgee is shown in Figure 4.7.

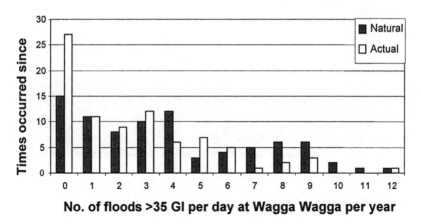

No. of floods >35 Gl per day at Wagga Wagga per year

Notes   A flow of 35 Gl per day at Wagga Wagga is considered sufficient to fill approximately one-third of floodplain wetlands.

Source   Unpublished DLWC preliminary flow modeling data

Figure 4.5   Comparison of natural and actual flows at Wagga Wagga 1913–1996

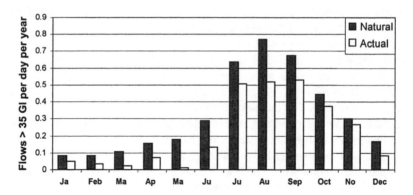

Notes   A flow of 35 Gl per day at Wagga Wagga is considered sufficient to fill approximately
          one-third of floodplain wetlands.

Source Unpublished DLWC preliminary flow modeling data.

Figure 4.6 Seasonal comparison of flows >35 Gl per day at Wagga Wagga

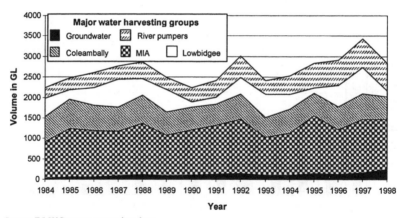

Source DLWC water extraction data.

*Figure 4.7 Extraction of surface and groundwater in the mid and lower
          Murrumbidgee catchment*

In summary, use of water from the Murrumbidgee for irrigation has had
three important impacts on wetland areas in the study area:

1. irrigation dams have reduced or removed minor to moderate floods
   (which historically occurred twice a year to once in three years), reducing
   the frequency of inundation in some wetlands (approximately 469 km²);

2. high flows and construction of weirs for irrigation has led to some wetland areas within the Murrumbidgee River and the MIA becoming more permanent (approximately 15 km^2); and

3. the seasonal wetting and drying of some wetlands has been altered significantly.

MRF flora resources

Wetland vegetation varies according to the frequency and duration of inundation. Across the study area wetland inundation duration varies from less than one month to near permanent and inundation frequency from annual to rare. Typical wetland vegetation in the MRF includes river red gum wetlands, shallow open water and deep billabong or anabranch wetlands. Black box wetlands, Lignum/Nitre goosefoot wetlands and tall reeds/rush swamps are also found in the MRF but are much less common.

Flooding of areas currently or previously forested with river red gums remains too regular for agricultural options to extend beyond grazing or forestry in most parts of the study area. The fertile riverine floodplain within the MRF provides a valuable source of fodder for grazing enterprises but is a major threat to wetland ecosystems and values (Buchan 1995b). Degradation of these wetlands due to grazing follows three related forms:

1. direct impacts of grazing animals on wetlands via consumption of wetland vegetation and trampling leading to disturbance of sediment and resulting higher turbidity, higher water temperature and reduced shelter among other impacts (Robertson 1997);

2. altered hydrology of some wetland areas through works to induce more rapid drainage or flood prevention (for example by constructing a levee or drains). Other wetlands have been modified to hold water over a longer period to supply stock or irrigation water (for example by constructing a dam) (see for example Thornton and Briggs 1994); and

3. many wetlands in the MRF are either forested or fringed by forest. In the past many trees were killed to facilitate increased fodder production from grazing (Buxton 1967).

The ongoing use of wetlands in the region for grazing and timber production has reduced or removed the shrub understorey in many red gum forests and led to the replacement of perennial and annua native species with annual introduced pasture and weed species.

River red gum forestry remains an important activity in MRF wetlands and many wetlands have been selectively logged or cleared completely. A significant proportion of the remaining river red gum forests are publicly owned and managed for the multiple objectives of timber production, grazing production, recreation, and in a few cases, nature conservation. These uses have also reduced the coarse woody debris remaining on the wetland floor that provide habitat for a variety of fauna species.19

MRF fauna resources

The fertile nature of the MRF, along with the presence of water in an otherwise dry landscape, provides habitat for a wide range of terrestrial and aquatic species. Seven threatened waterbird species have been recorded in the MRF and over twenty waterbird species have been recorded breeding (Maher 1988; Grose and Holics 1994; Briggs, Thornton and Lawler 1997; Grose and Makewita 1997). Wetlands in the region are also important habitat for woodland bird species and provide habitat for threatened species such as the bush thick-knee and superb parrot (Grose and Holics 1994; Grose and Makewita 1997). Wetlands between Narranderra and Carrathool within the MRF are listed in the 'Directory of important wetlands in Australia', in part for their value as water bird habitat (Environment Australia 2001).

Eighteen native fish, two shrimp, two crayfish and three mussel species have been identified in the MRF. Eleven species are regarded as rare, restricted or threatened in the MRF. Four feral fish species are found in the MRF of which common carp are now the predominant species (Harris 1995). Many fish species require major flooding to facilitate breeding. In addition several species undertake major migrations prior to spawning (Cadwallader and Lawrence 1990). Most native fish spawn in spring/summer – when flows are now reduced but flooding historically occurred in the Murrumbidgee. Cadwallader and Lawrence (1990) and Kingsford (2000) indicate the main management changes affecting fish are: reduced flows; altered seasonality of flows; reduced frequency of flood flows; altered river levels; increased rate of fall of river levels; thermal pollution; and barriers to migration. Fewer minor and moderate floods reduce fish spawning opportunities. Weirs and dams alter river flows, heights and water temperature in addition to breaking up migratory pathways. Irrigation management alters seasonal flows and river levels.

Eighteen native mammal species, 13 amphibian and 26 reptile species have been observed in the MRF. A number of mammal species are listed as vulnerable or rare at the national level but there is inadequate knowledge of amphibians and reptiles for a comprehensive comparable listing. Some of these species are associated with wetlands (for example eastern brown snake, eastern tiger snake, red-bellied black snake, platypus and water rat) while others shelter in remnant vegetation away from water (Grose and Holics 1994). A number of feral species have also been observed in the MRF including rabbits, foxes, cats, goats, pigs, rats and mice. A five-year study by

Bennison and Suter (1990) found 439 different macro-invertebrate taxa in the Murray River. A similar number of taxa would be expected in the Murrumbidgee.

Historically, MRF grazing industries have been based on wool production. A shift towards cattle grazing across much of the region has occurred in recent times due to low wool prices but sheep grazing has generally remained dominant (MCMC 1998).

MRF socio-economic, cultural and infrastructure resources
The study area contains three main towns (total population 22 500), while two larger towns lie just outside the study area. Approximately 70 farmers own wetlands on the floodplain and 2500 farmers irrigate from the Murrumbidgee River. Major highways cross the region, facilitating rapid transport of irrigated horticultural produce to domestic markets in Melbourne and Sydney and internationally.

The wetlands in the region are important social and cultural resources. Over a quarter of a million day visits to the Murrumbidgee River (including associated wetlands) are undertaken in the region each year (Forestry Commission of NSW 1986). Overnight wetlands based tourism in the region is relatively limited due to the large distance from potential target markets and wetland product consistency (because wetlands are ephemeral and are only at their best at unpredictable times). Significant aboriginal cultural values remain in many wetland areas where canoe trees, ceremonial trees, camp sites and other artifacts remain. Duck hunting is banned in NSW.

4.2.3 MRF Resource Allocation Scenario Development

As with USE wetlands in Section 4.1.3, the biophysical impacts of alternative management strategies (including the current allocation) must be identified and quantified in order to facilitate estimation and comparison of relative economic values. A scenario based approach to defining alternative management strategies and consequent outcomes is taken because the relationships underlying the biophysical modelling are not sufficiently well understood to facilitate the estimation of a continuous relationship.

The biophysical model must cover a sufficient time period to allow the impacts of resource reallocation to be assessed. However, some impacts may not be complete for over 100 years (in the case of river red gums forming nesting hollows). Furthermore, the continual ecological succession in flood-pulse wetland systems makes it difficult to select an appropriate point to measure the biophysical impacts. Most impacts of changing resource allocations will be evident in thirty years time and continue for the foreseeable future, hence outcomes are forecast for thirty years.

MRF biophysical outcomes from continuing current management (BAU)

The major reallocation of water from wetlands to irrigated agriculture in the MRF over the last 100 years has directly and indirectly degraded much of the wetland resources in the MRF. Irrigation dams have reduced the number and duration of flood-pulses in MRF wetlands. These impacts have been exacerbated by roads, levees and other floodplain structures.

The change to hydrology has led to many wetlands being linked to each other and the river much less regularly while a small proportion are now almost permanently linked. The hydrologically impaired wetlands mostly remain present in the region but are subject to continuing pressures and threats including pest and weed invasion, domestic livestock grazing and timber harvesting that pose barriers to natural ecological succession. The reduced number of floodplain linkages has caused a decline in native aquatic species and favoured some feral species (such as carp) thus increasing competition for native species and further reducing populations. Continuation of current management is likely to lead to further reductions in native fish populations.

Other species, such as water and woodland birds, are reliant on the maintenance of habitat in and around wetlands in combination with the flood-pulse. Continued degradation of wetland habitat through grazing and timber harvesting will further reduce the population of woodland birds within the region. While the total population of water birds is determined by events outside the catchment, the number of breeding events and the population of any one species present in the region at any one time is also dependent on local habitat maintenance and flood pulses.20

Wetland degradation may favour weeds and production of nuisance insects. Socio-economic interactions with wetlands are also likely to be adversely affected by a decline in the visual appearance of the wetlands and their amenity as recreation sites. There are not anticipated to be any significant impacts to cultural artefacts in the short to medium term but continued degradation will remove or reduce their integrity over the longer term. The BAU biophysical impacts are summarised in Table 4.4.

Several biophysical impacts could not be predicted due to knowledge, cost or time constraints. The impacts of these values on the bio-economic model are not anticipated to be significant but can be taken into account via threshold value analysis of the model results. In the MRF the factors not quantified were carbon sequestration (insufficient knowledge), benefits to grazing from flooding (insufficient knowledge) and the cost to farmers and the Gundagai community of additional floods (cost and time constraints).

Potential resource reallocation in the MRF

A number of threats and pressures imposed on MRF wetlands by the current management framework can be addressed via resource reallocations based on the application of conservation reserve design and planning and restoration ecology principles. These reallocations are designed to:

- facilitate a more natural flood-pulse and reduce the impacts of dams on wetlands;
- restore interaction between floodplain wetlands and the Murrumbidgee River;
- alleviate pressures on native vegetation caused by grazing, timber harvesting, weed competition, and enhance natural succession towards the desired state and output mix;
- alleviate pressures on native fauna from feral animals and competition by domestic livestock; and
- facilitate increased resilience to natural shocks such as disease and fire.

Four alternative resource allocations were developed from these goals:

1. improved hydrological management of water (termed 'water management');
2. improved grazing management practices in wetlands and buffer areas (termed 'grazing management');
3. improved management of timber harvesting practices in wetlands (termed 'timber management'); and
4. combining the three different options into a single strategy creates a fourth option (termed 'combined strategies');

The first three options are considered separately and the fourth is an additive combination of the individual resource reallocations as shown in Figure 4.8. The outcomes of the 'combined strategies' option are not a simple summation of the components because of synergistic responses to resource allocations.

Business as usual	Water management	Grazing management	Timber management	Combined strategies
				Timber management
				Grazing management
	Hydrological management	Grazing management	Timber management	Hydrological management
BAU	BAU	BAU	BAU	BAU

Figure 4.8 Structure of MRF modelling strategies

The four potential wetland management options could be achieved via a combination of reallocating resources that were historically combined in wetlands and the input of additional resources. Specific resource allocations that must be quantified are:

- changes in the intensity of landuse for grazing and/or timber production;
- shifts in water use from irrigation to flooding wetlands;
- capital works required to achieve changes in landuse (such as fencing);
- capital works required to re-institute the natural flood-pulse (such as construction/removal of earthworks);
- capital works required to facilitate ecological restoration or part thereof once land and water resources are combined (such as revegetation works and adding snags to wetlands and rivers); and
- upfront and ongoing pest and weed control in wetlands.

4.2.4 MRF Resource Reallocation Descriptions

The potential resource reallocation scenarios defined for the MRF are described in more detail in this section. These reallocations are summarised in Table 4.4 together with the anticipated ecological outcomes.

Water management
The 'water management' strategy diverts 50 Gl of water from irrigation in five out of six years in order to create a single artificial flood in these years between May and November as depicted in Figure 4.9.21 The flood would fill wetlands across approximately one third of the floodplain (or 258 km² of wetlands) significantly improving wetland connectivity and health. In order to maximise the impacts of the flood, approximately five km² of deep wetlands that are currently 'too wet' are rehabilitated. Despite the relatively small area rehabilitated it is anticipated that this type of wetland has a disproportionate impact on river-floodplain interactions and on conservation of native fish species in particular. Furthermore, five km² of rehabilitated deep wetlands equates to approximately twelve per cent of all deep wetlands in the MRF. The reallocation of resources from irrigated agriculture production to wetland protection will require allocation of a number of infrastructure resources. Specifically, 'water management' will require:

- engineering works to facilitate natural wetting and drying in rehabilitated deep wetlands;
- replacement of the water storage attributes of some wetlands; and
- ongoing management and maintenance to reduce the threats posed by weed and pest infestation.

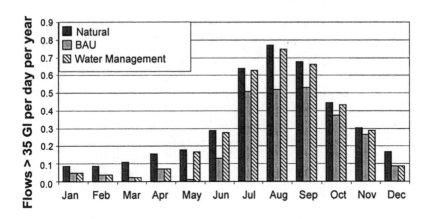

Figure 4.9 Historical, BAU and potential minor flood seasonality on the MRF

Table 4.4 MRF BAU and alternative resource allocation biophysical outcomes

Descriptive attributes	Unit	BAU	Water management	Grazing management	Timber management	Combined strategies
Aggregate MRF totals						
Water reallocated	Gl	0	50	0	0	50
Grazing productivity	'000 dse	55	55	40	55	40
Timber – saw logs	m^3	20,600	20,600	20,600	11,600	11,600
Timber – residue	m^3	41,200	41,200	41,200	23,100	23,100
Timber – firewood	m^3	2,000	2,000	2,000	1,600	1,600
Recreation trips	No.	500,000	503,000	507,500	500,000	512,500
Healthy wetlands	km^2	23	50	90	23	135
Native bird population	% pre 1800 population	40	60	60	50	70
Native fish population	% pre 1800 population	20	30	25	25	40

Table 4.4 Continued

Descriptive attributes	Unit	BAU	Water management	Grazing management	Timber management	Combined strategies
Marginal change from BAU						
Water reallocated	Gl	n.a.	50	0	0	50
Grazing productivity	'000 dse	n.a.	0	-15	0	-15
Timber – saw logs	m^3	n.a.	0	0	-9,000	-9,000
Timber – residue	m^3	n.a.	0	0	-18,100	-18,100
Timber – firewood	m^3	n.a.	0	0	-400	-400
Recreation trips	No.	n.a.	3,000	7,500	0	12,500
Healthy wetlands	km^2	n.a.	27	67	0	112
Native bird population	% change	n.a.	33	20	20	75
Native fish population	% change	n.a.	50	25	25	100
Fencing required	km	n.a.	0	2,406	0	2,406
Alternate stock water	km^2	n.a.	0	120	0	120
Rehabilitation works	km^2	n.a.	6	5	0	11
Ongoing management	km^2	n.a.	27	67	0	112

Grazing management
The 'grazing management' strategy involves reducing the impact of grazing on wetlands. Under the strategy, grazing is eliminated from approximately 106 km^2 of wetlands and the grazing management of a further 83 km^2 is altered to a rotational program that would improve conservation outcomes. Reallocation of land from grazing to conservation also includes reallocation of buffer strips.

A significant allocation of infrastructure resources is also required for this strategy, specifically: 22

- construction of fences to manage livestock in wetlands;
- revegetation works in five per cent of wetlands;
- alternative stock water supplies to substitute for wetlands or river frontage; and
- pest and weed control in rehabilitated wetlands on an ongoing basis.

Timber management
The 'timber management' strategy involves reallocating timber from consumptive harvest uses to providing conservation habitat as live trees or coarse woody debris and snags. Under the 'timber management' strategy timber harvesting is eliminated from 82 km^2 of wetlands, firewood collection from six km^2 and management of approximately 20 km^2 of remaining forests is changed from unsustainable to more sustainable timber production. No additional infrastructure or resources are anticipated to facilitate adoption of the 'timber management' strategy.

Combined strategies
'Combined strategies' is the additive combination of the resource reallocations proposed above. Hence, it involves reallocation of water, grazing and timber resources in the region as defined for the three previous strategies along with the additional fencing and other capital inputs.

4.2.5 MRF Resource Reallocation Biophysical Outcomes

The reallocation of resources is intended to achieve an increase in the biophysical outputs from wetlands relative to BAU. The overall impact is a reduction of consumptive values generated by grazing, timber yields and water harvested under alternative strategies compared to BAU. Non-consumptive values such as those provided by native wetland and woodland birds, native fish and aesthetically appealing wetlands are also increased. The socio-economic interactions with wetlands are also likely to be increased because wetlands will be relatively more attractive visually and as recreation sites. A summary of the biophysical modelling outcomes for the BAU and alternative resource management options developed for the MRF is presented in Table 4.5. For example, the resource reallocation under the 'water management' option results in 50 km^2 of healthy wetlands, which is 27 km^2 more than the BAU area but requires reallocation of 50 Gl of water, rehabilitation works on six km^2 and ongoing management of 27 km^2 of wetlands.

4.3   CONCLUSION

Biophysical definitions of the current resource allocation (BAU) and alternative resource allocations have been specified in this chapter. These quantitative biophysical definitions serve as a basis for the estimates of values that are derived in the next three chapters using the methodologies described in Chapter 3. For the purpose of value estimation these values can be divided into three groups: priced and unpriced direct use values and ecological function values and non-use values. In the next three chapters the focus is on the estimation of these values based on the physical quantification of alternative resource allocations and outcomes in Tables 4.2 and 4.4. Estimation of these values is undertaken using the methodologies described in Chapter 3. These valuations are drawn together in Chapter 8 to test Hypotheses One.

NOTES

1. The initial conditions are defined as at 1998.
2. Most publicly owned land is managed for conservation as nature reserves and national parks. Other publicly owned land comprises road corridors and undesignated crown lands.
3. The salt arises from the marine heritage of the region and that contained in rainfall containing salt crystals blown inland from the ocean by the prevailing winds (Blackburn 1983). Soil salinity is increasing as a result of heightened recharge from reduced deep-rooted perennial vegetation cover on both interdunal flats and adjacent ranges reducing transpiration (MacKenzie and Stadter 1992).
4. Wetlands and Wildlife is a not for profit organisation that owns and manages a large area of wetlands in the USE region.
5. The 'Wetlands Waterlink' comprises part of the dryland salinity and flood management scheme that is directed towards improving wetland health in the region.
6. Personal communications with Roger Ebsary (Primary Industries and Resources South Australia), Brenton Grear and Tim Croft (Department of Environment, Heritage and Aboriginal Affairs, South Australia) and Janice White (Wetlands and Wildlife).
7. Vegetation classes are intact systems of native vegetation comprising the full range of grasses, herbs, shrubs and trees that make up the natural vegetation structure.

8. Personal communication Keith Frost (Wetlands and Wildlife).
9. Based on a survey reported in Whitten and Bennett (2000c) and personal communications with Roger Ebsary (Primary Industries and Resources South Australia) and Brenton Grear (Department of Environment, Heritage and Aboriginal Affairs, South Australia).
10. The relationships between resource allocations and the biophysical outcomes are not sufficiently well understood, in part because there are likely to be discontinuities in the relationship. For example, the number of species lost may depend on the relative habitat specificity of different threatened species, or threshold habitat sizes may generate significant increases in ecosystem resilience and thus species protection.
11. Similar concepts are applied to native vegetation protection in the region in order to increase production of wetland protection outputs dependent on contributions from remnant vegetation.
12. Five per cent of wetlands remain degraded due to edge effects caused by lack of an adequate remnant vegetation buffer strip. Appropriate hydrology cannot be restored to five per cent that lie outside of the dryland salinity and flood management scheme.
13. Extrapolated from Wetlands Waterlink wetland rehabilitation data provided by Brenton Grear (Department of Heritage, Environment and Aboriginal Affairs, South Australia).
14. Extrapolated from Wetlands Waterlink wetland rehabilitation data provided by Brenton Grear (Department of Heritage, Environment and Aboriginal Affairs, South Australia) and personal communications Matt Giraudo (USE Wetlands Extension Officer, Primary Industries and Resources South Australia).
15. Extrapolated from Wetlands Waterlink wetland rehabilitation data provided by Brenton Grear (Department of Heritage, Environment and Aboriginal Affairs, South Australia) and personal communications Matt Giraudo (USE Wetlands Extension Officer, Primary Industries and Resources South Australia).
16. The specific boundary of the MRF case study is defined as the height of the 1974 flood and is not shown in Figure 4.4, however the general location is identified.
17. Thornton and Briggs (1994) data is adjusted for an assumed 15 km^2 of small wetlands that were not included in their survey specifications.
18. A flow of 35 Gl per day at Wagga Wagga is considered a minor flood and will cover approximately one third of the floodplain.
19. Coarse woody debris are fallen timber which is slowly decomposing on the floodplain. Large coarse woody debris exceed ten centimetres in diameter and one metre in length. A threshold value of approximately 50 tonnes of coarse woody debris per hectare is required for many mammal species (MacNally 1998, 1999). The current average coarse woody debris load is approximately 20 tonnes per hectare.
20. Personal communication Dr. Richard Kingsford (NSW National Parks and Wildlife Service)
21. Total water required to create an artificial flood is 70 Gl but 20 Gl are assumed to be in-stream flows at the time of the flood. Hence, only an additional 50Gl is required to create the flood.
22. Sources: Whitten and Bennett (1999) and personal communications with Leigh Meyers (NSW State Forests Narranderra), Greening Australia Murray and Murrumbidgee region, Mark Rowe (Farmer, Narimba Station), John Irwin (NSW Agriculture District Livestock Officer), Ted O'Kane ('Bidgee Banks' Project Officer) and Dr Amy Jansen (Charles Sturt University).

5. The Private Values of Wetlands

The concept of total economic value described in Chapter 3 is used to separate the economically relevant biophysical impacts of the management options described in Chapter 4 between use and non-use values. Use values can be subdivided into direct use values and ecological function values. Direct use values can be further divided between marketed and non-marketed benefits. In this chapter changes to marketed values from changing wetland management are estimated from data generated in existing markets. Some other direct use values are estimated using market data for equivalent products.

The estimation of the private and social values of wetlands is dependent on completing the process of identifying the economically relevant biophysical impacts that was commenced in Chapter 4. Hence, the first section of this chapter involves the definition of the economically relevant biophysical impacts before the monetary valuation and discounting steps in the economic model are undertaken. The remainder of this chapter is then devoted to the estimation of changes to marketed values for the USE and MRF case study areas respectively. These marketed values can be divided into three broad groups. First, changes to wetland management may reduce or discontinue some existing valued wetland uses such as timber harvesting or grazing. Discontinuing wetland uses may also change the existing costs of producing the existing outputs, for example costs associated with pasture management. Second, changing wetland management may introduce a different set of wetland management costs such as revegetation and weed control. Finally, changing wetland management may generate some new or expanded wetland uses that can be sold thus increasing the private values of wetlands. For example, changing wetland management may enhance tourism in a region.

In estimating these values a question arises as to the geographic extent of the relevant surplus. Specifically, a decision must be made about whether the impact of changing wetland management is limited to wetland owners or extends to a broader population. Existing market prices are the appropriate basis for valuation where individual and aggregate changes are not sufficiently large to impact on markets and thus on prices or consumers' surpluses. This is the case for the estimates presented in this chapter. A similar argument applies to the cost of additional resources to facilitate changes to wetland management. That is, where the additional quantities of resources required do not impact on market prices, then market prices can be used as the basis for resource valuation in alternative uses. Likewise, where costs are avoided by discontinuing current wetland uses, these resources are valued at the next highest use value.

Throughout this and the ensuing chapters the estimates of economic value are subject to a number of assumptions and considerable uncertainty. The potential impacts of relaxing these assumptions or the impacts of uncertainty are assessed in Chapter 8 via extensive sensitivity analysis.

5.1   ECONOMICALLY RELEVANT PROJECT IMPACTS

The biophysical changes identified and modelled in Chapter 4 must affect the well being of one or more individuals if they are to generate an economic impact. This step in the bio-economic modelling process is explicitly anthropocentric as only the biophysical changes that impact on humans are considered. Several values were not physically quantified in Chapter 4 because either no impacted population existed or the likely degree of biophysical change would not impact on values. For example, the population impacted by changes to flood mitigation benefits from wetlands in the USE region is extremely small. Likewise, the water quality impacts as a result of wetland rehabilitation in the USE and MRF may be measurable but are unlikely to impact on the values of the impacted population because the change is insufficient to impact water uses.

The identity of the population affected and the nature of the impact of the biophysical changes modelled in Chapter 4 are shown in Table 5.1. For example, a change to the amount of timber harvested from wetlands will impact on the marketed values of wetland owners in the MRF, but is judged to be insignificant in the USE. Some biophysical changes will generate economically relevant impacts to more than one group of individuals. For example, tourism impacts generate a producers' surplus to tourism operators and a consumers' surplus to tourists.

Selection of discount rate
Changing wetland management causes a series of costs and benefits now and into the future that need to be discounted to account for the time preferences of individuals. The discount rate applied to calculate the net present value

(NPV) of the marketed impacts of wetland resource allocations is seven per cent. This rate was chosen to be comparable to the real interest rate on capital investment on private agricultural lands that wetland owners face when making decisions about alternative investment strategies. This rate is varied as part of the sensitivity analysis described in Chapter 8.

5.2 MARKETED IMPACTS OF DISCONTINUED WETLAND USES

The marketed impacts of discontinued or reduced wetland uses were shown in Table 5.1. The value of these impacts is estimated in this section.

5.2.1 USE Marketed Impacts of Discontinued Wetland Uses

Adopting the wetland management options shown in Table 4.2 would lead to several impacts on USE agricultural productivity defined by:

- the total area of agricultural pastures;
- the mix of agricultural pasture types; and
- the grazing management of wetlands and remnants.

These changes to agricultural management lead to the following costs and benefits that must be estimated:

1. a reduction to producers' surpluses due to reduced agricultural production from grazing in wetlands and remnants. The reduction to producers' surplus is measured via the adjusted gross margin to producers from discontinuing current wetland grazing uses; and
2. avoided pasture establishment and maintenance costs due to a conversion of some pastures to wetlands. Agricultural gross margins are net of marginal costs specific to that enterprise. Hence, non-enterprise specific costs (such as the cost of improving pastures) avoided must also be estimated for completeness.

Table 5.1 Economic values generated by USE and MRF wetlands

Biophysical change	Type of value	Population[a]	
		USE	MRF
Future investments in pasture	marketed	wetland owners	insignificant
Grazing productivity	marketed	wetland owners	wetland owners
Timber – saw logs	marketed	insignificant	wetland owners
Timber – residue	marketed	insignificant	wetland owners
Timber – firewood	marketed	insignificant	wetland owners
Healthy wetland	non-marketed (non-use)	community	community
Degraded wetland	non-marketed (non-use)	community	community
Healthy remnants	non-marketed (non-use)	community	not applicable
Degraded remnants	non-marketed (non-use)	community	not applicable
Waterbirds hunted	marketed / non-marketed (non-use & use)	duck hunters/ community/ wetland owners	not applicable
Water reallocated	Marketed	insignificant	irrigators
Hydrological management works	Marketed	wetland owners	wetland owners
Revegetation management works	Marketed	wetland owners	wetland owners
Fencing required	Marketed	wetland owners	wetland owners
Alternate stock water	Marketed	wetland owners	wetland owners

Table 5.1 Continued

Biophysical change	Type of value	Population[a]	
		USE	MRF
Ongoing management – wetlands	Marketed	wetland owners	wetland owners
Ongoing management – remnant vegetation	Marketed	wetland owners	not applicable
Hunting trips	marketed / non-marketed (non-use & use)	duck hunters/ community/ wetland owners	not applicable
Total tourist/recreation numbers	non-marketed (use) / marketed	tourists / tourism operators	recreation users
Improved conservation status of species	non-marketed (non-use)	community	not applicable
Native bird population	non-marketed (non-use)	not applicable[b]	community
Native fish population	non-marketed (non-use and use)	insignificant	community

Notes a Community includes wetland owners. In some cases the values generated to some members of the population may be positive and negative to other members. For example, duck hunting may generate negative values for many in the community while it will generate positive values to duck hunters.

  b Improved conservation status of species in the USE is defined to include impacts on native bird populations in the region.

123

Net cost of reduced agricultural production

Grazing productivity is reduced where improved or unimproved pasture is converted to wetlands or native vegetation. Similarly, grazing productivity is reduced in rehabilitated wetland and remnant vegetation areas because these areas are assumed not to be grazed except for short periods during drought conditions.

To estimate the costs of lost productivity to producers' surpluses the following assumptions are made:

1. the mix of sheep and cattle enterprises in the region will not change significantly over the next 30 years;
2. the proportion of improved pastures to total pasture will remain the same as modelled by Barber (1993) for the BAU scenario; and
3. the gross margin as at 1999 will be maintained for all enterprises over the next 30 years.[1]

Warren and Wurst's (1999) gross margin estimates for the region are adjusted by subtracting the cost of labour inputs to provide an estimate of producers' surpluses resulting from grazing enterprises. The adjustment for labour costs is made because gross margins are not a good indicator of producers' surpluses, but are a comparison of the alternative uses of a given set of farm resources (including labour, pastures and fixtures). Hence, the labour component of grazing enterprises would become available for alternative uses.[2] Costs of existing fixtures such as shearing sheds and fencing are treated as sunk costs as discussed in Chapter 3. Hence, they do not affect future producers' surpluses. The resulting estimates of per production unit and aggregate producers' surplus are reported in Table 5.2. The aggregate estimates assume that changes to management would be phased in over a ten-year period. For example, implementing the 'wetlands and remnants' strategy would cause an agricultural production loss of about 250 000 dse per year in ten years time or approximately $18.3 million (present value) in total.

Table 5.2 USE enterprise margins and changes to agricultural surplus

Enterprise	Gross margin / dse	Labour cost / dse	Producers' surplus / dse
Prime Lambs	$16.38	$2.17	$14.22
Merino Ewe flock	$10.24	$2.17	$8.07
Merino Wethers	$6.14	$2.17	$3.98
Cattle production	$11.78	$5.42	$6.36
Change to agricultural production	**Wetland retention**	**Pro-wetlands**	**Wetlands and remnants**
Productivity difference per year in 30 years (dse)	−16 000	−79 000	−257 000
Total present value production loss	−$1,166,000	−$5,672,000	−$18,332,000

A significant area of existing pastures is converted to wetlands or native vegetation, under the 'Pro-wetlands' and 'Wetlands and Remnants' strategy as indicated in Table 4.2. Future costs associated with managing improved pastures are avoided in these cases. Not all costs are avoided; some are diverted to improve other pasture areas while the remainder are saved. It is assumed that the proportion of improved pastures to total grazed area remains constant at the existing level of 61 per cent of pastures. Only pasture improvement costs that are saved are included within the economic model.

Barber (1993) provides estimates of the costs of establishing and maintaining improved pasture.[3] These avoided costs include the construction and maintenance of on-farm costs of 'neighbourhood' drains to connect farms to the regional dryland salinity and flood management scheme, and additional fencing related to intensive management of improved pasture.

The costs that would be avoided as a result of the changes in the physical area of pasture are reported in Table 5.3. Costs are estimated assuming that changes to management (and hence costs avoided) would be undertaken over a ten-year period and discounted to a present value. For example, the pro-wetlands strategy reduces the area of pasture by 126 km^2 comprising three types of improved pasture and an area of unimproved pasture. Farmers would save a NPV of $2.5m that would otherwise have been spent to establish and maintain the improved pasture.

Table 5.3 USE pasture costs saved compared to BAU

Pasture type	Wetland retention	Pro-wetlands	Wetlands and remnants
Salt tolerant grasses – category 5	$ 0	$1,327,000	$1,334,000
Salt tolerant grasses	$ 0	$548,000	$630,000
Two stage salt mix	$ 0	$587,000	$674,000
Two stage salt mix – category 2	$ 0	$0	$33,000
Non-saline pasture mix	$ 0	$0	$95,000
Lucerne	$ 0	$0	$219,000
Total	$ 0	$2,462,000	$4,963,000

Notes   Cost savings are incurred over a ten-year period and discounted to a present value.

5.2.2 MRF Marketed Impacts of Discontinued Wetland Uses

Adopting a wetland management option from those shown in Figure 4.8 would lead to changes to grazing and timber harvesting in wetlands that were quantified in Table 4.4. These changes to agricultural management would lead to the following costs and benefits that must be estimated:
1. a reduction to producers' surpluses due to reduced grazing in wetlands;
2. a reduction to producers' surpluses due to reduced timber harvesting in wetlands; and
3. the additional costs of providing alternative stock water supplies to facilitate continued grazing away from wetlands.

Cost of lost agricultural production to MRF wetland owners
Grazing in floodplain wetlands would be reduced if some wetland management options shown in Table 4.4 were adopted. To estimate the costs of lost production the following assumptions are made:

1. the mix of sheep and cattle enterprises in the region will not change significantly over the 30 year period; and
2. the gross margin as at 1999 will be maintained for all enterprises over the next 30 years.

Sensitivity analyses of these assumptions are reported in Chapter 8.

Agriculture NSW (2001) provides estimates of gross margins for the region that were adjusted for the cost of labour inputs (as was the case in the USE). The production changes (in dse) and the NPV cost estimates of these changes to MRF landowners are reported in Table 5.4. Cost estimates are calculated assuming that changes to management would be linearly undertaken over a ten-year period. For example, implementing the 'grazing management' strategy would cause an agricultural production loss of about 19 000 dse per year in ten years time or a total present value cost of $3.1 million.

Table 5.4   MRF changes to agricultural production producers' surplus

Change to production	Water management	Grazing management	Timber management	Combined strategies
Productivity difference / year in 30 years (dse)	0	−19,000	0	−19,000
Present value of production loss	$ 0	−$3,137,000	$ 0	−$3,137,000

Cost of lost timber production to MRF wetland owners
The wetland resource allocations shown in Table 4.4 would reduce the total quantity of timber harvested at any one point in time but may also reduce the period between harvests under some options. That is, changing wetland management may lead to more frequent but lower yield timber harvesting in some wetlands.

A brief summary of forestry practices is useful to understand the changes in yield and income to wetland owners. Timber harvesting in the MRF yields a mix of sawn timber (used for furniture and construction) and residue (used as woodchips or dried for use as firewood). The total quantity of timber and residue harvested depends (among other factors) on the age of the forest and the harvesting method. Clear felling generates the maximum absolute yield at 80-year intervals, while a 'sustainable' harvesting regime yields less than half as much but at 25-year intervals.[4] Firewood harvesting of fallen timber is generally conducted at 10-year intervals.

The changes in the physical quantities of timber that would be produced under each option were reported in Table 4.4 and the estimated cost of these changes is shown in Table 5.5. Costs are estimated assuming that changes to management would be linearly adopted over a ten-year period. For example, implementing the 'timber management' strategy would cause a sawn timber loss of about 208,000m^3 or approximately \$3.6 million in present values.

Table 5.5 MRF timber producers' surplus changes

Cost to wetland owners (NPV)	Water management	Grazing management	Timber management	Combined strategies
Sawn timber	\$ 0	\$ 0	\$3,568,000	\$3,568,000
Residue	\$ 0	\$ 0	\$1,071,000	\$1,071,000
Firewood	\$ 0	\$ 0	\$39,000	\$39,000
Total	\$ 0	\$ 0	−\$4,678,000	−\$4,678,000

Cost of alternative stock watering points in the MRF

Where stock are excluded from wetlands they may also be excluded from their current water supply, particularly when exclusion from wetlands includes exclusion from access to the Murrumbidgee River and its tributaries and anabranches.[5] Alternative water supplies would be required in these cases. The cost of alternative watering supplies will vary according to the additional infrastructure required (including pumps, pipes and tanks), the number of watering points to be installed and the distance from a water source. The Forest Creek Management Plan Committee (unpublished) proposed a large-scale watering scheme for a similar region that facilitates transfer of the costs to the MRF region. Estimates of the costs of alternative water supplies for each strategy are shown in Table 5.6.

Table 5.6 MRF NPV cost of alternative water supply compared to BAU

Description	Water management	Grazing management	Timber management	Combined strategies
Alternative water supply	0 km^2	120 km^2	0 km^2	120 km^2
Capital cost of water supply	\$ 0	\$192,000	\$ 0	\$192,000
Ongoing cost of water supply	\$ 0	\$7,000	\$ 0	\$7,000

Source Adapted from Forest Creek Management Plan Committee (unpublished). Costs are the NPV of costs over the next 30 years.

5.3 MARKETED WETLAND MANAGEMENT IMPACTS

The focus in this section is on the additional capital and labour resource inputs required to implement the wetland management options in the USE and MRF. These include the upfront costs of remedial earthworks, structures, revegetation and fencing along with the ongoing maintenance costs. These impacts also include the net costs of water reallocated to flood wetlands in the MRF.

5.3.1 USE Marketed Wetland Management Impacts

Adopting the wetland and remnant vegetation strategies modelled in Chapter 4 requires the following additional resources for which values must be estimated:

1. capital costs of changing water management in wetland areas;
2. the capital and labour costs of revegetating some wetland and remnant areas;
3. the capital and labour costs of fencing wetlands and remnants to facilitate changes to stock management; and
4. the ongoing labour and input costs of maintaining wetland and remnant vegetation areas.

In each case the demand for additional resources is assumed not to impact on resource prices. All estimates incorporate the assumption that changes to management would be undertaken over a ten-year period.

Where wetlands are to be recreated or rehabilitated, substantial capital costs may be involved in removing levees and ensuring appropriate flows of water through the wetland area. In the USE these costs can be estimated by extrapolating existing schemes such as the 'Wetlands Waterlink' component of the USEDSFMP. The per-unit capital costs of engineering works to manage water in existing and recreated wetlands are reported in the first two rows of Table 5.7 and the aggregate costs in Table 5.8. The engineering works to recreate wetlands are more complex in areas that have been drained and converted to pasture and thus impose approximately double the cost of works to rehabilitate existing wetlands. For example, the present value cost is $506,000 for the 126km^2 hectares that would be recreated over ten years under the 'pro-wetlands' strategy.

Table 5.7 USE marketed costs of changing management

Description	Basis	Cost / km²
Upfront capital costs		
Works in existing wetlands	once-off	$2,853
Wetland recreation	once-off	$5,843
Re-establish wetland or native vegetation	once-off	$56,320
Fencing existing wetlands	1 in 30 yrs	$7,000
Fencing recreated wetlands	1 in 30 yrs	$8,000
Fencing remnants and revegetation	1 in 30 yrs	$4,800
Labour costs		
Fencing remnants and revegetation	1 in 30 yrs	$3,984
Fencing existing wetlands	1 in 30 yrs	$5,810
Fencing recreated wetlands	1 in 30 yrs	$6,640
Wetland maintenance	annual	$1,275
Remnant vegetation maintenance	annual	$563
Ongoing materials costs		
Existing wetland maintenance	annual	$167
Recreated wetland maintenance	annual	$169
Remnant vegetation maintenance	annual	$1,035

Notes   The difference between the cost of maintaining existing and recreated wetlands is due to slightly more additional fencing being maintained around recreated wetlands.

Source   Brenton Grear (Department of Environment and Heritage SA) provided preliminary cost estimates of implementing the 'Wetlands Waterlink' component of the USE Dryland Salinity and Flood Management Scheme.

Some USE wetlands have been drained for pasture and may not contain viable wetland flora 'seed-banks' (see for example Brock and Casanova 1997 or 2000). Reallocating land to remnant vegetation may not regenerate without active revegetation. Many wetlands do retain viable seed-banks even many years after draining. Hence, it is assumed that only some recreated wetlands would require revegetation – specifically woodland and tea-tree wetlands.[6] All recreated areas of native vegetation are assumed to require revegetation. All degraded wetlands and remnants that would be rehabilitated are assumed to contain viable seed-banks.

The cost to revegetate wetlands and native vegetation areas under the 'Wetlands Waterlink' component of the regional dryland salinity and flood management were used as a proxy. These costs are reported in Table 5.7 and the aggregate costs in Table 5.8. For example, to revegetate the 171 km^2 of native vegetation over ten years under the 'wetlands and remnants' strategy would cost \$56,300 per km^2 for a present value total of \$6.8m.

Table 5.8 USE marketed costs of changing management compared to BAU

Cost description	Wetland retention	Pro-wetlands	Wetlands and remnants
Capital costs			
Works in existing wetlands	\$253,000	\$253,000	\$250,000
Wetland recreation	\$ 0	\$506,000	\$506,000
Re-establish wetland vegetation	\$ 0	\$3,864,000	\$3,864,000
Re-establish remnant vegetation	\$ 0	\$ 0	\$6,761,000
Fencing wetlands	\$621,000	\$1,331,000	\$1,486,000
Fencing remnants and revegetation	\$ 0	\$ 0	\$1,729,000
Labour Costs			
Fencing remnants and revegetation	\$ 0	\$ 0	\$1,435,000
Fencing wetlands	\$516,000	\$1,105,000	\$1,234,000
Wetland maintenance	\$1,427,000	\$2,855,000	\$2,968,000
Remnant vegetation maintenance	\$ 0	\$ 0	\$5,793,000
Maintenance Costs			
Fencing wetlands	\$15,000	\$31,000	\$35,000
Fencing remnants and revegetation	\$ 0	\$ 0	\$42,000
Wetland maintenance	\$172,000	\$345,000	\$358,000
Remnant vegetation maintenance	\$ 0	\$ 0	\$699,000
Total	\$3,004,000	\$10,290,000	\$27,159,000

Notes   Capital costs would be incurred over a ten-year period and maintenance costs over all years following construction.

Fencing remnants and wetlands facilitates changes to grazing management. Unit costs of fencing are drawn from fencing undertaken under the 'Wetlands Waterlink' project. Aggregate costs are shown in Table 5.8. For example, the present value costs of fencing 253 km^2 of wetlands over ten years under the 'pro-wetlands' strategy are \$1.3m for materials and \$1.1m for labour inputs.

Rehabilitated and recreated wetlands and native vegetation require ongoing action to control pests (such as rabbits) and weeds, manage fire risks and maintain additional fences. The costs of such activities are not well documented. As a proxy, the per hectare material and labour costs of management of conservation lands in the South East Region by SA National Parks and Wildlife Service are used for rehabilitated and recreated wetlands, while half this cost is used for rehabilitated and recreated native vegetation.[7] The per-hectare costs are reported in Table 5.7. For example, maintaining an existing wetland is projected to cost $167 per km^2 for materials and $1,275 per km^2 for labour per-year. Hence, the present value of the total costs of wetland maintenance for the 126 km^2 that would be rehabilitated over ten years under the 'wetlands retention' strategy is $1.6m.

5.3.2 MRF Marketed Wetland Management Impacts

Rehabilitating MRF wetlands imposes the same range of additional wetland management costs on wetland owners as in the USE. Additional costs would be imposed on irrigators by the reallocation of water from irrigated agriculture to flood wetlands on the MRF. A summary of the unit and aggregate costs is shown in Tables 5.9 and 5.10. Cost estimates assume that changes to management would be undertaken over a ten-year period and water acquisition over a five-year period.

Table 5.9 MRF marketed costs and benefits of wetland management

Description	Basis	Unit	Cost
Capital costs			
Water acquisition	one-off	ML	$408
Irrigation drainage removal	one-off	km^2	$677,122
Irrigation pumping removal	one-off	km^2	$108,919
Levees removal	one-off	km^2	$5,843
Revegetation	one-off	km^2	$56,320
Fencing wetlands	1 in 30 yrs	km	$1,125
Labour costs			
Fencing wetlands	1 in 30 yrs	km	$1,375
Other			
Ongoing costs of irrigation pumping removal	Annual	km^2	$3,622
Wetland maintenance	Annual	km^2	$2,000
Future water sales income	1/6 per year	ML	$34

Sources are provided in the text.

Table 5.10 MRF marketed NPV costs of changing wetland management

Cost description	Water management	Grazing management	Timber management	Combined strategies
Capital costs				
Water acquisition	$18,161,000	$ 0	$ 0	$18,161,000
Irrigation drainage removal	$209,000	$ 0	$ 0	$209,000
Irrigation pumping removal	$940,000	$ 0	$ 0	$940,000
Levees removal	$3,000	$ 0	$ 0	$3,000
Revegetation	$ 0	$209,000	$ 0	$209,000
Fencing existing wetlands	$ 0	$694,000	$ 0	$694,000
Labour costs				
Fencing existing wetlands	$ 0	$567,000	$ 0	$567,000
Other				
Ongoing costs of irrigation pumping removal	$88,000	$ 0	$ 0	$88,000
Wetland maintenance	$478,000	$1,187,000	$ 0	$1,985,000
Less future water sales income	$6,246,000	$ 0	$ 0	$6,246,000
Total	$13,633,000	$2,657,000	$ 0	$16,609,000

Notes   Management would be changed over a ten-year period, water acquired over a five-year period and ongoing costs incurred over the remainder of the thirty-year period commencing at the point of management change.

Water acquisition costs – MRF

Under the 'water management' and 'combined strategies' options, sufficient water will be required to facilitate an artificial flood as reported in Table 4.5. The quantity of water required under the 'water management' and 'combined strategies' is 50 GL, or approximately two per cent of current diversions for irrigation.[8] Current modelling indicates that allocations are approximately 92 per cent of licences in a median year and 88 per cent in a dry year.[9] Hence, water licences totalling 54.3 GL are required to access 50 GL of water. Diversion of this quantity of water will impact on future irrigation growth in the region but not on current irrigation levels, thus imposing an opportunity cost in the form of reduced growth of future irrigation opportunities rather than in reduced current output.[10] This is because the quantity of water acquired is less than the total savings of over 71 GL targeted under the MIA and Districts Community Land and Water Management Plan (MIA and Districts Community Land and Water Management Plan 1998). Kemp and Hafi (2001) also found water savings of up to 27 GL per year in the MIA would generate increased returns to irrigators. In addition, diversions to the MIA account for less than half of the total diversions from the Murrumbidgee River and further cost-effective water savings are likely from river pumpers and the Coleambally Irrigation Area. Hence, water diversions for an artificial flood are unlikely to reduce total production in the region and may induce regional benefits from the substantial cash injection if water licences were purchased from local irrigators.

An estimate of the present value of the future opportunity cost imposed on future irrigators is not readily available because the future surpluses generated by water inputs to future production are not known. Furthermore, the impacts of water reforms underway in NSW increase the uncertainty about future returns. Economic theory suggests that the expected future surpluses generated by water inputs are capitalised into the current price of water access licences in competitive markets. That is, the price of water access licences is an expression of the willingness to pay for the next best use of the water (if it is not used for the public good of an artificial flood). Hence, the cost of acquiring sufficient water licences to create an artificial flood is estimated as a proxy for the opportunity cost of lost production from diverting water savings from future irrigation to environmental uses.[11] The per-unit capital costs of acquiring water licences are reported in Table 5.9 and the aggregate cost in Table 5.10. For example, the approximate cost of acquiring licenses is $408 per ML.[12] The total present value cost is $18.2m for the 54.3 GL of water licences that would be purchased over five years under the 'water management' and 'combined strategies' options.

Wetland rehabilitation and management costs – MRF

Where wetlands are to be rehabilitated, capital costs may be involved in reducing irrigation drainage inflows, providing alternative irrigation supply systems, removing levees and undertaking revegetation works. Removing and recycling irrigation drainage water involves large-scale earthworks. As an example, the cost of the Murrumbidgee Wetland Working Group's project to rehabilitate Turkey Flat and several other wetlands on the MRF is approximately $677,100 per km^2.[13] Using these cost estimates, the cost of removing irrigation drainage from 0.3 km^2 under the 'water management' and 'combined strategies' options is calculated at $209,000.

The cost to relocate pumping from deep billabongs on the floodplain involves construction of pipes, buffer storage dams and pumping from the Murrumbidgee River. These costs are estimated at $108,900 per km^2. Additional ongoing costs of $3,622 per year for each square kilometre of wetlands rehabilitated are associated with pumping water from the Murrumbidgee River rather than deep billabongs.

Some wetlands that have been drained or levied off from the floodplain could also be restored. Rehabilitation actions would require the removal or relocation of levees and blockages to floodplain flow-paths. The total area of these wetlands under the 'water management' and 'combined strategies' options is very small. Hence, estimates of these costs are transferred from the USE case study as reported in Section 5.3.1.

Revegetation may be required where wetlands have lost their seed-banks due to being too wet or dry over long periods. Revegetation can only be implemented in areas where livestock are excluded. In Chapter 4, it was estimated that 5 per cent of wetland areas from which grazing is excluded would require revegetation (approximately 0.5 km^2). USE case study costs (shown in Table 5.7) were used because no data relating to the costs of revegetation in the Murrumbidgee case study area are available. These cost estimates can be transferred to the Murrumbidgee based on the assumption that the main cost components are similar. That is, a similar number of tube-stock or seeds are required per unit area (at a similar cost) and the labour costs of planting and management are similar. The present value of revegetation costs under the 'grazing management' and 'combined strategies' in the MRF is $209,000.

Fencing wetlands (and buffer strips) facilitate the changes to grazing management under the 'grazing management' and 'combined strategies' options defined in Chapter 4. Costs of fencing are drawn from fencing undertaken in floodplain wetland areas by NSW State Forests.

Rehabilitated wetlands will require ongoing management to control pests and weeds, manage fire risks and maintain fences. The costs of such activities are not well documented so NSW State Forests estimated per km^2 costs of MRF State Forest management are used. For example, the present value of wetland maintenance for the additional 27 km^2 of healthy wetlands resulting from adoption of the 'grazing management' resource allocation reported in Table 5.10 is $1.2m.

Income from future water sales
The artificial flood created under the 'water management' and 'combined strategies' options is only created in five out of six years. Hence, the water acquired for this purpose could be sold one in six years thus reducing the opportunity costs of creating an artificial flood. As the year in which water will be sold cannot be predicted in advance it is assumed that one sixth of total water acquired to create an artificial flood is sold each year.[14] All water acquired would be temporarily traded during the five-year period that water licences would be being purchased to create a sufficiently large volume to create an artificial flood, further reducing the opportunity costs of environmental use of water in an artificial flood. Under these assumptions the estimated net present value of the income generated under the 'water management' and 'combined strategies' options by temporarily selling water is $6.2m.

Marketed costs not estimated – MRF
The detail of the biophysical modelling was insufficient to allow the quantification of several potential costs in the USE. None of these costs is likely to be significant and they are likely to cancel each other out to some extent. They are briefly discussed and defined below to demonstrate the type of baseline information required to facilitate a threshold value analysis of their potential importance. These costs can also be viewed as a potential source of increased wetland management costs that are assessed within the sensitivity analysis in Chapter 8.

The release of an artificial flood under the 'water management' and 'combined strategies' options may require farmers to raise irrigation pumps and move stock from flood prone areas more frequently than would otherwise occur. These costs are expected to be relatively low because of the small number of farmers affected and rare flood occurrence. The costs would be offset by the (uncosted but relatively small) positive impact of a flood on flood prone pastures. Hence, the net costs are expected to be neutral although they may be distributed to differing farmers (that is, the farmers that raise their pumps may not necessarily be the same farmers who gain from a flood).

Institutional constraints currently prevent an artificial release of sufficient water to create an artificial flood due to the impacts on stakeholders in the confined upper sections of the Murrumbidgee River. The constraint is generically referred to as the 'Gundagai choke'. Costs may be imposed on a limited number of landholders and the Gundagai community for the lost use of the floodplain to grow crops and use of sports fields for a short time period. No estimates of compensation costs are included in this chapter but it is anticipated that the cost would be small when compared to the total costs of adopting the potential management strategies.

There are also no cost estimates included should carp control programs be required to facilitate an increase in native fish numbers. This is because the response of carp to conditions that would improve wetland health is unknown. Carp may be so dominant that control and fish stocking programs are needed to allow native fish populations to expand.

5.4 MARKETED IMPACTS OF NEW OR EXPANDED WETLAND USES

Reallocating resources in the USE also has impacts for new or expanded wetland uses including marketed duck hunting and wetland tourism. It is unlikely that a substantial tourism benefit would be generated in the MRF and duck hunting is illegal in NSW. Therefore, the focus in this section is on the estimation of the marketed duck hunting and tourism benefits (producers' surpluses) in the USE case study area.

Wetland based tourism generates producers' surpluses to wetland owners who charge entry fees and businesses supplying accommodation and tour services. These businesses may or may not be run by wetland owners but the returns received are directly related to wetland visits. Less direct relationships such as profits on the sales of fuel, food and associated spillover impacts are not included. While these impacts are likely to be small in aggregate they may be important to the small USE towns. However, estimation of such impacts was beyond the scope of the study.

Producers' surplus estimates are not available for the very small accommodation, tour and parks industries in the USE region. Producers' surplus estimates from a region that has similar industries and distance from its main tourist markets were used as proxies.[15] The potential for substantial variation between the producers' surplus of the regions is taken into account in the sensitivity analysis in Chapter 8. The resulting per-day and aggregate producers' surplus estimates that were calculated for the USE are reported in Table 5.11. For example, adoption of the pro-wetlands strategy is forecast to increase the tourism related producers' surplus in the USE by $1.8m (present value).

Table 5.11 USE tourism producers' surplus by service provided

Service	Total daily expenditure	Proportion producers' surplus*	Producers' surplus per day
Farm stay	$60	10.5%	$6.30
Specialised tours	$70	54.4%	$38.08
Mini-resort	$140	10.5%	$14.70
Charged day visits	$20	75.0%	$15.00
Camping	$10	10.5%	$1.05
Self-catering	$30	10.5%	$3.15

Service	Wetland retention	Pro-wetlands	Wetlands and remnants
Farm stay	$128,000	$262,000	$262,000
Specialised tours	$206,000	$424,000	$641,000
Mini-resort	$168,000	$419,000	$503,000
Charged day visits	$205,000	$633,000	$804,000
Camping	$1,000	$4,000	$10,000
Self-catering	$18,000	$36,000	$72,000
Total	$726,000	$1,778,000	$2,292,000

Notes * Changes to tourist numbers occur over a 20-year period. Hence, the growth in surpluses occurs over a 20-year period. The proportion of total daily expenditure that comprises producers' surplus is adapted from CARE (1998) except charged day visits which are estimated at 75% due to very low input and management costs.

USE marketed duck hunting impacts

Adoption of a strategy leading to increased areas of healthy wetlands will generate additional opportunities to hunt ducks in the USE region. In some instances, such as 'Wetlands and Wildlife' organised shoots, a hunting fee is payable ($20 in the case of 'Wetlands and Wildlife'). The hunting fee can be used as a suitable proxy for producer's surpluses where a fee is charged because the marginal expenses incurred in organising and running the hunt (such as labour, access construction and hunt management) are a trivial amount. The estimated NPV of the change to the future stream of producers' surplus generated from 'Wetlands and Wildlife' hunts as a result of reallocating wetland resources is reported in Table 5.12.

Table 5.12 USE duck hunting producers' surplus changes

	Unit	Wetland retention	Pro-wetlands	Wetlands and remnants
Extra duck hunting trips	No.	443	692	762
in 2030	(%)	52%	81%	90%
Producers' surplus	$	$26,000	$66,000	$72,000
	(%)	9%	22%	24%

Notes Changes to duck hunting occur over a ten-year period and are discounted to a present value.

5.5 CONCLUSIONS

Changing the allocation of wetland resources in the both the USE and MRF impose monetary costs on wetland owners and, in the MRF, also on irrigators due to the reduction in extractive wetland marketed outputs and the increased costs of wetland management. In contrast the marketed outputs from wetlands increase relatively little due to tourism and duck hunting in the USE and are not expected to change significantly in the MRF. However, the total economic value generated by reallocating wetland resources also includes use and non-use benefits and costs. These benefits and costs are the focus in the next two chapters. All the benefit and cost estimates are combined for the integration phase of the bio-economic modelling in Chapter 8.

NOTES

1. The 1999 gross margin is approximately consistent with the long-term trend for sheep and cattle. Sensitivity tests are used to vary this assumption in Chapter 8.
2. Labour input estimates were provided by Adrian Barber and Denice Rendell (PIRSA Regional Livestock Officers) and labour cost adjustments are made using the award rate of pay for a senior station hand and indexed to year 2000 using Australian Bureau of Statistics (2001) 'Prices paid by farmers for materials and services'. The senior station hand wage is used to incorporate some management input.
3. 1993 prices are adjusted to year 2000 prices using the ABS (2001) index of 'Prices paid by farmers for materials and services'.
4. Sustainable harvesting is defined in this context as harvesting timber according to a management plan that incorporates environmental objectives. Environmental objectives include retention of habitat trees, retention of trees critical for bank stabilisation, timing harvest to avoid bird breeding events and harvesting when wetlands are dry.

5. In flat areas rivers typically separate into several channels each of which are termed 'anabranches'. In some cases anabranches may lie many kilometres apart before eventually rejoining the main channel.
6. Janice White (The University of South Australia and 'Wetlands and Wildlife', a not for profit group that owns and rehabilitates wetlands in the USE) provided this information.
7. Brenton Grear (National Parks and Wildlife Service, SA) supplied these data.
8. Total water required to create an artificial flood is 70GL but 20 GL are assumed to be instream flows at the time of the flood. Hence, only an additional 50GL is required to create the flood.
9. Dry year allocations will be used to forecast water sales later in this section. Allocation is as at the final announcement on January 1 each year. If predicted allocations are different to the January 1 allocation, water will need to be borrowed from future years or past credits (at an assumed overall neutral cost). Source: Mark Foreman (Department of Land and Water Conservation Regional Hydrologist).
10. It is explicitly assumed in this Section that water acquired and used for an artificial flood could have been used for irrigation. Hence, the appropriate opportunity cost is irrigation. The possibility also exists that an alternative environmental use is valued more highly than irrigation. In that case, the environmental use would be the appropriate opportunity cost. If the water used for the artificial flood could not be used for irrigation (for example, it is already an environmental allocation), then the appropriate opportunity cost is the next highest valued environmental use.
11. It is assumed that water licences will be acquired from irrigation over the next five years. Water savings are assumed over the same period. Hence, the opportunity costs of changing water use and the savings from efficiency improvements are generated over the same period negating any additional discounting. This approach assumes that the relatively small increase in irrigation area that would otherwise result from water savings causes no spillover impacts on the regional economy.

    Water licences acquired to create an artificial flood are assumed to involve fixed (licence charges) and variable (usage charges) costs. These charges would be paid by the organisation – government or non-government – that acquires the water licences for the flood. Without the artificial flood, irrigators would pay the charges. Hence, there is no change to the total costs involved, only to who is paying the costs.
12. P. Killen (Department of Land and Water Conservation, Murrumbidgee Region, Water Access and Licensing) provided water licence cost estimates. High security licences are approximately $450/ML and normal security $400/ML, weighting by 85 percent normal and 15 percent high (per ratio of licences) generates $408/ML.
13. The cost per hectare for drainage removal (and total hectares over which it is averaged) also includes the costs of rehabilitating nearly 100 ha of wetlands that are too wet through use as a buffer storage for irrigation. Jonathon Streat (Murrumbidgee Wetlands Working Group Project Officer) provided these estimates.
14. As noted under water purchases, dry year allocations are used to forecast water sales (88 percent versus 94 percent in a normal year).
15. Estimates were derived from the 'other value added' component in the input-output tables for the Central West Region of New South Wales – further details can be found in CARE (1998).

6.   Non-market Use Values of Wetland Resources

In this chapter the value of a second component of the total economic value of wetlands is considered – the non-market use values of wetland resources. Non-market use values of wetlands include some recreational values, landscape aesthetic values and cultural values of wetlands as detailed in Chapter 2. Reallocating wetland resources as discussed in Chapter 4 generates changes to several biophysical attributes that impact on the non-market use values of wetlands. Estimating these impacts in the USE and MRF is the focus in the first and second sections of this chapter respectively. Duck hunting and tourist recreation generate the major non-market use values in the USE while day recreation values are the primary source of MRF values. Wetland landscape aesthetic values are also discussed, but not estimated, for both the USE and MRF in this chapter. The estimation of those values is undertaken in Chapter 7.

6.1   USE NON-MARKET USE VALUES OF WETLAND RESOURCES

6.1.1 Recreational Values Generated by Duck Hunting

The estimation of the benefits enjoyed by duck hunters in the USE is detailed in this part.[1] First, the selection of an appropriate valuation methodology and a brief literature review are outlined. The methodology selected – the Travel Cost Method (TCM) – is developed in the second section including the design and implementation of the survey instrument. The resulting estimates of the consumers' surplus from duck hunting are reported in the third section.

Method selection
The benefits enjoyed by duck hunters are mostly generated outside the operation of markets. They are, therefore, non-market benefits. However, they are directly related to actions in the market place. For example, the decision to hunt dictates spending money on fuel, food, hunting fees and

other items in order to enjoy the sport. The TCM is a technique that enables the valuation of non-market goods such as hunting, based on the assumption 'that the incurred costs of visiting a site in some way reflect the recreational value of that site' (Turner, Pearce and Bateman 1994, p. 116). By estimating this relationship, the value of the wetlands as a site for a recreational activity (for example, hunting) can be estimated. Hence, the TCM method is suited to the estimation of consumers' surpluses from duck hunting in the USE.

An especially attractive aspect of the TCM application to hunting is the cost-effectiveness of data collection during registration for duck hunting events organised by 'Wetlands and Wildlife' – a not-for-profit company that owns over 100 km^2 of wetlands in the USE.[2]

The TCM involves the estimation of the relationship between the recreational services provided (in this case duck hunting) and the purchase and use of goods and services by duck hunters who travel to the site. The TCM assumes weak complementarity between the expenditure on goods and services and the recreational service (Hanley and Spash 1993). The implication of this assumption is that when consumption expenditure is zero, the marginal utility (and hence consumers' surplus) of the good is also zero. In other words, the consumers' surplus of the furthest distant wetland visitor approaches zero because the costs of the visit almost equal the benefits enjoyed from the trip. People living further away, with higher costs, do not visit because they would not enjoy any surplus. The utility function of duck hunters is also assumed separable (Hanley and Spash 1993). That is, the demand for duck hunting can be estimated independently of the demand for other activities (both recreational and non-recreational). Finally, the TCM method used makes no distinction between a 'good' hunting trip and a 'bad' hunting trip. That is, there is no difference in the value estimated if the number of ducks shot per hunter is high or low. This is because the TCM methodology is based on hunters' expectations of trip quality.

The TCM relationship estimated is between the number of people hunting per head of population and the costs of travelling to and from that site. This gives the trip generation function (TGF):

$$H = f \text{ (travel costs)} \tag{6.1}$$

The rate of participation in duck hunting (H) is expected to fall as the travel costs, potentially including the travel time, increase. Hence, the number of duck hunters per head of population in a particular geographic area is dependent on the costs of participating in the hunt. Under the TCM assumptions, the imposition, or increase, of a participation fee would increase the travel costs and reduce the rate of duck hunting. By simulating the effects of an increase in the participation fee, travel costs are increased and the impacts on total visitor numbers estimated. That is, a demand curve is derived (the relationship between quantity of duck hunters and price of duck hunting). The value of hunting to duck hunters (their consumers' surplus) is equal to the area under the demand curve and above the fee charged to participate in duck hunting.

Research design

Travel costs are defined as the opportunity costs incurred by hunters in order to participate in duck hunting in the USE. Costs can be split between time costs and other costs of travelling (Bateman 1993). Time costs can be further split between travel time and on-site time. Bateman suggests three cost calculation options for travel costs:

1. fuel and additional costs only (marginal costs);
2. full car costs (that is fuel, insurance, maintenance costs, etc.) and full additional costs (food and ammunition supplies etc.); and
3. perceived costs as estimated by respondents.

Use of option (2) will increase travel costs above (1), and hence increase the resulting consumers' surplus estimates. Bateman argues that the correct cost is that perceived by respondents as pertaining to their visit and this definition was used for the USE application. For example, respondents may perceive daily insurance and maintenance costs as sunk costs that are not traded off against alternative uses.

Inclusion of the cost of time spent travelling to the hunting site is debated in the TCM literature. Hunters participating in duck hunting are giving up the opportunity to participate in some other activity but they may also enjoy the trip. Bateman (1993) suggests that, where time costs are thought to be important, a sensitivity analysis should be conducted using values of 0.25, 0.5, 0.75 and the full wage rate. Time spent on-site is exogenously determined. At the margin, time spent on-site is expected to generate utility equal to that from alternative activities. Hence, time spent on-site is treated as having no impact on the consumers' surplus estimates.

The relationship between the frequency of duck hunting and travel costs can be analysed using either individual visitor data or data averaged across a number of population groups referred to as zones. The zonal approach defines the visitation rate as the proportion of hunters from the population of a specific geographic area, per pre-specified time-period. The individual visitation rate is the number of visits per individual per time-period. A trade-off arises between the benefits to model accuracy of the additional detail that is captured by the individual approach and the difficulties of obtaining sufficiently detailed data and variability in the number of visits undertaken by individuals to achieve model validity. The zonal approach was used in the USE application because data were collected at a single hunt and it was believed that most hunters make relatively few hunting trips to the USE in a single year (tested via including a question about trip numbers and destinations in the survey).

A basic assumption of the TCM is that each hunter makes the trip solely to hunt ducks in the USE. The majority of hunters are hypothesised to be travelling only to participate in duck hunting in the USE because duck hunting is primarily a weekend recreational activity and because the ducks that are taken need to be frozen relatively quickly. The presence of substitute sites can also impact on visitor demand via their travel costs (or price), their entry fees and their relative quality (Bateman 1993). A question was included in the survey to determine whether the issue of substitute sites is a problem.

Survey design and implementation

A TCM study of duck hunting in the USE region ideally would involve the collection of data from all hunters over a complete hunting season. Data collection over several seasons would be required to average out the impact of individual hunting seasons on the overall visitation patterns. For example, 2000 was the fifth in a succession of dry years. A suitable substitute for data collection from all hunters is collection from hunters participating in 'Wetlands and Wildlife' organised hunts. 'Wetlands and Wildlife' own by far the largest area of wetlands suitable for duck hunting in the USE and hold several large-scale organised hunts in a typical season. The largest numbers of duck hunters usually participate in the season opening shoot organised by 'Wetlands and Wildlife'. A survey was therefore designed for implementation at the year 2000 event.

The intended survey methodology determines, in part, the design and structure of the questionnaire. In order to maximise response rates and minimise respondent cost the questionnaire was kept to one page and distributed to all duck hunters as part of the registration procedure at the year 2000 'Wetlands and Wildlife Organised Shoot'. Completed questionnaires were collected immediately or prior to hunters leaving the event.

As the survey was being distributed as part of registration procedures minimal introduction of the questionnaire and explanation of the purpose of the survey was required in the document. The questionnaire, which was based on Bennett's (1995) suggested simplified format,[3] consisted of the following sections:

- a short preamble including who is collecting the information and the use of that information;
- seven questions gathering the data required for a TCM analysis;
- a short section thanking respondents and indicating who to contact for additional information; and
- opportunity for additional feedback.

Results

A total of 294 hunters attended the year 2000 'Wetlands and Wildlife Organised Shoot'. Questionnaires were distributed to hunters during registration procedures on 12th February 2000. One hundred and ninety-one useable responses were received giving a response rate of 65 per cent across all hunters attending the shoot.

The zonal TCM requires estimation of the relationship between the costs of travelling to the shoot and the proportion of the population from each zone travelling to the shoot (the TGF). Prior to undertaking this analysis, the zones must be established from the respondent data. The goal in combining respondents into zones is to establish composite zones containing sufficient respondents for averaging, but which are also relatively homogeneous in terms of distance from the shoot and socio-economic composition. A pragmatic response means that trade-offs need to be made between these goals – especially between homogeneity and sample size. The final zones used for the USE duck hunting TCM are shown in Table 6.1. In Figure 6.1, the travel time is plotted against the cost of attending the hunt. As shown in Table 6.1, the population of the zones varies significantly.[4]

The dependent variable in the TGF is the number of duck hunters per head of population from each zone. The population for the analysis is the population of males aged over 15 years in each zone because only males attended the 'Wetlands and Wildlife Organised Shoot'. The population for each zone was calculated using the Australian Bureau of Statistics data from the 1996 census (ABS 2001). The visitation rate is calculated by dividing the number of visits from each zone by the number of males over 15 living in each zone.

Table 6.1 USE duck hunting TCM zones

Zone (normal place of residence)	Males over 15 years[a]	Hunters	Mean cost	Mean travel time[b]
1. Local	2,845	24	$153	1.281
2. Naracoorte and districts (includes Murray Bridge)	19,789	39	$162	1.949
3. Adelaide	428,248	27	$180	3.206
4. Lower South East	12,577	18	$171	3.389
5. Horsham and district	9,893	28	$190	3.107
6. Central and Northern Victoria	125,805	18	$262	5.083
7. Melbourne and surrounds	1,297,696	14	$313	7.107
8. North Wimmera	9,290	11	$181	3.364
9. Hamilton and districts	14,019	12	$163	3.458

Notes a The male population is used as only male shooters attended the 'Wetlands and Wildlife Organised Shoot'.
   b Travel time is in hours and fractions of hours.

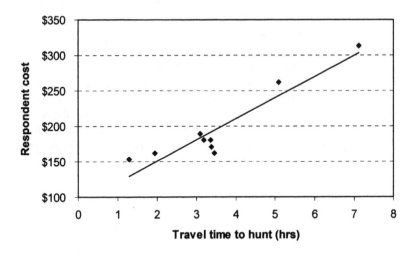

Figure 6.1 Duck hunter travel time and cost

Travel costs

Respondents were asked to provide an estimate of their monetary costs of attending the hunt. The respondent estimate is of the marginal monetary costs of attending the hunt. It does not include the opportunity costs of attending the hunt. As respondents were also asked to include an estimate of travel time, a proxy for the opportunity cost of travel time can be included. The proxy can be used to test the sensitivity of the consumers' surplus estimates to alternative values of time as per Bateman (1993). The time values for sensitivity analysis were 0.5 and full value of time estimated using the mean male weekly wage (in February 2000 from the ABS 2001) divided by the mean number of hours worked by males in 1998–99. The hourly wage rate calculated using this methodology was \$19.09 per hour. Hence, three alternative measures of the travel cost to participate in the hunt were generated.

The potential for multiple purpose trips to affect cost estimates was also raised in the section on research design. Only three hunters indicated that participating in the hunt was not either the sole purpose of the trip or very important to the trip. Therefore, the data were not adjusted for multiple purpose trips, as it was considered unlikely that the three observations would bias the results.

The travel cost relationship

The TGF was estimated by regressing the visitation rate against the mean travel cost for each zone.[5] Three alternative functional forms were investigated:

a. Semi-log dependent: log (visit rate)   = a + b travel cost
b. Semi-log independent: visit rate   = a + b log (travel cost)
c. Double log: log (visit rate)   = a + b log (travel cost)

The choice between (a) and (c) can be made using model validity, R-squared and accuracy of predicted hunter numbers. Scaling the dependent variable allows likelihood ratio tests between (b) and (a) or (c) (Rao and Miller 1971, p. 107). Model validity can be used to assist in making decisions between (b) and (a) or (c). Christensen and Price (1982) note that accurate prediction of current hunter numbers is not a suitable criterion if it leads to incorrect model specification and incorrect consumers' surplus estimates. That is, a model that incorrectly predicts the current number of hunters but more accurately predicts hunters' responses to a change in costs may be preferred over a model that accurately predicts current hunter numbers. Hence, model validity is the primary selection criterion and predicted current hunter numbers the secondary criterion.

Preliminary regressions were undertaken using ordinary least squares (OLS). Predicted hunter numbers from all models indicated that the visit rate from Adelaide was substantially different from the other zones and was poorly predicted (over 100 hunters versus just 27 in reality). This was possibly due to differences in population preferences between capital cities and rural areas. Because of the large differences, Adelaide acted as an outlier on remaining predictions. A dummy variable for capital cities (Adelaide and Melbourne) was therefore included in the model to eliminate the capital city effect and improve model validity.

The dependent variable semi-log model was not significantly different from the double log model (models (a) and (c)). Model (a) was selected due to simplicity of estimating results and model validity over model (b). The Rao and Miller (1971) scaled likelihood ratio test indicated no significant difference between models (a) and (c), but both models (a) and (c) were significantly different from (b) at the 1 per cent level. The preliminary model estimated was:

Log (visit rate) = a + b . travel cost + c . capcity dummy   (6.2)

With no time costs included, the OLS estimated TGF is:

Log (visit rate) = $-2.604 - 2.10E-2$. travel cost $- 2.785$. capcity dummy
              (1.243)   (0.007)   (0.801)

Notes   numbers in brackets are standard errors

Model R^2 adjusted = 0.847, F probability = 0.002

Cooper and Loomis (1993) indicate that potential heteroscedasticity due to zones with differing population sizes is likely to be minimised by the logged dependent variable.[6] A simple test for heteroscedasticity involves plotting prediction error against population for the logged dependent variable. This test indicated that there was little likelihood of its presence in the model. This finding was confirmed by a Breusch-Pagan test.

In Table 6.2 the three models estimated in order to test the sensitivity of the results to the inclusion of a cost for travel time are reported. The TGF can also be estimated using the maximum likelihood non-linear least squares (NLSQ) method. This method of estimation eliminates some concerns regarding the OLS estimation of the TGF relationship.[7] The results, which are reported in Table 6.3, are very similar to the OLS methodology used above but exhibit smaller standard errors.

Table 6.2 OLS models for travel time cost sensitivity

Coefficients	Travel time cost		
	Base	**0.5 cost**	**Full cost**
A	–2.604	–2.859	–3.065
	(1.243)	(1.088)	(0.997)
B	–2.10E-2	–1.69E-2	–1.40E-2
	(0.007)	(0.005)	(0.004)
C	–2.785	–2.717	–2.685
	(0.801)	(0.770)	(0.755)
R^2 adjusted	0.847	0.861	0.867
F (Sig.)	0.002	0.001	0.001

Notes Bracketed numbers are standard errors

Table 6.3 Non-linear least squares models for travel time cost sensitivity

Coefficients	Travel time cost		
	Base	**0.5 cost**	**Full cost**
A	–2.455	–2.657	–2.925
	(0.995)	(0.858)	(0.760)
B	–2.36E-2	–1.95E-2	–1.61E-2
	(0.005)	(0.004)	(0.003)
C	–2.990	–2.876	–2.832
	(0.437)	(0.412)	(0.404)
R^2 adjusted	–0.452	–0.289	–0.228

Notes Bracketed numbers are asymptotic standard errors, R^2 adjusted is not bound in {0,1}.

Other modelling issues
Respondents were asked to indicate where and how many times they had been hunting in five pre-specified areas and to nominate any other areas they had been duck hunting. The proportion of hunters from each zone who had hunted in specified regions is shown in Table 6.4. A majority of hunters from all zones except two (Lower South East remainder and Melbourne and

Table 6.4 Proportion of hunters hunting in substitute areas by zone

Zone	Proportion of hunters hunting in each area in last 12 months							
	USE	LSE	Lower SA Murray[a]	Upper SA Murray[b]	Victoria	Other	Substitutes[c]	
1.	91.7%	4.2%	8.3%	0.0%	4.2%	4.2%	0	
2.	74.4%	23.1%	2.6%	2.6%	10.3%	20.5%	0	
3.	51.9%	3.7%	29.6%	7.4%	7.4%	11.1%	0	
4.	31.6%	47.4%	10.5%	15.8%	52.6%	10.5%	2	
5.	46.4%	28.6%	3.6%	3.6%	78.6%	35.7%	2	
6.	61.1%	5.6%	0.0%	0.0%	100.0%	55.6%	2	
7.	28.6%	7.1%	0.0%	0.0%	71.4%	28.6%	1	
8.	81.8%	27.3%	0.0%	0.0%	90.9%	63.6%	2	
9.	53.8%	7.7%	0.0%	0.0%	84.6%	23.1%	1	

Notes a   Lower SA Murray is the Murray River and floodplain below Murray Bridge including Lakes Alexandrina and Albert.
b   Upper SA Murray is the Murray River and floodplain above Murray Bridge.
c   Substitutes are defined as more than one third of hunters from the zone have hunted in that area in the previous twelve months.

surrounds) had hunted in the USE in the last twelve months. For many hunters this would have been one or more of the 1999 'Wetlands and Wildlife Organised Shoots'. Table 6.4 shows there were very few substitute sites within South Australia during the last twelve months. Only South Australian hunters resident within the Lower South East area had a strong substitute site outside the USE (the Lower South East area). The 'substitutes' variable shown in Table 6.4 was tried within the model in an attempt to include the effects of substitutes but was insignificant and showed the incorrect sign. This is potentially because the duck hunting open seasons in South Australia and Victoria overlap rather than occurring at the same time.

The proportion of hunters who travelled with friends was also considered as a potential explanatory variable, however its coefficient was insignificant. It is likely that the impacts of the variable were incorporated in the self-estimated travel costs as respondents were asked to indicate the costs of their trip (rather than group costs).

Consumers' surplus estimation
Estimation of consumers' surplus is undertaken via a two-stage approach in most TCM applications. The TCM consumers' surplus is the area under the Marshallian demand curve. The first stage utilises the TGF to simulate demand for hunting under different pricing conditions: that is, to derive a demand curve for duck hunting. The second stage is to estimate the area under the demand curve at the current level of hunting fees. For some functional forms, the consumers' surplus can be estimated directly from the TGF (see for example, Hanley and Spash 1993 and Offenbach and Goodwin 1994). In the case of the OLS log-linear form applied in this study the average per-capita consumers' surplus is:

$$CS = -1 / \text{(travel cost coefficient)} \tag{6.3}$$

Hence, for the base (OLS) relationship:

$$CS = -1/ 0.210E{-}2$$
$$= \$47.73 \text{ per visit}$$

A 95 per cent confidence interval is calculated as follows:

$$-1 / (0.210E{-}2 - 1.96SE) < CS/visit < -1 / (0.210E{-}2 + 1.96SE)$$

where: SE = standard error of travel cost coefficient

Hence, the 95 per cent confidence interval is:

$$\$29.58 < CS/visit < \$123.50$$

To estimate the total consumers' surplus for the 'Wetlands and Wildlife Organised Shoot', the per-visit consumers' surplus is multiplied by the total number of participants (294). Hence, the base level total consumers' surplus for the 2000 Shoot is $14,033. The equivalent estimate for the NLSQ method is slightly lower at $12,439 or $42.31 per visit.

To estimate the sensitivity of the model to inclusion of costs for travel time, the above calculations were repeated for the alternative models. The results of these are reported in Table 6.5. There are large differences between the estimates. The full cost estimate is 50 per cent larger than the base model estimate. The difference between the models shows the importance of the treatment of the costs of travel time to consumers' surplus estimates. The consumers' surplus estimates from the NLSQ estimation are also included in Table 6.5. NLSQ estimates are around 12 per cent lower than the OLS estimates and have much tighter confidence intervals.

Table 6.5 Sensitivity of estimates to inclusion of cost of travel time

OLS Estimate	Base	0.5 cost	Full cost
Individual CS	$ 47.73	$ 59.20	$ 71.39
95% upper	$123.50	$138.17	$159.46
95% lower	$ 29.58	$ 37.67	$ 45.99
Total CS*	$14,033	$17,406	$20,987
NLSQ Estimate	Base	0.5 cost	Full cost
Individual CS	$ 42.31	$ 51.33	$ 62.03
95% upper	$ 76.14	$ 87.04	$101.81
95% lower	$ 29.30	$ 36.40	$ 44.61
Total CS*	$12,439	$15,092	$18,238

Notes * Total consumers' surplus for Wetlands and Wildlife opening shoot in 2000.

Calculation of a net present value of USE duck hunting

The final steps in the analysis of consumers' surplus are to extrapolate the consumers surplus drawn from the 'Wetlands and Wildlife Organised Shoot' in 2000 to duck hunting across the USE and to estimate the net present value of hunting benefits across the 30 year time horizon of the case study. The total number of duck hunting trips undertaken under alternative resource allocations was estimated in Chapter 4. The extrapolation of the USE consumers' surplus under BAU compared to that under alternative resource allocations is shown in Table 6.6 for the NLSQ model incorporating travel costs at 50 per cent of average wage levels.[8]

The extrapolation of the survey data assumes similar travel costs and quality of the hunting experience. This assumption is not as unlikely as it may seem because participants in the 'Wetlands and Wildlife Organised Shoot' do not know which of several wetlands they will be allotted for hunting. Each of these wetlands may also be some distance from the centralised meeting point. However, the inclusion of hunting trips to wetlands other than those owned by 'Wetlands and Wildlife' in Table 6.6 is subject to a number of uncertainties. The hunters participating in trips to other wetlands may enjoy a higher average consumers' surplus because the main participants (friends and neighbours) often live close by (and are subject to low travel costs) and no fee is charged for participation. The possibility also exists that the average consumers' surplus for these additional trips could be lower than for the Wetlands and Wildlife organised hunt. For example, a small benefit from participation less even smaller transport costs leaves a small but positive consumers' surplus. Hence, the consumers' surplus estimate derived from the Wetlands and Wildlife organised shoot is conservatively attributed to the estimated number of additional trips in the extrapolation performed in Table 6.6. Sensitivity tests of the NPV of consumers' surpluses from duck hunting in the USE are undertaken in Chapter 8.

Table 6.6 Recreational duck hunter consumers' surplus from resource reallocation

	Unit	BAU	Wetland retention	Pro-wetlands	Wetlands and remnants
Total hunting trips	No.	1,100	1,700	2,000	2,100
Consumers' surplus	$	$980,000	$1,065,000	$1,199,000	$1,218,000
Marginal change					
Hunting trips	No.	n.a.	600	900	1,000
Consumers' surplus	$	n.a.	$85,000	$220,000	$238,000

Notes   The number of ducks hunted is based on the number of trips undertaken by hunters and hence is not affected by bag limits.
Changes to duck hunting occur over a ten-year period and are discounted to a present value.

Conclusions

The estimates reported in this section comprise the non-market use values generated to the duck hunting community. It must be recognised that the generation of these values may impose negative non-market costs on other members of the community via their distress over the killing of waterfowl. These costs will be considered in Chapter 7. Furthermore, the benefits generated to wetland owners (as reported in Chapter 5) and those estimated in this chapter may result in the maintenance of wetland habitat that generates other social benefits to the community. These benefits include maintenance of habitat and protection of endangered species that in turn generate other non-market use and non-use values to the community. These values are, in part, the focus in the remainder of this chapter and Chapter 7.[9]

6.1.2 USE Tourism Consumers' Surplus

Tourism generates non-market use values to the tourists in the form of a consumers' surplus (benefits to tourists of visiting net of costs). Tourism also generates marketed values to wetland owners and others in the community via producers' surpluses that were estimated in Chapter 5.[10] Current visitor numbers to USE wetlands are small (see Chapter 4). A survey of wetland owners in the region found that just two wetland owners currently undertake commercial recreation or hunting in their wetlands (Whitten and Bennett 2000c). However, 43 per cent of wetland owners recognise that their wetlands provide potential opportunities for tourism and recreation activities, and the USE lies along a major tourism corridor between Melbourne and Adelaide that includes the Coorong, Coonawarra Wine Region, Grampian Ranges and Great Ocean Road. Hence, with reallocation of wetland resources it is anticipated that a significant increase in visitor numbers would be generated over the next thirty years as detailed in Chapter 4.

No estimates of the consumers' surplus that would be generated by tourism are available for the USE region. Furthermore, extrapolation from current visitors, as was undertaken for duck hunting in Section 6.1.1, poses a number of problems given the relatively large changes in biophysical conditions and relatively small number of tourists currently visiting the region. Benefit transfer from other studies may provide a potential method for including values in the analysis.

The benefit protocols were discussed in Chapter 4 and include (Desvousges, Naughton and Parsons 1992 and Brouwer 2000):

1. empirical rigour in the valuation study from which benefit estimates are transferred;

2. the type and quantity of the environmental goods produced is similar;
3. the populations and market characteristics are similar for both locations; and
4. stakeholder acceptance of the use of benefit transfer.

Potential studies considered for benefit transfer

Read Sturgess and Associates (2000) estimated the recreational benefits to tourists of visiting a number of Victorian National Parks by applying the TCM to several years of data for the late 1990s. The most similar of these parks to the USE is Hattah-Kulkyne National Park near the Murray River in north-west Victoria. Hattah-Kulkyne includes a number of large wetland areas and mallee vegetation including tea tree that are similar to the wetlands of the USE region, but includes a lesser variety of wetland ecosystems overall. The park is further from its main markets than the USE (580km versus 250km) and smaller in total area (48,000 ha versus more than 100,000 ha). The Murray River is the major tourist drawcard in the region that is anticipated to act somewhat similarly to other tourist drawcards in the USE region. Appraisal of the methodology employed in the Read Sturgess document indicated that the principles of undertaking a TCM study specified in Section 6.1.1 had been adhered to (including data selection, modelling of costs, estimate of the TGF and the resulting consumers' surplus estimate). Hence, the Read Sturgess and Associates study was judged to meet adequately the specified criteria for benefit transfer to the USE region.[11]

The consumers' surplus of visitors to Hattah-Kulkyne National Park was estimated at $20.52 per person per day (in 2000 dollars) (Read Sturgess and Associates 2000). Total consumers' surplus is estimated by multiplying by the number of visitors by the consumers' surplus estimate and subtracting entrance fees, if any. There are no entrance fees for Hattah-Kulkyne. However, in the USE region, 'Wetlands and Wildlife' charge an entry fee of $15 to day visitors at their open days.[12] Hence, the entrance fee must be subtracted from the consumers' surplus of day visitors as it represents an additional cost not levied on Hattah-Kulkyne visitors.[13] Estimates of consumers' surplus are reported in Table 6.7. For example, adoption of the 'wetlands and remnants' strategy is predicted to generate an additional 35 150 extra visitor days per year in 20 years time yielding additional consumers' surplus of $1.5m (present value).

*Table 6.7 Difference between tourism consumers' surplus under the BAU
and alternative strategies in the USE*

Descriptive attributes	Unit	Wetland retention	Pro-wetlands	Wetlands and remnants
Extra tourists (visitor days per year)	No.	11,900	26,150	35,150
	%	187	412	553
Marginal tourism consumers' surplus	$	$531,000	$972,000	$1,492,000
	%	45	82	126

6.1.3 Aesthetic Wetland and Remnant Values

Reallocating wetland resources in the USE case study area will also change
other non-market use values of wetlands and remnant vegetation. Aesthetic
non-market use values of wetlands are primarily generated by the area and
balance between healthy and degraded wetlands and remnant vegetation in
the region and the quantity and type of fauna they support. The most
important of these is the landscape aesthetic value of wetlands. Aesthetic
values of wetlands are of importance to both wetland owners and the wider
community (see for example Whitten and Bennett 2000c). Estimation of the
non-market use value of aesthetic benefits in the USE is complicated by two
factors:

1. some aesthetic use values of tourists and duck hunters are captured in the
   tourism and duck hunting consumers' surpluses that were estimated in
   Sections 6.1.2 and 6.1.1 respectively. Hence, any estimation procedure
   must avoid double counting of these surpluses; and
2. separation of aesthetic non-market use values from other marketed and
   non-market, use and non-use values generated by USE wetlands is
   difficult because they are often consumed in combination.

The combination of these estimation difficulties implies that a pragmatic
approach is to estimate the as yet uncounted aesthetic non-market use values
as part of a larger bundle of wetland values. This approach is undertaken
with respect to non-use values and aesthetic non-market use values in
Chapter 7.

6.2 MRF NON-MARKET USE VALUES OF WETLAND RESOURCES

Non-market use values in the MRF include those generated by the recreation and aesthetic impacts in MRF wetlands. No marketed producers' surplus benefits are directly generated by recreation activities in MRF wetlands. Economic modelling of recreation non-market use values is the focus in this section. Economic modelling of aesthetic values is discussed but estimation is left until Chapter 7.

6.2.1 Recreation Consumers' Surpluses

Recreational activities that take place in or near MRF wetlands include fishing, swimming, picnicking and nature watching. These activities generate a consumers' surplus to participants. There are over a quarter of a million visits to MRF wetlands each year (Forestry Commission of NSW 1986). The majority of visits to MRF wetlands are day visits to beaches and picnic areas within the NSW State Forest managed areas. These visits generate benefits in the form of a consumers' surplus (benefits to visitors net of costs). In addition, 73 per cent of wetland owners in the MRF also use their wetlands for pleasure or recreation.[14] Increasing the area of healthy wetlands by changing wetland management is likely to generate two benefits; firstly increased benefits for existing visitors, and secondly, an increased number of visits. Only an increased number of visits are considered in this section due to the difficulty in estimating willingness to pay for improvements to existing visit experiences. However, sensitivity analysis of the improved quality of visitor benefits is undertaken in Chapter 8.

There are no current estimates of the number of users of wetlands and rivers in the MRF (the most recent data relate to 1986). Likewise, there are no estimates of the consumers' surplus generated by additional visits to the Murrumbidgee River and wetlands. Despite the large number of total visitors to MRF wetlands, management changes are anticipated to impact on a relatively small proportion of activities undertaken in or around wetlands. Hence, it was judged that the likely benefits of conducting a study to estimate user values would be outweighed by the costs of data collection and analysis. Therefore, other studies of wetland recreation values were examined in order to determine the potential for transfer of benefits to the MRF case study according to the benefit transfer principles summarised in Section 6.1.2.

Potential studies considered for benefit transfer

Estimates of the willingness to pay (WTP) for recreation in the Ovens and King Basin in Victoria were reported by Sinden (1989). The sites for which recreation is valued in the Ovens and King Basin range from similar sites (billabong and river beach recreation areas), to those upstream of the MRF study area. Recreational activities conducted in the Ovens and King basin were also similar and included fishing, swimming and general recreation. The source of visitors in the two regions differs because less than half of all visitors are attributed to the local area in the Ovens and Kings Basin while most MRF visitors are likely to be local. The significant difference in beneficiaries between the two regions may signify that the Ovens and King Basin generates larger values to potential users than the MRF. The impacts of this possibility are considered as part of the sensitivity analysis conducted in Chapter 8.

Sinden (1989) estimates the WTP at $27.80 ($22.00 in 1989 converted to 2001 dollars using Australian Bureau of Statistics 2001). The change in consumers' surplus is estimated by multiplying an estimated increase in visitor numbers by the WTP.[15] The change to visitor numbers under potential resource allocations in the MRF was reported in Chapter 4. The increase in visitor numbers is reported in Table 6.8 along with the estimate of consumers' surplus generated. For example, adopting the 'grazing management' strategy stimulates 7 500 additional visits that generate $1.8m in consumers' surplus.

Table 6.8 Difference between recreation consumers' surplus under the BAU and alternative strategies in the MRF

	Unit	Water management	Grazing management	Timber management	Combined strategies
Extra visitors	No.	3,000	7,500	0	12,500
	(%)	*1.2%*	*3.0%*	*0.0%*	*5.0%*
Consumers' surplus	$	$742,000	$1,842,000	$0	$3,078,000

6.2.2 Aesthetic Wetland Values

Reallocation of wetland resources in the MRF will change the aesthetic values generated to wetland owners (see for example Whitten and Bennett 2000a) and the wider community. As in the USE, a pragmatic approach is to estimate the previously uncounted aesthetic non-market use values as part of a larger bundle of wetland values. This approach is undertaken with respect to non-use values and aesthetic non-market use values of wetlands in Chapter 7.

6.3 CONCLUSIONS

Changing the allocation of wetland resources in the USE and MRF generates significant recreational benefits to visitors including day visitors, overnight visitors and duck hunters. These benefits are larger than the marketed benefits but do not outweigh the marketed costs of resource reallocation that were estimated in Chapter 5. However, the total economic value generated by reallocating wetland resources also extends to non-use values. Aesthetic non-market use values of wetlands also extend beyond the recreation values estimated in this chapter. Furthermore, some uses may impose non-market costs on others in the community – for example as a result of the distress caused to some members of the community by duck hunting. These benefits and costs are the focus of the next chapter. The benefits estimated in this section are combined with the outputs of Chapters 5 and 7 in the bio-economic integration phase of the bio-economic modelling in Chapter 8.

NOTES

1. This section is substantially based on Whitten and Bennett (2002).
2. There are over 630 km^2 of wetlands in the USE region. However, the majority of these wetlands are unsuitable for duck hunting.
3. We are grateful to Keith Frost, Janice White and Michael Lewis of Wetlands and Wildlife, and Brenton Grear of the SA Department of Environment and Heritage for reviewing the draft questionnaire.
4. Heteroscedasticity is potentially present because the unequal zonal populations generate differing variances for each observation (see Bowes and Loomis 1980).
5. There are a number of alternative functional forms available (semi-log, double log and quadratic) and two alternative methods of estimation (maximum likelihood and ordinary least squares). Furthermore, the non-constant variance of the dependent variable suggested that a weighted estimation procedure could be appropriate to estimate the relationship (weighted maximum likelihood or weighted least squares).

6. Furthermore, using weighted least squares or generalised least squares (as per Bowes and Loomis 1980) would expose the methodology to the criticisms made by Christensen and Price (1982). That is, the greatest weighting is given to zones further from the hunting site by virtue of their larger populations. Hence, the weighting procedure suggested by Christensen and Price was not suitable for the data even if heteroscedasticity were present.

7. The dependent variable of the TGF is both truncated and censored (Hanley and Spash 1993). It is argued that ordinary least squares estimates will therefore be inappropriate but the literature is divided on this point. For example, Smith and Desvouges (1986) and Willis and Garrod (1991) argue maximum likelihood is more accurate while Kling (1987, 1988) and Smith (1988) argue for OLS.

8. The tighter confidence intervals surrounding the NLSQ estimates suggest a more robust model than the OLS model while the travel time is likely to have imposed at least some costs on participants (that is, it is not likely to have been an entirely enjoyable experience).

9. Duck hunters from outside the USE region may also generate other social benefits from any beneficial direct or spillover impacts on local businesses due to purchases of provisions or accommodation. These benefits are not estimated by the TCM method or in this dissertation.

10. The inclusion of a value for tourism in the bio-economic model presents the question of whether the extra net tourism revenue to a region should be considered as a net economic benefit or whether it merely represents a redistribution from present tourist and recreation expenditure in other areas. The approach here is to include tourism as net benefits, but the policy results derived in Chapter 9 should be considered in the light of the caveat relating to the possible redistribution of benefits.

11. As in all cases, benefit transfer decisions are subject to an element of judgement on the part of the researcher.

12. Wetlands and Wildlife levy a differential access charge on hunters and tourists.

13. Entry charges are only subtracted from day visitor consumers' surplus. This is because charges to overnight visitors are assumed included in accommodation costs, as this is the current practice for visitors to Wetland and Wildlife wetlands.

14. Data from a survey of MRF wetland owners conducted in 1999 and reported in Whitten and Bennett (2000a).

15. Similar caveats about whether these benefits are additional or transferred apply to the MRF.

7.   Non-use Values of Wetland Resources

The focus in this chapter is estimation of non-use values of wetland resources. Some aesthetic and future option values for duck hunting could not be estimated using the revealed preference methodologies demonstrated in Chapter 6. Estimation of these use values is therefore included in this chapter for methodological ease. The non-use values of wetlands estimated in this chapter include option values associated with future potential uses, existence values from the knowledge that healthy wetland ecosystems and the values they support remain, and bequest values for the passing of these values to future generations. Reallocating wetland resources as discussed in Chapter 4 will change the biophysical drivers of each of option, existence and bequest non-use values as well as aesthetic and duck hunting unpriced use values.

The approach followed involves the use of choice modelling (CM) to estimate these values in each case study area. Hence, the two case study areas are considered concurrently in the next two sections of this chapter. In section 7.1 a discussion of the method selection and rationale is provided. The application of CM in the USE and MRF is the focus in the second part of the chapter. The results of the economic valuation exercises are reported in the final two sections for the USE and MRF respectively.

7.1   NON-USE VALUE METHOD SELECTION AND RATIONALE

The techniques available to estimate the changes to values associated with the outcomes of changing wetland management can be divided into two main groups as indicated in Chapter 3: those using revealed preferences, and those using stated preferences. The non-use values for which estimates of economic values are estimated in this chapter do not rely on marketed goods in any way. The unpriced aesthetic and duck hunting values also estimated were judged in Chapter 6 to not be sufficiently related to consumption of marketed goods to facilitate their estimation separately from non-use values. Hence, demand for these outcomes is not revealed in the market place and cannot be estimated via revealed preference methods.

Two stated preference methods, contingent valuation (CV) and CM, were suggested in Chapter 3 as potentially suitable methods for estimating non-market values of wetlands. The alternative resource allocations considered in Chapter 4 generate a range of biophysical outcomes in each case study area according to the scale and scope of resource reallocation from the BAU scenario. For the USE, management strategies and biophysical outcomes are defined for the BAU and three alternative options. Similarly, for the MRF, the outcome of BAU and four alternative options are defined. The CV approach would require a separate survey comparing the BUA and each alternative outcome in each case study area (a minimum of seven surveys).[1] However, the CM methodology allows multiple biophysical outcomes to be compared against the BAU outcome using a single survey instrument for each case study area. The CM approach also allows other, potentially superior, biophysical outcomes to be compared. Hence, the costs and practicalities of estimating the non-use values generated by alternative wetland resource allocations indicate that CM is superior to CV for this application.

7.2   CHOICE MODELING METHODOLOGY

The focus in this section is on describing CM methodology and its application to estimating the non-use values of wetlands resources in the USE and MRF case study areas. CM studies normally follow a series of steps outlined by Adamowicz, Louviere and Swait (1998) and Bennett and Adamowicz (2001):

1. characterisation of the decision problem / establishing the issue;
2. attribute and level selection;
3. questionnaire development;
4. experimental design development;,
5. sample size and data collection;
6. data preparation and model estimation; and
7. analysing the results / policy analysis.

Step 1 was undertaken in Chapter 4. Steps 2 to 6 and the analysis of results are the focus in of the remainder of this chapter. The policy analysis phase is undertaken in Chapter 9.

7.2.1 Overview of Choice Modelling Theory

CM, in the context of estimating environmental non-use values for inclusion in the bio-economic modelling process, is based on Lancastrian consumer theory, information processing in decision making and random utility theory (Adamowicz, Louviere and Swait 1998). Lancaster (1966) suggested that the utility derived from a good or service is dependent on its characteristics or attributes. Hence, a good can be described by the characteristics that generate utility or disutility to individuals. Information processing theory indicates how individuals trade-off differing levels of attributes and form preferences about different alternatives (see for example Anderson 1982). Random utility analysis states that consumers make choices that would lead to their utility being maximised conditional on their constraints (attributed to Thurstone 1927 – see for example McFadden 1974).

CM is therefore based on consumers choosing option 'A', if, and only if, option 'A' generates at least as much utility as any other option, with utility being assessed by trading off the attributes of the alternative options available. The utility generated by an option is dependent on the characteristics or attributes of the good (X), the characteristics of the individual (S) and an unobservable component (e). The unobservable component is generally assumed random and independently and identically distributed (IID). Hence, the utility of option 'A' can be specified:

$$U_A = V(X_A, S_A) + e_{A1} \tag{7.1}$$

where: 'V' is an indirect utility function.

Hence, the probability that an individual 'i' will choose option 'A' from the set of choices 'J' is:

$$P(A|A, A \in J) = P[(V_{Ai} + e_{Ai}) > (V_{Ji} + e_{Ji})] \tag{7.2}$$

That is, the probability that an individual will choose 'A' from the set of options 'J' is equal to the probability that the utility they obtain from 'A' (including the random component) is higher than for any other element of 'J'.

Selection of the appropriate methodology for estimation of choice probabilities is dependent on the distribution of the random error component 'e'. Louviere (2001) indicates that errors are usually assumed either independent and identically distributed (IID) Gumbel random variables, or not independent or randomly distributed normal random variables.[2] Louviere notes that it is difficult to distinguish which is the appropriate assumption. Furthermore, the choice between assumptions about errors is a matter of preference or computational simplicity rather than strong theoretical grounds. Hence, errors are assumed IID in this application because this simplifies estimation and many previous studies have also taken this approach (see for example Morrison, Bennett and Blamey 1999). An IID error term facilitates estimation using a binary or multinomial logit model depending on the number of alternatives that respondents are choosing between, expressed as follows:

$$P_{Ai} = \exp(\lambda V_{Ai}) / \Sigma \exp(\lambda V_{Ji}) \qquad (7.3)$$

where: $J = 1,...,n$ choice alternatives
V = the systematic component of utility
λ = a scale parameter that is usually arbitrarily set to 1

Multinomial logit models rely on the independence of irrelevant alternatives (IIA). IIA arises from the assumed independence and identical distribution (IID) of the error term. IIA means that the probability of choosing an alternative is dependent only on the options from which a choice is made, and not on any other options that may exist. If IIA is violated, the estimates derived from the model could be biased and may not generate accurate values for inclusion in a bio-economic model. IIA violations can be corrected for via the use of more complicated nested logit models. Nested logit models relax the IID condition across differing subsets of options but preserve the IID condition within each subset (Louviere, Henscher and Swait 2000). Louviere, Henscher and Swait (2000, p. 16) describe the nested logit model as 'essentially a set of hierarchical multinomial logit models, linked by a set of conditional relationships'. The conditional relationships are defined by the nesting structure that is employed.

Recalling Equation 7.1, the V_J are assumed to be additive functions of the attributes, socio-economic/attitudinal characteristics and an alternative specific constant as shown in Equation 7.4.

$$V_{Ai} = ASC_i + \Sigma_m \beta_m . X_m + \Sigma_l \beta_l . ASC_i . S_l \qquad (7.4)$$

where: $m = 1,...,n$ attributes
$l = 1,...,n$ socio-economic or attitudinal characteristics
β = the coefficient associated with each of the attributes and socio-economic or attitudinal characteristics

The alternative specific constant takes up the remaining systematic variation that cannot be explained by either the attribute levels or the socio-economic characteristics (Bennett and Adamowicz 2001).[3] Bennett and

Adamowitz also note that the inclusion of socio-economic or attitudinal characteristics facilitates consideration of the impacts of respondent heterogeneity and reduces the potential for violation of MNL assumptions. However, because respondent characteristics are constant across the 'J' choice sets they must be interacted with either the ASC terms or the attributes. Similarly, the ASC terms can only be included in a maximum of (J–1) of the V_J utility equations else perfect multi-collinearity would arise thus confounding estimation (Louviere, Henscher and Swait 2000).

7.2.2 Non-use Values Research Design

The most critical elements underlying the research design are the definition of the BAU and alternative biophysical outcomes that were set out in Chapter 4. These elements define the change in attributes that is to be valued. Bennett and Adamowicz (2001) indicate two further questions regarding research design that need to be answered:

1. are there specific features of the biophysical outcomes to be valued that might change the values associated with other features? For example, the inclusion of water skiing in a survey primarily relating to the fishing and passive recreation in an area might lead to a significant reduction in the value of fishing or other passive recreation; and
2. what is the geographic extent of the values to be estimated? That is, how far from the wetlands do the benefits extend?

In the USE case study, the inclusion of increased hunting as a potential outcome of changed management may cause a problem. This is because some individuals may view the inclusion of hunting as eliminating values associated with other outcomes such as increased areas of healthy wetlands or improved conservation of endangered species. In the MRF, the perceived impact of the outcomes on farm viability (mainly due to reduced irrigation water availability) could lead to similar impacts. In both cases, the use of focus groups to define the nature and likely significance of these effects is important. The findings of the focus groups undertaken for this study are discussed in Sections 7.2.3 and 7.2.4.

The geographic extent of the values to be estimated is unclear for both the MRF and the USE. Other estimates of wetland non-use values indicate that the values associated with wetlands with similar characteristics extend beyond the region within which they are located (see for example Morrison, Bennett and Blamey 1998, Bennett, Blamey and Morrison 1997 and Stone 1992). In some circumstances, for example, where migratory birds are involved, the values may extend beyond Australia. The likelihood of low per capita values and the practicalities of overseas surveys effectively limit the estimation of values to those held within Australia.[4]

The treatment for the potential scope of values and attribute trade-off problems is to conduct parallel surveys. The surveys differ in terms of outcomes and in terms of the population sampled. This strategy can be expensive. So the trade-offs associated with ensuring an appropriate research design versus cost-effective valuation must be carefully considered. The use of focus groups can be instructive in determining these trade-offs.

7.2.3 Attribute Selection

The aggregate biophysical outcomes of alternative resource allocations must be defined succinctly in a fashion that allows alternative value sets to be assessed and compared in a stated preference survey. The biophysical outcomes to be valued were identified and defined in Chapter 4. Comparison is achieved via the application of Lancastrian demand theory to define a comprehensive and representative set of attributes from these outcomes. Lancastrian demand theory specifies that any 'product' can be defined by its attributes, and that these attributes determine the utility or value of the good or service to individuals (Lancaster 1966). Furthermore, combining different goods together may generate different attributes and therefore values to individuals (Lancaster 1966). Bennett and Adamowicz (2001) indicates the attributes that are selected must have the following characteristics:

1. measurable in order to communicate the biophysical changes that are being valued;
2. representative of the scale and scope of the full range of values of importance to individuals; and
3. able to be incorporated into policy development processes.

At least one attribute must represent a monetary measure of cost (or compensation). Inclusion of the monetary attribute facilitates estimation of the monetary willingness to pay (or to be compensated) for changes to the values generated to individuals by different resource allocations.

Focus groups
Focus groups are used to increase certainty that the attributes selected are representative of the scale and scope of the full range of values of importance to individuals and to assist in designing survey instruments (Morrison, Bennett and Blamey 1997). Focus groups are a planned discussion guided by a facilitator and involving between eight and ten participants. Participants are

recruited from the population that is hypothesised to hold values.[5] Two focus groups were recruited for each case study area.[6] The focus groups were structured into three sections: attribute selection and ranking; assessment of information provided to respondents; and tests of questionnaire design.

The attributes selected for inclusion in the CM survey instrument following the focus groups are shown in Table 7.1. The MRF attributes include an attribute describing the number of 'farmers leaving' due to management changes. This attribute is included because the nature of the wetland management changes proposed was taken by focus group participants to imply an adverse impact on farmers in the case study area. Hence, the 'farmers leaving' attribute was effectively a dummy attribute that was designed to increase the plausibility of the survey to respondents. The attribute was included despite the biophysical modelling indicating a very small impact on aggregate farm production when non-wetland areas are included.

Table 7.1 USE and MRF survey attributes

Attributes for USE survey	Attributes for MRF survey
• Cost to respondent	• Cost to the respondent
• Area of healthy wetlands	• Area of healthy wetlands
• Area of healthy remnants	• Population of native water and
• Threatened species that benefit	woodland birds
• Number of ducks hunted	• Population of native fish
	• Number of farmers leaving

7.2.4 Choice Modelling Survey Design

Choice modelling surveys can be delivered via a number of different mechanisms including face-to-face, drop-off and pick-up and mail-based surveys. The design and structure of the questionnaire is determined, in part, by the intended survey methodology. Preliminary price quotations from a number of market research firms indicated that any type of individual approach would require a budget considerably larger than that available for the study (including face to face, drop-off pick-up and drop-off mail-back). The detailed information that respondents consider along with the inherently difficult nature of the trade-offs required in the CM process also precluded telephone-based surveys. Hence, the selected survey delivery mechanism was mail-out, mail-back. The survey consisted of the following sections (based on Bennett and Adamowicz 2001):

- letter of introduction;
- preamble including background and contextual information (framing information);
- statement of the problem;
- statement of the potential solution;
- introduction to the choice sets;
- the choice sets;
- debriefing questions;
- socio-economic and attitude based questions; and
- opportunity for additional feedback.

Each of the sections was developed and refined in three main phases:

1. an initial survey draft was designed based on questionnaire designs from Blamey et al. (1997) and Morrison, Bennett and Blamey (1997);
2. draft surveys were refined following feedback from each focus group. Focus group discussions targeted the preamble, statements of the issue and solution and the choice sets; and
3. the final questionnaire was formatted into the layout required to undertake a mail-based survey.[7]

Discussion of the most important section, the choice sets, is the focus in the remainder of this section.8

The choice sets

The choice sets are the heart of any CM questionnaire. They are designed to elicit the trade-offs that individuals make between attributes and to facilitate the estimation of values for each attribute and thus for alternative biophysical outcomes. The trade-offs that are expected of respondents are difficult. Therefore, simplicity and clarity are two key aspects of choice set presentation and a number of alternative formats were designed and trialled during the focus groups. Choice set methodology followed Bennett and Adamowicz (2001). Choice sets were generically labelled (except the BAU option) and a 'blocked' fractional factorial design was used in the survey. A draft choice set format was developed based on previous CM surveys from Blamey et al. (1997) and Morrison, Bennett and Blamey (1997).

The final choice set design is shown in Figure 7.1. Key features of the design are:

| 6. Suppose options A, B and C are the ONLY ones available, which would you choose? | I Pay | What I get | | | | I would choose |
	Levy	Healthy wetlands	Healthy remnant vegetation	Threatened species that benefit	Ducks hunted	Tick one box only
Option A: No Change	NIL	🌾	🌳	NIL	🦆🦆	☐
Option B	20	🌾🌾	🌳🌳	🦜	🦆🦆	☐
Option C	50	🌾🌾	🌳🌳	🦜🦜🦜🦜	🦆🦆	☐

Notes   The symbols were related to the quantitative numbers in the preamble of the survey and respondents were reminded of the key to the symbols in the introduction to the choice sets.

Figure 7.1 Choice set design for USE questionnaire

1. the labels 'What I pay' and 'What I get' clarify the trade-offs facing respondents;
2. the choice options are read horizontally; and
3. icons represent the attribute levels. The icon levels were shown in a 'Symbol key' that folded out to allow respondents to view it while completing the choice sets (shown for the USE in Figure 7.2).

Participants in the final focus group indicated they had no particular problems answering the question, commenting it was 'clear enough' and 'easy to answer'. Despite the confidence achieved that respondents would have few difficulties answering the choice set, several debriefing questions were included to assess any such difficulties.

Symbol key

Healthy wetlands		= 22 000 Hectares (55 000 acres)
Healthy remnant vegetation		= 25 000 Hectares (60 000 acres)
Threatened species that will benefit		= 6 Species
Ducks hunted		= 3 000 Ducks

A summary of the situation

Healthy wetlands	44 000 Ha
Healthy remnant vegetation	50 000 Ha.
Total number of threatened species	24*
Ducks hunted	6 000

* *Includes several species that would become extinct in the Upper South East (but not Australia)*

Figure 7.2 Foldout symbol key used in questionnaire

7.2.5 Survey Implementation

The sample frame determines who is to be surveyed. Previous studies have indicated that the values held for wetlands are likely to differ in relation to the geographic proximity of the respondent (see for example Rolfe and Bennett 2000) while the focus groups indicated wetland values are held outside the case study areas. Hence, USE surveys[9] were undertaken in the Naracoorte (800), Adelaide (800) and ACT (400). For the MRF, surveys were undertaken in Griffith (800), Wagga Wagga (800), ACT (800) and Adelaide (400). The cross-samples can be used to test hypotheses about the effects of distance on values.

Both the USE and MRF surveys were undertaken as mail-out/mail-back. This survey format decision was based on the relative costs of obtaining a suitable sample size and feedback received in focus groups. The publicly available residential telephone directory 'Australia on Disk' was used to derive a sample of some 2 000 names and addresses for the USE surveys and 2,800 for the MRF surveys. Samples were randomly selected from sub-samples within the 'Australia on Disk' database to reflect a broad socio-economic cross section of the target communities.[10] Due to the costs associated with survey printing, only one mail-out of the survey followed up by two reply reminders spaced at two and three and a half weeks after the initial mail-out were undertaken.

The next phase of the research is to prepare and analyse the data received from the questionnaires. These steps are discussed in the next two sections of this chapter.

7.3   USE NON-USE VALUES

In this section, the survey response rate, sample characteristics, choice model estimation and results are discussed for the USE survey. These results are then used to generate estimates of the non-use values for each of the potential resource reallocations discussed in Chapter 4.

7.3.1 Survey Response Rate, Sample Characteristics and Representativeness

The response rate for the USE is summarised in Table 7.2. A total of 2,000 surveys were mailed out, 247 were returned to sender and 542 completed surveys were returned for a response rate of 31 per cent excluding undelivered surveys. The response rate is relatively consistent across all samples and questionnaire versions. The response rate compares favourably with other mail-out CM surveys in Australia such as Rolfe and Bennett (2000) and Lockwood and Carberry (1998).

Respondent characteristics are shown in Table 7.3. Seventy-eight per cent of respondents had visited the USE region. ACT residents were much less likely to have visited the region (37 per cent) or to visit the region in the future (26 per cent). Only a small proportion of respondents indicated they are likely to hunt ducks in the future. The mean age of respondents was 51 years (median 50) and 58 per cent of respondents were male. The median age of respondents was uniformly six to nine years older than the population. The income level of respondents was also generally higher than the wider population. The education qualifications of respondents were skewed towards higher levels with 27% having tertiary or higher qualifications. The median income bracket is $36,400 to $51,999. This is higher than the national median of just over $34,322. The ACT sub-sample is higher again at $52,000 to $77,999, which is comparable to the difference between ACT incomes and the national average.

Table 7.2 Response rate for USE survey

Sample	Number mailed out	Undelivered*	Successful	Response rate
Adelaide	800	98	225	32.1%
Naracoorte	800	78	207	28.7%
ACT	400	67	110	33.0%
Total	*2 000*	*247*	*542*	*30.8%*

Notes   *   Undelivered surveys were those returned to sender.

7.3.2 USE Choice Model Estimation

The variables included during estimation of the USE CM are defined in Table 7.4. Tests of preliminary models indicated that the 'assumption of independence of irrelevant alternatives' was violated (IIA violation).[11] The practical conclusion of IIA violations is that the estimated model may not generate accurate choice predictions. A nested logit model (NLM) is the suggested treatment where IIA violations occur (Louviere, Henscher and Swait 2000). The NLM 'partitions the choice set to allow alternatives to

Table 7.3 Summary of USE respondent demographics and sample representativeness

Sample characteristics	ACT	Adelaide	Naracoorte	Aggregate sample
Median age	48	49	50	50
Sex (%Male)	50.5%	59.9%	61.1%	58.1%
Median annual income	$52,000 to 77,999	$36,400 to 51,999	$36,400 to 51,999	$36,400 to 51,999
Tertiary educated	46.1%	29.7%	16.0%	27.4%
Population characteristics	**ACT**	**Adelaide**	**Naracoorte**	**Australia**
Median age	39	43	43	42
Sex (%Male)	48.7%	47.8%	51.0%	48.9%
Median income	$48,699	$30,971	$28,647	$34,322
Tertiary educated	23.9%	10.4%	5.1%	11.0%

Wetland and remnant vegetation visitation	Yes	No	Maybe
Have you visited the USE region?	78.4%	21.6%	n.a.
Do you think that you will visit the USE in the future?	63.7%	8.9%	27.4%
Have you ever hunted ducks?	15.2%	84.8%	n.a.
Do you think you will hunt ducks in the future?	4.7%	95.3%	n.a.

Notes   Age and percentage male is reported for individuals over 17 years of age.
For all samples, the sample is significantly different from the population age at the 95 per cent level of confidence, except for gender in the ACT.

share common unobserved components among one another compared with a non-nested alternative' (Louviere, Henscher and Swait 2000). Louviere, Henscher and Swait note that the partitioning occurs as a result of the primary conditions imposed on the unobserved effects in each indirect utility function and that the specification of the partitioning structure can often be assisted by intuition about the behaviour of respondents due to the number of nesting structure options available.

The results for the NLM are reported in Table 7.5 and the tree diagram for the model in Figure 7.3. The coefficients for all of the attributes in the choice sets, except the area of healthy wetlands, are significant at the one per cent level. All coefficients except wetland area have the expected sign.[12] The overall model result is also significant at the one per cent level as shown by

Table 7.4 Definition of all variables included in the USE modelling process

Variable	Definition
Cost	Size of one-off levy on income via income tax
Wetlands	Area of healthy wetlands (hectares)
Remnants	Area of healthy remnant vegetation (hectares)
Species	Number of threatened species that benefit
Duck hunt	Number of ducks hunted
ASC1	Alternative specific constant equals 1 for options 2 and 3 else zero
ASC2	Alternative specific constant equals 1 for option 2 else zero
Age	Age of respondents
Sex	Gender of respondent (1 for female, 0 for male)
Income	Log of respondent income
Canberra	Dummy variable equals 1 for ACT else zero
Naracoorte	Dummy variable equals 1 for Naracoorte else zero
Tert	Dummy variable equals 1 for tertiary education else zero
Trade	Dummy variable equals 1 for diploma/trade qualification else zero
Hschool	Dummy variable equals 1 for high school qualifications else zero
Other	Dummy variable equals 1 for other educational qualifications else zero
Visit	Dummy variable equals 1 for respondents who visited the region else zero
Intended visit	Dummy variable equals 1 for respondents who intend to visit the region else zero
Hunt	Dummy variable equals 1 for respondents who reported hunting ducks else zero
Green	Dummy variable equals 1 for respondents who preferred conservation in decisions between conservation and development else zero
NDT	Dummy variable equals one for respondents who do not trust government to make levy one-off or protested against the payment vehicle on other grounds else zero
Confusion	Dummy variable equals one for respondent reporting they were confused about survey design or information else zero
Wgreen	Green * Wetlands
Dhhunt	Hunt * Duck hunt

Table 7.5 Results of USE nested logit model

Variables	Coefficient	Standard error
Utility functions		
ASC2	0.203E+0[a]	0.695E–1
Cost	–0.131E–1[a]	0.536E–5
Wetlands	–0.161E–4[a]	0.414E–5
Remnants	0.121E–4[a]	0.416E–5
Species	0.632E–1[a]	0.617E–2
Duck hunt	–0.572E–4[a]	0.121E–4
Wgreen	0.359E–4[a]	0.616E–5
Dhhunt	0.968E–4[a]	0.314E–4
Branch choice equations		
ASC1	7.624E+0[a]	1.153E+0
Income	–0.683E+0[a]	0.993E–1
Intended visit	–0.510E+0[a]	0.158E+0
Age	-0.147E–1[a]	0.479E–2
Confusion	0.381E+0[a]	0.141E+0
NDT	2.357E+0[a]	0.150E+0
Canberra	–0.338E+0[b]	0.190E+0
Inclusive value parameters		
Support	0.995E+0[a]	0.618E–1
No support (fixed parameter)	1.000E+0	
Model statistics		
N (choice sets)	2385	
Log L	–1337.703	
Adjusted rho-square (%)	32.882	
Chi-square (constants only)	1329.599[a]	

Notes a   indicates significance at the one per cent level; and
b   indicates significance at the ten per cent level.

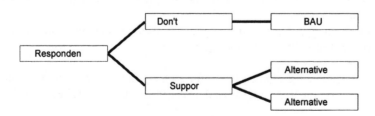

Figure 7.3 Tree diagram for nested logit model

the chi-squared statistic. The explanatory power of the model is very high with an adjusted rho-squared of 32.8 per cent.[13]

The negative cost coefficient indicates that respondents are less likely to choose options as cost increases. Likewise, respondents are less likely to choose options with larger numbers of ducks hunted but more likely to choose options with larger numbers of endangered species protected and larger areas of healthy remnant vegetation. The positive *Wgreen* coefficient indicates that respondents who indicated they favour conservation over development also value increased wetland area. The positive *Dhhunt* coefficient indicates that duck hunters value increased duck hunting harvests.

Theory provides guidance as to the expected sign of the socio-economic and attitudinal variables. Respondents who indicated they were confused by the questionnaire, did not trust the government, or protested against the payment vehicle (the levy) would all be more likely to support the BAU approach and hence possess a positive coefficient when predicting the likelihood of supporting BAU. The significance of these variables indicates that despite the careful design and proofing of the survey a statistically significant element of respondent confusion and protest against the payment vehicle remained. Individuals with higher incomes should be more likely to support the proposal hence a negative income coefficient.[14] Intending visitors would also be expected to support changed management as a reflection of their option values for future visits, again a negative coefficient is expected. Education, gender and location dummies were insignificant with the exception of the Canberra dummy. Variables that were insignificant at the 15 per cent level were removed and the model re-estimated. Movements in the adjusted rho-squared were used to assist decisions about the explanatory value of the variables removed.

7.3.3 Estimation of Willingness to Pay

The results of the CM estimation can be used to estimate two types of values:

1. implicit prices – the willingness to pay for a unit change in a single attribute; and,
2. compensating surplus – the change in welfare, measured in dollars, resulting from a change in management.

In this section, the implicit prices for each attribute and the compensating surplus for the potential USE wetland management strategies are estimated.

Implicit price estimates
Implicit prices (IP) are the marginal rates of substitution between the non-marketed attributes and the monetary attribute. The marginal rates of substitution are derived as the partial differentiation of the attribute of interest with respect to utility. Hence, in a model without any socio-economic interactions with the attributes, they are estimated as the ratio of the coefficient of a non-monetary attribute and the coefficient of the monetary attribute:

$$IP = ß_{\text{non-monetary attribute}} / ß_{\text{monetary attribute}} \qquad (7.5)$$

Confidence intervals can also be calculated for the implicit price estimates following the procedure developed by Krinsky and Robb (1986).[15] Implicit price and confidence intervals for the USE attributes are presented in Table 7.6. The results indicate that on average, respondents are willing to pay $0.92 for an extra 1 000 hectares of remnant vegetation and $4.81 to benefit an additional threatened species. Respondents who indicated they were pro-conservation were willing to pay $2.73 more for an additional 1 000 hectares of wetlands than other respondents. That is, $1.51 for an additional 1 000 hectares of healthy wetlands. Remaining respondents were willing to pay minus $1.22 and the average willingness to pay across the whole sample was minus $0.61 per additional 1 000 hectares of healthy wetlands. The average willingness to pay for an additional 1 000 hectares of healthy wetlands was not significantly different from zero at the 95 per cent level. Similarly, duck hunters were willing to pay $7.37 more than non-hunters for an additional 1 000 ducks hunted for a net price of $3.01. Respondents who had not hunted ducks were willing to pay $4.35 to have 1 000 fewer ducks hunted for an average of minus $1.79 per additional 1 000 ducks hunted. The willingness to pay of duck hunters and the average willingness to pay were not significantly different to zero at the 95 per cent level.[16]

The marginal rates of substitution can also be used to estimate the trade-offs between differing attributes. For example, respondents are willing to trade-off:

- 1 additional threatened species benefits = 5,219 ha of extra remnant vegetation = 2,684 fewer ducks hunted

Table 7.6 Estimates of USE implicit prices

Attribute	Mean IP	95% Confidence Interval	
		Upper	Lower
Wetland area (non-green respondents per 1,000 ha)	–$1.22	–$0.53	–$1.92
Wetland area (green respondents per 1,000 ha)	$1.51	$2.35	$0.66
Wetland area (average per 1,000 ha)	–$0.61*	$0.05	–$1.24
Remnant area (per 1,000 ha)	$0.92	$1.54	$0.25
Species (per species)	$4.81	$5.70	$3.94
Ducks hunted (non hunters per 1,000)	–$4.35	–$2.62	–$6.07
Ducks hunted (hunters per 1,000)	$3.01*	$7.35	–$1.34
Ducks hunted (average per 1,000)	–$1.79*	$0.06	–$3.49

Notes * Implicit price is not significantly different from zero at the 95 per cent level of confidence.
Prices are in Australian dollars at year 2000 levels estimated at the sample mean.

Compensating surplus estimates
Compensating surplus is the appropriate estimate of the willingness to pay for a change from the current situation.[17] The willingness to pay for a change from the current situation incorporates other reasons why respondents might (or might not) choose to support the management change that are incorporated in the ASCs, socio-economic and attitudinal variables. Estimates of the average compensating surplus per individual are calculated using:[18]

$$CS = -1 \text{ / marginal utility of income} * (V_C - V_N) \quad\quad (7.6a)$$
$$CS = -1 / \beta_{cost} * (V_C - V_N) \quad\quad (7.6b)$$

where: V_C represents the utility of the BAU option
V_N represents the utility of the new option

BAU utility (VC) is estimated by substituting the coefficients and attribute levels (except cost) for the current situation. The calculation of the utility of the BAU situation also includes the other determining factors (ASC, socio-economic and attitudinal variables). Hence, VC is estimated as follows:

$V_{C(USE)}$ = ASC + ($\beta_{\text{wetland area}}$ * wetland area + $\beta_{\text{remnant area}}$ * remnant   (7.7)
area + β_{species} * species + $\beta_{\text{ducks hunted}}$ * ducks hunted +
β_{wgreen} * wetland area * proportion respondents green +
β_{Dhhunt} * ducks hunted * proportion duck hunters) + Σ
($\beta_{\text{socioeconomic \& attitudinal}}$ * Socio-economic and attitudinal)

where the socio-economic and attitudinal values are entered at population
levels or average respondent measures where population measures are
not available.19

The new utility is calculated by multiplying the IV parameter by the new
attribute levels after adopting the change to management:

$V_{N(USE)}$ = IV parameter * (ASC_1 / 2 + $\beta_{\text{wetland area}}$ * wetland area +   (7.8)
$\beta_{\text{remnant area}}$ * remnant area + β_{species} * species + $\beta_{\text{ducks hunted}}$
* ducks hunted + β_{wgreen} * wetland area * proportion
respondents green + β_{Dhhunt} * ducks hunted * proportion
respondents who hunt)

The average per-individual compensating surplus estimate calculated
must be extrapolated across the population to estimate the total value from
changing wetland management. Extrapolation requires a number of
assumptions about the proportion of the population that hold the values
estimated in the survey and about how these values may change into the
future. Initial assumptions used to calculate the aggregate estimates reported
in Table 7.7 are:

- only 30.8 per cent of the SA population hold values for wetlands in the
  USE (that is, values are only extrapolated across the response rate of
  the survey);
- no values are held by non-SA residents; and
- no growth in the SA population over the next 30 years.

Table 7.7 Environmental values from adopting alternative USE management strategies compared to the BAU strategy

Attributes and values	Wetland retention	Pro-wetlands	Wetlands and remnants
Individual CS estimate	$42.01	$42.49	$111.01
Confidence interval – lower 95%	$7.15	$6.39	$79.86
Confidence interval – upper 95%	$60.40	$55.44	$121.88
Extrapolated population	610,600	610,600	610,600
Aggregate CS estimate	$8,029,000	$8,120,000	$21,217,000

The implications of relaxing these assumptions are discussed in the sensitivity analysis in Chapter 8. The environmental values are not discounted to a present value because respondents were asked to place their current value on an outcome that would occur in 30 years time. Hence, individuals implicitly discounted their future values by providing present values for a future outcome.[20]

Confidence intervals can be estimated for the CS using the same methodology as for the IP. For example, the 95 per cent confidence interval for the CS resulting from adopting the 'wetlands and remnants' strategy is $80 to $122. These values are input into the sensitivity testing procedure in Chapter 8.

7.4   MRF NON-USE VALUES

Estimation of the MRF choice model is the focus in this section. The MRF modelling procedure was the same as the USE with the exception of the final functional form selected. The resulting value estimates are the final component of the economic modelling for the MRF case study area.

7.4.1 Survey response rate, sample characteristics and representativeness

The response rate for the MRF survey is summarised in Table 7.8. Two thousand eight hundred surveys were mailed out, 378 were returned to sender and 732 surveys were returned for a response rate of 30 per cent when undelivered surveys were excluded. The response rate is relatively consistent across all samples except the Griffith sample (22%). The relatively low Griffith response rate is partly due to a survey assembly error that was not discovered until responses were being processed.[21] The response rate compares favourably with other mail-out CM surveys in Australia such as Rolfe and Bennett (2000) and Lockwood and Carberry (1998).

Table 7.8 Response rate for MRF survey

Sample	Mailed out	Undelivered*	Returned	Response rate
Griffith	800	113	151	22.0%
Wagga Wagga	800	96	232	33.0%
ACT	800	121	229	33.7%
Adelaide	400	48	120	34.1%
Total	2,800	378	732	30.2%

Notes * Undelivered surveys were those returned to sender.

Respondent characteristics are shown in Table 7.9. Seventy-seven per cent of respondents had visited the MRF region. As would be expected the proportion of respondents who had visited the region was highest for towns adjoining the case study area (Wagga Wagga and Griffith at 93%) and lower in the ACT (67%) and Adelaide (47%). Likewise Adelaide residents are much less likely to visit the region in the future (33% say they won't versus less than ten per cent for the remainder of the sample). The mean age of respondents was 51 years (median 50) and 61 per cent of respondents were male. The median age of respondents was uniformly eight to eleven years older than the population. The education qualifications of respondents were skewed towards higher levels with 38 per cent having tertiary or higher qualifications. The median income bracket is $36,400 to $51,999, which is higher than the wider population. The ACT sub-sample is higher again at $52,000 to $77,999, which is comparable to the difference between ACT incomes and the national average.

7.4.2 MRF Choice Model Estimation

The same data preparation was undertaken with the MRF survey data as for the USE. Definitions of the variables used in the modelling process are provided in Table 7.10.

Table 7.9 Summary of MRF respondent demographics and sample representativeness

Sample characteristics	ACT	Wagga Wagga	Griffith	Adelaide	Aggregate sample
Median age	48	49	52	52	50
Sex (%Male)	61.8%	55.8%	66.2%	60.2%	60.9%
Median income	$52,000 to $77,999	$36,400 to $51,999	$36,400 to $51,999	$36,400 to $51,999	$36,400 to $51,999
Tertiary educated	52.3%	28.4%	26.0%	42.5%	37.9%

Population characteristics	ACT	Wagga Wagga	Griffith	Adelaide	Australia
Median age	39	39	41	43	42
Sex (%Male)	48.7%	48.5%	50.3%	47.8%	48.9%
Median income	$48,699	$32,850	$33,163	$30,971	$34,322
Tertiary educated	23.9%	8.9%	6.1%	10.4%	11.0%

Wetland visitation	Yes	No	Maybe
Have you visited the Murrumbidgee River or floodplain?	77.4%	22.6%	n.a.
Do you think you will visit the Murrumbidgee River or floodplain in the future?	63.3%	10.5%	26.3%

Notes   Age and percentage male is reported for individuals over 18 years and over.
Income is median annual income.
For all samples, the sample is significantly different from the population age at the 95 per cent level of confidence.

182

Table 7.10 Definition of all variables included in the MRF modelling process

Variable	Definition
Cost	Size of levy
Wetlands	Area of healthy wetlands (hectares)
Birds	Number of native birds as a percentage of pre-1800 populations
Fish	Number of native fish as a percentage of pre-1800 populations
Farmers leaving	Number of farmers who leave as a result of management changes
ASC1	Alternative specific constant equals 1 for options 2 and 3 else zero
ASC2	Alternative specific constant equals 1 for option 2 else zero
ASC	Alternative specific constant for options 2 and 3
Age	Age of respondent
Sex	Gender of respondent (1 for female, zero for male)
Adelaide	Dummy variable equals 1 for Adelaide else zero
Canberra	Dummy variable equals 1 for ACT else zero
Griffith	Dummy variable equals 1 for Griffith else zero
Visit	Dummy variable equals 1 for respondents who visited the region else zero
Intended visit	Dummy variable equals 1 for respondents who intend to visit the region else zero
Income	Log of respondent income
Tert	Dummy variable equals 1 for tertiary education else zero
Trade	Dummy variable equals 1 for diploma/trade qualification else zero
Hschool	Dummy variable equals 1 for high school qualifications else zero
Other	Dummy variable equals 1 for other educational qualifications else zero
NDT	Dummy variable equals 1 for respondents who do not trust government to make levy one-off or protested against the payment vehicle on other grounds else zero
Confusion	Dummy variable equals 1 for respondents confused about survey design or information else zero
Levy	Dummy variable equals 1 where respondent indicated levy is not a good idea else zero

Data analysis
Once the data were prepared, an initial series of models was run using the LIMDEP software package on an equivalent generic model to the USE. A number of alternative model structures were also tested on the MRF data because:[22]

1. there were no interaction terms (such as *wgreen* and *dhhunt* in the USE model) providing a computationally simpler model structure; and
2. the range over which the attribute levels was estimated was larger for the MRF than the USE. Theory indicates declining marginal utility from additional units of goods. Because a linear function yields identical additional amounts across the range estimated it is less likely to be appropriate for estimates across a large change in attribute levels.

The generic model structure selected was:

Status quo: $V_1 = ß_1 . Cost + ß_2 / Wetlands + ß_3 / Birds + ß_4$ (7.9a)
                 $/ Fish + ß_5 . Farmers leaving$

Alternative 2: $V_2 = ß_{ASC1} . ASC + ß_1 . Cost + ß_2 / Wetlands +$ (7.9b)
                 $ß_3 / Birds + ß_4 / Fish + ß_5 . Farmers leaving$
                 $+ ß_i . ASC1 . (socio\text{-}economic$ and
                 attitudinal variables$)$

Alternative 3: $V_3 = ßASC1 . ASC + ß_1 . Cost + ß_2 / Wetlands$ (7.9c)
                 $+ ß_3 / Birds + ß_4 / Fish + ß_5 . Farmers$
                 $leaving + ß_i . ASC1 . (socio\text{-}economic$ and
                 attitudinal variables$)$

The generic model structure uses a $1/x$ form for the *wetland area*, *birds* and *fish* attributes and gave the best fit for the data. The $1/x$ form allows diminishing marginal values for progressive increases in the healthy wetlands, native bird and native fish population attribute levels. That is, as the increase in the attribute grows larger the willingness to pay for additional increases grows smaller. Note that the *farmers leaving* and *cost* attributes remain linear due to the zero starting coefficients.

A NLM was developed using the same methodology as for the USE survey data due to IIA violations. The results for the NLM are reported in Table 7.11. The coefficients for all of the attributes in the choice sets are significant at the one per cent level. All coefficients have the expected sign. The overall model result is also significant at the one-per cent level as shown by the chi-squared statistic. The explanatory power of the model is very high with an adjusted rho-squared of 33.6 per cent.

Table 7.11 Results of MRF nested multinomial logit model

Variables	Coefficient	Standard error
Utility functions		
ASC	0.120E+0[b]	0.532E–1
Cost	–0.122E–1[a]	0.570E–3
1 / Wetlands	–7.831E+3[a]	8.293E+2
1 / Birds	–0.508E+0[a]	0.110E+0
1 / Fish	–0.328E+0[a]	0.495E–1
Farmers leaving	–0.700E–1[a]	0.892E–2
Branch choice equations		
ASC	5.809E+0[a]	0.992E+0
Income	–0.345E+0[a]	0.716E–1
Intended visit	–0.444E+0[a]	0.109E–1
Age	0.101E–1[a]	0.349E–2
Tertiary education	–0.216E+0[c]	0.112E+0
NDT	1.553E+0[a]	0.106E+0
Levy	2.111E+0[a]	0.110E+0
Griffith	0.539E+0[a]	0.124E+0
Adelaide	–0.228E+0	0.141E+0
Inclusive value parameters		
Support	0.465E+0[a]	0.686E–1
No support (fixed parameter)	1.000E+0	
Model statistics		
N (choice sets)	3148	
Log L	–2400.297	
Adjusted rho-square (%)	33.58	
Chi-square (constants only)	2445.566[a]	

Notes   a   indicates significance at the one per cent level;
          b   indicates significance at the five per cent level; and
          c   indicates significance at the ten per cent level.

The negative cost coefficient indicates that respondents are less likely to choose options as cost increases. Likewise, respondents are less likely to choose options with more farmers leaving. The negative coefficients for wetland area, birds and fish are a reflection of the functional form and indicate respondents are more likely to pay for options with more healthy wetlands, birds and fish, but at a decreasing rate.

Respondents who could not afford to pay the levy or did not trust the government would all be more likely to support BAU and hence possess a positive coefficient. The significance of these variables indicates that, as for the USE survey, the careful design and proofing of the survey was not sufficient to eliminate protest. Respondents who consider the levy a bad idea will also be more likely to choose the BAU branch. Individuals with higher incomes or who intend to visit the wetlands should be more likely to support the proposal hence a negative income coefficient. There are no strong priors for the age coefficient. Respondents with tertiary education were also hypothesised to support changed management (a result also shown in other surveys such as Rolfe and Bennett 2000). The negative tertiary coefficient supports this hypothesis but is only significant at the 10 per cent level.

Adelaide residents are more likely to support changes to management despite the distance from the wetlands.[23] The Griffith location dummy variable is also significant and negative, indicating a lower willingness to pay for Griffith residents. Due to the low response rate from Griffith, the model was examined carefully prior to inclusion of this dummy variable. Specifically the model was re-estimated with the Griffith data only and with the Griffith data excluded. The coefficients did not differ significantly in these models so the Griffith data and dummy variable were included. Other education and location dummies were insignificant and were removed from the final model. Variables that were insignificant at the 15 per cent level were removed and the model re-estimated. Movements in the adjusted rho-square were used to assist decisions about the explanatory value of the variables removed.

7.4.3 Estimation of Willingness to Pay

Implicit price estimates
The CM results can be used to estimate both implicit prices and the compensating surplus associated with a change in management. Implicit prices are estimated as the rate of change in the attribute divided by the rate of change of the cost coefficient. The rate of change is found by differentiating the utility function with respect to the specified attribute. Hence the implicit price formula (given the $1/x$ inverse functional form) for wetland area, birds and fish attributes is:

$$IP = - \left(-\beta_{\text{non-monetary attribute}} / (\text{attribute level})^2 \right) / \beta_{\text{monetary attribute}} \qquad (7.10)$$

Because the implicit price is related to the level of the attribute, the implicit price will change across the range of areas evaluated. The implicit price estimate for the *farmers leaving* attribute is calculated using the same formula as used in Section 7.3.3. Implicit price and confidence intervals for the MRF attributes are presented in Table 7.12. The estimates for *wetland area, birds* and *fish* are evaluated at the midpoints of the attribute levels evaluated in the survey. The results indicate that respondents are willing to pay $11.39 for an extra 1 000 hectares of healthy wetlands, $0.55 for a one per cent increase in the number of native birds, $0.34 for a one per cent increase in the number of native fish and $5.73 to have one less farmer leave. As indicated, the IP for *wetland area, birds* and *fish* vary in relation to the size of the attribute. For example, at the midpoint (7,500 hectares of healthy wetlands) the *wetland area* IP is $11.39 per 1 000 hectares. At the BAU level (2 500 hectares of healthy wetlands) the willingness to pay is $102.53 for an additional 1 000 hectares, while at the maximum level in the questionnaire (12 500 hectares of healthy wetlands) the IP is $4.10 for an additional 1 000 hectares.

Table 7.12 Estimates of MRF implicit prices

Attribute	Mean IP	95% Confidence Interval	
		Upper	Lower
Wetland area (per 1 000 ha)	$11.39	$13.92	$8.97
Number of native birds (per 1% population change)	$1.15	$1.68	$0.63
Number of native fish (per 1% population change)	$1.68	$2.12	$1.17
Farmers leaving (per farmer)	−$5.73	−$4.46	−$7.15

Notes Prices are in dollars at year 2000 levels and evaluated at the midpoint of the levels surveyed. Confidence intervals are estimated using the Krinsky and Robb (1986) random draw procedure outlined in Section 7.3.3.

The marginal rates of substitution can also be used to estimate the trade-offs between differing attributes. For example, at the survey midpoints respondents are willing to trade-off:

- 1 more farmer leaving = 503 ha of extra healthy wetlands = 10.4% extra native bird numbers = 17.0% extra native fish numbers

Compensating surplus estimates
Compensating surpluses are calculated using the methodology explained in Section 7.3.3 and using equation 7.6b. The utility levels are estimated using

the functional forms shown in equations 7.9a, b and c. Hence, VC and VN in the MRF are defined as 7.11 and 7.12:

$$VC_{(MRF)} = ASC + (\beta_{\text{wetland area}} / \text{Wetlands} + \beta_{\text{birds}} / \text{Birds} + \beta_{\text{fish}} / \quad (7.11)$$
$$\text{Fish} + \beta_{\text{farmers leaving}} * \text{Farmers leaving}) + \Sigma$$
$$(\beta_{\text{socioeconomic \& attitudinal}} * \text{Socio-economic and}$$
$$\text{attitudinal})$$

where the socio-economic and attitudinal values are entered at population levels or average respondent measures where population measures are not available.[24]

$$V_{N(MRF)} = \text{IV parameter} * (ASC\_1 / 2 + \beta_{\text{wetland area}} / \text{Wetlands} + \quad (7.12)$$
$$\beta_{\text{birds}} / \text{Birds} + \beta_{\text{fish}} / \text{Fish} + \beta_{\text{farmers leaving}} * \text{Farmers}$$
$$\text{leaving})$$

The average per-individual compensating surplus estimate calculated must then be extrapolated across the population. Extrapolation requires a number of assumptions about the proportion of the population that hold the values estimated in the survey and about how these values may change into the future. Initial assumptions used to calculate the aggregate MRF estimates reported in Table 7.13 are:

- only 29.6 per cent of the population of the Murrumbidgee Catchment (including the ACT) hold values for wetlands in the MRF (that is, values are only extrapolated across the response rate of the survey);
- no values are held by non-Murrumbidgee Catchment residents; and
- no growth in the Murrumbidgee Catchment population over the next 30 years.

The implications of relaxing these assumptions are discussed in the sensitivity analysis in Chapter 8. The environmental values are not discounted to a present value because respondents were asked to place their current value on an outcome that would occur in 30 years time. Hence, individuals implicitly discounted their future values by providing present values for a future outcome.

Confidence intervals can be estimated for the CS using the same methodology as for the IP. For example, the 95 per cent confidence interval for the CS resulting from adopting the 'grazing management' strategy is $123 to $164. These values are used as part of the sensitivity testing procedure in Chapter 8.

Table 7.13 Environmental values from adopting alternative MRF management strategies compared to the BAU strategy

Attributes and values	Water management	Grazing management	Timber management	Combined strategies
Individual consumers' surplus	$131.55	$143.26	$46.91	$184.02
Confidence interval – lower 95%	$114.12	$123.84	$20.21	$160.11
Confidence interval – upper 95%	$148.04	$164.00	$79.53	$210.05
Extrapolated population	64,300	64,300	64,300	64,300
Total consumers' surplus	$8,459,000	$9,212,000	$3,016,000	$11,832,000

7.5 CONCLUSIONS

Changing wetland management in both the USE of SA and the MRF in NSW generates significant non-monetary benefits. Wetland owners and the wider community enjoy these non-monetary benefits. However, these non-monetary benefits must be integrated with the other benefits and costs experienced by wetland owners in reallocating resources in these wetland areas that were estimated in Chapters 5 and 6. The aggregate trade-offs are the focus of the bio-economic integration phase of the model in Chapter 8.

NOTES

1. Strict application of the contingent valuation approach would require each outcome to be compared against BAU and against each other in order to determine whether one biophysical outcome is superior over another. This would require a total of six surveys for the USE and ten surveys for the MRF.
2. IID of the error term means that it has an 'extreme value error distribution' (Ben-Akiva and Lerman 1993).
3. The questionnaire design along with the underlying assumptions about respondents determines the number of ASCs that are required. For example, labelled choice sets require individual ASCs for (J-1) alternatives. However, non-labelled sets can be estimated via a generic model with a common ASC for (J-1) alternatives.

4. While low per capital values may generate large aggregate values, there will be little perceived respondent benefit from participating in the CM exercise and hence a low response rate.
5. Focus groups are selected to cover a broad cross section of the community in terms of socio-economic characteristics such as age and sex that potentially signal differing attitudes and values.
6. Market research companies were employed to recruit four focus groups. Each group consisted of 8 to 10 people that were loosely representative of the population eligible to vote in terms of age and sex. Groups were convened in Canberra (two groups), Adelaide and Griffith. During the recruitment of participants incentive payments ($35 per participant) were mentioned after the person had agreed to attend. Groups were convened in Canberra (two groups), Adelaide and Griffith. Groups were audio recorded to allow opinions expressed to be examined in detail.
7. A graphic design artist undertook the final questionnaire preparation phase in close consultation with the authors in order to improve the presentation of the questionnaire and increase the response rate.
8. A copy of the questionnaire and accompanying material is available from the authors on request.
9. Sample sizes are given in brackets for each sub-sample area.
10. While the electoral role is the preferred sample source it is not available in electronic form and is thus much more expensive to use.
11. Testing of the best performing multinomial logit model using the test procedure developed by Hausman and McFadden (1984) showed IIA violations at the 1 per cent level. More information on the Hausman and McFadden test is also provided in Louviere, Henscher and Swait (2000).
12. A potential explanation for a negative wetland coefficient is that many respondents may be recalling the (undesirable) appearance of saline wetlands that can be seen from the major roads through the region.
13. Rho-squared adjusted is similar to R^2 in standard regression analysis. It is equal to one minus the ratio of the unrestricted log-likelihood ratio over the restricted log-likelihood ratio. Rho-squared adjusted values between 20 per cent and 40 per cent are considered extremely good fits (Henscher and Johnson 1981). Louviere, Henscher and Swait (2000) suggest that the inclusive value parameter should be significantly different from one in order to justify use of NLM structures – this is clearly not the case for the USE model shown in Table 7.5. The NLM model is used because use of the NLM structure has significantly improved the explanatory power as measured by Rho-squared adjusted (.32 versus .27), the Hausman and McFadden test indicate IIA violations, and, for consistency with the MRF model discussed in Section 7.4.
14. The expected sign of the coefficient depends on which branch of the nested logit model the socio-economic coefficients are placed. If they were placed on the change options rather than the BAU the expected sign would be the opposite to those above.
15. To estimate confidence intervals a random draw (of 200 in this case) of parameter vectors is made from a multivariate normal distribution with the mean and variance equal to the ß vector and the variance-covariance matrix from the estimated nested logit model.
16. The non-significance of the values held by duck hunters for additional ducks hunted is likely due to the relatively small number of duck hunters surveyed (82 of 542 respondents reported having hunted ducks).
17. Estimation of the consumers' surplus is consistent with the discussion in Chapter 3. The measure of compensating surplus calculated is the Hicksian surplus. The Hicksian surplus and the Marshallian surplus are equivalent if the marginal utility of income is assumed constant across the ranges estimated. The Marshallian surplus is commonly known as the consumers' surplus.

18. Estimation of consumers' surplus from CM results is based on the assumption that the cost coefficient (β_{cost}) equals the marginal utility of income.
19. An estimate of the true willingness to pay if there was no confusion or protest at the payment vehicle can also be made because measures of respondent confusion and protest against the payment vehicle are included in the model. This estimate is tested as part of the sensitivity tests in Chapter 8.
20. The time path of achieving the 30-year outcome was not specified in the CM questionnaire. Hence, it is difficult to infer the progression of benefits within the 30-year period.
21. Some pages of the questionnaire were stapled into the booklets upside down. The error was only present in MRF version 5 that were sent to Griffith and led to a response rate of 10 per cent for version 5 in Griffith.
22. Adamowicz, Boxall, Williams and Louviere (1998) explored the use of linear and quadratic functional forms and showed large differences in the resultant welfare measures, thus underlining the importance of functional form.
23. This could be due to a perceived impact on Adelaide water quality because Adelaide water is drawn from the Murray River, of which the Murrumbidgee is a major tributary.
24. Because measures of respondent confusion and protest against the payment vehicle are included in the model an estimate of the true willingness to pay if there was no confusion or protest at the payment vehicle can also be made. This estimate is tested as part of the sensitivity tests in Chapter 8.

8.   Bio-economic Integration

The focus of this chapter is the integration of the estimates of economic values changed by altering wetland management into a bio-economic model. The main object of the bio-economic model is to inform decisions involving the allocation of resources to those uses that generate the highest net value to the community. The criterion used to assess alternative allocations is referred to as the 'Net Present Value Test' (NPVT). The NPVT asks whether the sum of the discounted benefits from changing wetland management exceeds the sum of the discounted costs that are incurred as a result of wetland management changes.

Bio-economic integration comprises steps 7 to 9 of the bio-economic modelling process outlined in Chapter 3. The first of these steps involves aggregating the costs and benefits of changing wetland management. Aggregation of the discounted costs and benefits of changing wetland management facilitates a test of Hypothesis One using the net present value test (NPVT) as discussed in Chapter 3. Distributional analysis is the second step in bio-economic integration. Analysis of the distribution of the discounted costs and benefits across differing population sections and through time facilitates an assessment of the validity of the NPVT as a test of Hypothesis One and provides valuable policy information that may be used as an input into the Hypothesis Two test methodology. A 'best estimate' aggregation of the costs and benefits is subject to risk and uncertainty and is therefore only suitable as a weak test of Hypothesis One. Incorporation of risk and uncertainty via a sensitivity analysis is the last of the steps in the bio-economic modelling process. Elements of risk and uncertainty can be incorporated via a sensitivity analysis of the constituent discounted costs and benefits thus facilitating a stronger test of Hypothesis One.

The three steps in the bio-economic integration component of the bio-economic model, along with tests of Hypothesis One, are undertaken for the USE and MRF case study areas in the next three sections of this chapter. In the first section, aggregation of a 'best-estimate' integrated bio-economic model is undertaken for the USE and MRF along with a weak test of Hypothesis One according to the NPVT criteria. The distribution of the discounted benefits and costs aggregated in Section 8.1 is analysed in

Section 8.2. The impact of risk and uncertainty on the discounted costs and benefits is then assessed in the final part of the chapter via a series of sensitivity tests. The final section includes a stronger NPVT test of Hypothesis One for the USE and MRF using the output from the sensitivity tests.

8.1   INTEGRATION AND AGGREGATION

Aggregation of the values estimated in the economic modelling phase forms the base of the bio-economic model. It facilitates the comparison of alternative biological states created by the adoption of alternative wetland management strategies in terms of the net benefits they generate to society.

USE aggregation and weak test of Hypothesis One
The change to NPV that would result from the adoption of each strategy in the USE compared to the BAU scenario is shown in Table 8.1. The 'wetland retention' strategy generates a positive NPV ($5.2m) from the best-estimate assumptions set out in Chapters 5, 6 and 7. All other strategies generate a negative NPV. For example, the 'wetlands and remnants' strategy generates a NPV of –$15.2m. Hence, the weak test of Hypothesis One using the NPVT of the aggregate data in Table 8.1 indicates that the 'pro-wetlands' and 'wetlands and remnants' strategies are rejected while the 'wetland retention' strategy is accepted. Therefore, a net benefit to the community could be generated from at least some increase in the production of wetland outputs in the USE region.

Some value estimates included in the aggregation are considered to be conservative (such as the non-use environmental values).[1] The implications of the conservative nature of these estimates are discussed in Section 8.3 in which the sensitivity analysis is reported.

MRF aggregation and weak test of Hypothesis One
Estimates of the costs and benefits of adopting alternative wetland management strategies in the MRF are summarised in Table 8.2. Adoption of the 'grazing management' strategy is the only option that generates a positive NPV ($5.1m). The 'water management' (–$4.4m), 'timber management' (–$1.7m) and 'combined strategies' (–$9.7m) options each generate a negative NPV. Therefore, the 'grazing management' option is accepted under a weak test of Hypothesis One. This conclusion is subjected to more rigorous examination following incorporation of the impacts of risk and uncertainty in Section 8.3.

Table 8.1 NPV from adoption of alternative USE management strategies

Cost or benefit	Wetland retention	Pro-wetlands	Wetlands and remnants
Changes to agricultural activities			
Pasture establishment and management costs saved	$0	$2,462,000	$4,963,000
Cost of lost agricultural productivity	−$1,166,000	-$5,672,000	−$18,332,000
Sub-total	−$1,166,000	−$3,210,000	−$13,368,000
Management costs of wetlands and remnants			
Capital costs of wetland rehabilitation	$253,000	$4,624,000	$4,621,000
Capital costs of native vegetation rehabilitation	$0	$0	$6,761,000
Capital costs of fencing	$1,137,000	$2,436,000	$5,883,000
Ongoing management costs	$1,614,000	$3,231,000	$9,894,000
Sub-total	−$3,004,000	−$10,290,000	−$27,159,000
Environmental values generated – consumers' surpluses			
Duck hunting	$85,000	$220,000	$238,000
Tourism	$531,000	$972,000	$1,492,000
Non-use values	$8,029,000	$8,120,000	$21,217,000
Sub-total	$8,645,000	$9,312,000	$22,947,000
Environmental values generated – producers' surpluses			
Duck hunting	$ 26,000	$66,000	$72,000
Tourism	$726,000	$1,778,000	$2,290,000
Other wetland owner values		*Not estimated*	
Sub-total	$752,000	$1,844,000	$ 2,364,000
Total environmental values	$9,397,000	$11,156,000	$25,311,000
Total changes valued	$5,227,000	−$2,343,000	−$15,217,000

Notes   Values are net present values of benefit and cost streams over 30 years using a 7 per cent discount rate.

8.2   DISTRIBUTION OF IMPACTS

Aggregation across individuals for different types of values and across groups of individuals to estimate the NPV of changes to total economic value is reliant on several assumptions which were discussed in Chapter 3. First, it requires an assumption that income elasticities are similar for all individuals and that any changes in income distribution are small (Hanley and Spash 1993).   Second, valid aggregation also requires that the income distribution on which estimates are based be regarded as a sufficiently 'fair' base for making comparisons. These two issues are briefly discussed in this section with respect to the USE and MRF case studies.

8.2.1 USE Distributional Analysis

The distribution of the costs and benefits of adoption of the alternative wetland management strategies in the USE are shown in Table 8.3 (which is an alternative specification of Table 8.1). The majority of benefits from changing management accrue to the wider community in the form of non-marketed benefits, primarily generated by non-use values. In contrast, the majority of the costs imposed by changing wetland management are imposed directly on wetland owners. Wetland owners also receive a small monetary benefit from changing wetland management. A closer examination of the nature of the costs to wetland owners in the second part of Table 8.3 shows that the costs of implementing the wetland management strategies comprise upfront capital investment or natural resource repair expenses (such as re-establishing wetland hydrology), ongoing wetland maintenance costs (such as pest and weed control) and loss of income from foregone current uses. The corresponding gains to wetland owners' incomes from changing wetland management are insufficient to compensate for the loss of income from foregone current uses.

The implication of violating the assumptions of similar income elasticities and small changes to income is that the estimated NPV is not unique and the values estimated could be dependent on the particular distributional pattern from which it is drawn. Evidence for or against similar income elasticities was not collected. However, policy design can seek to leverage differences in income elasticities by use of market-based instruments. For example, from a similar starting point, a policy instrument that reduces the price of wetland outputs demanded by higher income elasticity individuals will be more effective than an equivalent policy instrument targeting lower income elasticity individuals, *ceteris paribus*.

Table 8.2 Aggregate cost-benefit analysis of MRF management strategies

Cost or benefit	Water management	Grazing management	Timber management	Combined strategies
Changes to agricultural activities				
Lost agricultural production	$0	–$3,137,000	$0	–$3,137,000
Cost of providing watering points	$0	–$198,000	$0	–$198,000
Lost timber production	$0	$0	–$4,678,000	–$4,678,000
Sub-total	$0	–$3,335,000	–$4,678,000	–$8,013,000
Management costs of wetlands				
Capital costs of water acquisition	–$18,161,000	$0	$0	–$18,161,000
Capital costs of wetland rehabilitation	–$1,151,000	$0	$0	–$1,151,000
Capital costs of fencing	$0	–$1,261,000	$0	–$1,261,000
Capital costs of wetland revegetation	$0	–$209,000	$0	–$209,000
Ongoing costs of wetland management	–$566,000	–$1,187,000	$0	–$2,072,000
Income from future water sales	$6,246,000	$0	$0	$6,246,000
Sub-total	–$13,633,000	–$2,657,000	$0	–$16,609,000

Table 8.2 Continued

Cost or benefit	Water management	Grazing management	Timber management	Combined strategies
Environmental values generated – consumers' surpluses				
Recreation	$742,000	$1,842,000	$0	$3,078,000
Non-use values	$8,459,000	$9,212,000	$3,016,000	$11,832,000
Sub-total	$9,201,000	$11,053,000	$3,016,000	$14,911,000
Other wetland owner values		*not estimated*		
Total changes valued	–$4,432,000	$ 5,061,000	–$1,661,000	–$9,711,000

Notes Values are net present values of benefit and cost streams over 30 years using a 7 per cent discount rate.

Table 8.3 Distribution of adoption costs and benefits of USE strategies

Distribution assessment	Wetland retention	Pro-wetlands	Wetlands and remnants
Monetary costs and benefits (wetland owners)			
Costs direct to owners	–$3,004,000	–$ 7,828,000	–$22,196,000
Other costs (in part to owners)	–$1,166,000	–$ 5,672,000	–$18,332,000
Benefits to wetland owners	$26,000	$66,000	$72,000
Other benefits (in part to owners)	$726,000	$1,779,000	$2,293,000
Net monetary benefits	–$3,418,000	–$11,655,000	–$38,163,000
Non-monetary benefits (wider community)			
Consumers' surplus – visits and non-use values	$8,645,000	$9,312,000	$22,947,000
Total net benefits	$5,227,000	–$ 2,343,000	–$15,217,000
Nature of costs and benefits of changing wetland management			
Capital investment/repair costs	–$1,390,000	–$4,597,000	–$12,301,000
Ongoing maintenance costs	–$1,614,000	–$3,231,000	–$9,894,000
Loss of income (owners only)	–$1,166,000	–$5,672,000	–$18,332,000
Gains to income (not only owners)	$752,000	$1,844,000	$2,364,000
Non-monetary consumers' surplus	$8,645,000	$9,312,000	$22,947,000
Total net benefits	$5,227,000	–$2,343,000	–$15,217,000

Notes   Values are net present values of benefit and cost streams over 30 years using a 7 per cent discount rate.

The evidence in Table 8.3 indicates that the changes to wetland owners' incomes as a result of changing wetland management may be significant – particularly given that there are 73 wetland owners within the region, many of whom may not change wetland management. Therefore, actual compensation (rather than the hypothetical compensation within the Kaldor-Hicks criterion) must be assumed within the bio-economic modelling framework in order to retain a so-called 'Pareto safe' outcome that avoids any potential misallocation due to distributional shifts. A notionally 'Pareto safe' mechanism may nevertheless violate the assumption of small changes to income if the current distribution of property rights and resource rents is regarded as unfair. While this outcome is not assessed in this section it should be considered in policy instrument development, particularly where redistributions of property rights are contemplated.

8.2.2 MRF Distributional Analysis

An alternative specification of Table 8.2 identifying the distribution of costs and benefits of changing wetland management in the MRF is shown in Table 8.4. The majority of the costs of all wetland strategies are imposed on wetland owners while no additional wetland owner income is generated from the changes to wetland management. The 'upfront' proportion of total costs varies significantly between strategies, comprising over 90 per cent of the 'water management' option costs but none of the 'timber management' option costs.

The implications of the distributional analysis are similar to those drawn for the USE in Subsection 8.2.1. The Kaldor-Hicks hypothetical compensation principle underlying the NPVT test can be made operational by paying actual compensation to the relatively small number of wetland owners (approximately 150) in order to ensure a 'Pareto safe' outcome. Similarly, if either the 'water management' or 'combined strategies' option is considered, the costs imposed on the wider community must be sufficiently widespread in order to reduce the income impacts to relatively small proportions of the community. Evidence of differing income elasticities was not collected for the MRF but can be considered as part of the sensitivity analysis and leveraged by appropriate policy instrument design in later chapters. The caveat raised in Subsection 8.2.1 regarding the perceived fairness of the current distribution of property rights and resource rents from wetland resource ownership and the implications for potential redistributions (even when 'Pareto safe') will also be considered when developing MRF wetland policy.

Table 8.4 Distribution of adoption costs and benefits of MRF strategies

Distribution assessment	Water management	Grazing management	Timber management	Combined strategies
Monetary costs and benefits (wetland owners)				
Costs direct to owners	–$1,717,000	–$5,992,000	–$4,678,000	–$12,706,000
Other costs (may also be to owners)	–$11,915,000	$0	$0	–$11,915,000
Net monetary benefits	–$13,633,000	–$5,992,000	–$4,678,000	–$25,622,000
Non-monetary benefits				
Consumers' surplus to wider community	$9,201,000	$11,053,000	$3,016,000	$14,911,000
Total net benefits	–$4,432,000	$5,061,000	–$1,661,000	–$9,711,000
Nature of costs and benefits of changing wetland management				
Costs imposed on wetland owners				
Capital investment/repair costs	–$1,151,000	–$1,661,000	$0	–$2,813,000
Ongoing maintenance costs	–$566,000	–$1,194,000	$0	–$2,079,000
Loss of income	$0	–$3,137,000	–$4,678,000	–$7,814,000
Costs and benefits imposed on wider community				
Capital investment/repair costs	–$18,161,000	$0	$0	–$18,161,000
Ongoing water management costs	$6,246,000	$0	$0	$6,246,000
Non-monetary consumers' surplus	$9,201,000	$11,053,000	$3,016,000	$14,911,000
Total net benefits	–$4,432,000	$5,061,000	–$1,661,000	–$9,711,000

8.3   IMPACTS OF RISK AND UNCERTAINTY

Risk and uncertainty arise from incomplete information within the biophysical and economic modelling components of the bio-economic model. Risk and uncertainty about the bio-economic model components translates into uncertainty about the output from the bio-economic integration – the aggregate NPV and the test of Hypothesis One. One way of addressing the specific uncertainty about the consequences to the aggregate NPV is to conduct sensitivity tests on the sources of risk and uncertainty within the biophysical and bio-economic models. To conduct the sensitivity tests, the assumptions about the sources of uncertainty are varied within their likely range. Sensitivity tests are undertaken for the USE and MRF biophysical and economic modelling in this section. These tests are then used as the basis for a stronger test of Hypothesis One.

8.3.1 USE Sensitivity Tests

Sensitivity tests were carried out on all values reported in Table 8.1. The ranges of values for which sensitivity tests are conducted are shown in Table 8.5. The base level in each case is that under the 'best-assumption' level defined and estimated in Chapter 5, 6 or 7.

The highest and lowest estimates that result from each of the variables for which sensitivity tests are conducted are reported in Table 8.6. The sensitivity tests reveal the relative impacts of differing sources of risk and uncertainty on NPVT outcomes. The breadth between the highest and lowest estimates for the tests indicates the likely range of variation in NPV due to risk or uncertainty about the target parameter. If the sensitivity tests indicate the potential for significant variation to aggregate outcomes there may be significant quasi-option values associated with obtaining additional information to reduce the level of risk and uncertainty.

In summary, the consumers' surplus of environmental non-use values has the highest leverage of the components of the NPV. A minimal relaxation of the estimation assumptions generates a positive NPV for all strategies (for instance, including 30% of non-respondents per Morrison (2000), or including ACT survey respondents). More extensive, but still relatively conservative, extrapolation to Victorian residents leads to positive NPVs for all strategies that were considered. On the other hand, using the lower 95 per cent confidence interval boundary of the initial extrapolation of willingness to pay (SA residents only and excluding predicted population growth) generates a negative NPV for all strategies. A second source of uncertainty in environmental non-use values is the extent of the benefits that management

Table 8.5 Schedule of sensitivity tests conducted for the USE case study

Parameter	Sensitivity test values
Discount rate	Base level (7%), 4%, and 10%.
Time period to complete management changes	Base level (10 years except tourism over 20 years), 5 years (10 years tourism), and 15 years (25 years tourism).
Pasture establishment and maintenance	Base level, Costs 30% higher, and Costs 30% lower.
Grazing productivity losses – unimproved pasture	Base level, 25% lower, and 25% higher.
Grazing productivity losses – improved pasture	Base level, 15% lower, 15% higher, and Coffey[a] suggested productivity.
Grazing productivity losses – wetlands and native vegetation	Base level, 25% lower, and 50% lower.
Grazing enterprise returns	Base level, 20% higher, and 20% lower.
Capital costs – fencing	Base level, 30% higher, and 30% lower.
Capital costs – engineering works	Base level, 30% higher, 30% lower, and include cost of potential additional infrastructure.
Capital costs – revegetation	Base level, all recreated areas require revegetation, 75% of recreated native vegetation, and no wetlands but 50% of recreated native vegetation.
Ongoing wetland and remnant management costs	Base level, 50% lower labour costs, 20% higher labour costs, 20% lower materials costs, and 20% higher materials costs.
Duck hunting benefits – alternative consumers' surplus estimates	Base level, log-log model in Whitten and Bennett 2002, and travel time cost excluded.
Duck hunting benefits – wetlands available for hunting	Base level, 20% of rehabilitated or re-created wetlands available, and 70% of rehabilitated or re-created wetlands available.
Tourism benefits – consumers' surplus	Base level, 50% higher, and 100% higher.
Tourism benefits – producers' surplus	Base level, 50% lower, 50% higher, and 100% higher.

Table 8.5 Continued

Parameter	Sensitivity test values
Tourism benefits – visitor number estimates	Base level, 50% less visitors, and 50% more visitors
Non-use environmental values – consumers' surplus confidence intervals (CI)	Base level, Upper 95% CI, and lower 95% CI.
Non-use environmental values – extrapolation of willingness to pay (WTP) estimates	Base level, include future population growth in SA, include 30% of non-respondents, include ACT population, include Victorian population at 50% of mean WTP, and protest free WTP estimates.
Non-use environmental values – endangered species outcomes	Base level, 50% less species benefit, 20% less endangered species benefit, and 20% more endangered species benefit.
Impacts of duck hunting on non-use environmental values	Base level, no duck hunting (duck hunting banned)[b], and no duck hunting in re-created and rehabilitated wetlands.

Notes   a   Productivity of pasture suggested by Coffey MPW Pty Ltd (Environmental Impacts Assessments Branch 1995).

          b   Caution should be exercised in interpreting this result as it lies outside the range of values included in the choice modelling survey reported in Chapter 7.

changes generate to endangered species. If these are only half as successful as initially predicted, the NPV is negative in all cases.

After environmental values, the category with the greatest leverage is the costs of rehabilitating and re-creating wetlands and native vegetation and their ongoing management. Revegetation and ongoing management costs are the two most important components of these costs. If revegetation costs are much lower than estimated, then the 'pro-wetlands' strategy NPV becomes positive. The cost to agricultural productivity of changing wetland and remnant management also has significant leverage but is not sufficient alone to alter any NPVT.

The sensitivity of the aggregate values to variations in multiple assumptions simultaneously was not assessed in this study. It is unlikely that a combination of changes would be large enough to alter the NPVT of the strategies with the exception of environmental values, rehabilitation and management of wetlands and remnants, and productivity of agricultural pastures. This is because all other values are relatively small and would require large changes in combination to be sufficient to alter the outcome of the NPVT.

The validity of the initial assumptions and the relaxation of these assumptions in the sensitivity tests will need to be judged by policy makers. In particular, policy makers will need to assess their ability to design policies that would access non-use environmental values outside the USE region or outside South Australia.

Hypothesis One – stronger USE test

A stronger test of Hypothesis One requires that all sensitivity tests generate a positive aggregate NPV, while a weak test would only require the 'best estimate' aggregate total to be positive. NPVT tests that are positive are in bold in Table 8.6. Negative NPVT are generated by the sensitivity tests of the non-use environmental values for all strategies. This result is generated by the lower 95 per cent confidence interval of willingness to pay for improvements to environmental outcomes in USE wetlands or if the management changes are only half as successful as predicted at improving threatened species outcomes. Hence, a stronger test of Hypothesis One is rejected for all USE wetland management options. However, despite the stronger test being rejected, the sensitivity testing procedure indicates that the 'wetlands retention' strategy is a low risk strategy and it is unlikely that a combination of risk and uncertainty in the bio-economic model would lead to a negative NPV.

Table 8.6 Summary of USE sensitivity test outcomes

Sensitivity test	Wetland retention	Pro-wetlands	Wetlands and remnants
Totals per Table 8.1	**$5,227,000**	–$2,343,000	–$15,217,000
Discount rate			
Highest NPV	**$5,753,000**	–$430,000	–$7,320,000
Lowest NPV	**$4,467,000**	–$5,122,000	–$27,496,000
Time period of adoption			
Highest NPV	**$5,448,000**	–$1,274,000	–$11,622,000
Lowest NPV	**$5,227,000**	–$2,881,000	–$19,709,000
Pasture establishment and maintenance costs			
Highest NPV	**$5,227,000**	–$1,605,000	–$13,728,000
Lowest NPV	**$5,227,000**	–$3,082,000	–$16,706,000
Grazing productivity losses			
Highest NPV	**$6,004,000**	–$1,209,000	–$11,207,000
Lowest NPV	**$5,227,000**	–$3,765,000	–$16,798,000
Grazing enterprise returns			
Highest NPV	**$5,460,000**	–$1,209,000	–$11,550,000
Lowest NPV	**$4,994,000**	–$3,478,000	–$18,883,000
Capital costs of wetland and native vegetation rehabilitation			
Highest NPV	**$5,568,000**	**$1,521,000**	–$7,972,000
Lowest NPV	**$4,886,000**	–$8,343,000	–$21,217,000
Costs of ongoing wetland and remnant management			
Highest NPV	**$5,941,000**	–$916,000	–$10,836,000
Lowest NPV	**$4,942,000**	–$2,914,000	–$16,969,000
Benefits from duck hunting			
Highest NPV	**$5,391,000**	–$1,922,000	–$14,759,000
Lowest NPV	**$5,166,000**	–$2,509,000	–$15,397,000
Benefits from tourism			
Highest NPV	**$6,248,000**	–$565,000	–$12,924,000
Lowest NPV	**$4,206,000**	–$4,111,000	–$17,501,000
Non-use environmental values			
Highest NPV	**$18,505,000**	**$18,596,000**	**$48,833,000**
Lowest NPV	–$1,436,000	–$9,243,000	–$21,172,000
Impacts of duck hunting on consumers' surplus estimates			
Highest NPV	**$9,803,000**	**$3,181,000**	–$9,416,000
Lowest NPV	**$5,227,000**	–$2,343,000	–$15,217,000

Notes The maximum and minimum variations for all strategies may not correspond with the same change of assumptions as each assumption may affect alternative strategies differently. Positive NPVs are in **bold** type.

8.3.2 MRF Sensitivity Tests

The sensitivity tests applied to the MRF value estimates are shown in Table 8.7. The base level in each case is that defined and estimated in Chapter 5, 6 or 7. There is a greater level of risk or uncertainty about some variables compared to others and this is reflected in the range of sensitivity levels used for each variable.

The highest and lowest estimates that result from each of the parameters for which sensitivity tests are conducted are reported in Table 8.8 (positive NPVT results are in bold type). The breadth between the highest and lowest estimates for the parameters indicates the likely range of variation in NPV due to risk or uncertainty.

The sensitivity tests show that the consumers' surplus of environmental non-use values has the highest leverage of the components of the NPV. Relaxing the assumptions minimally leads to a positive NPV for the 'water management' option.[2] Alternatively extrapolation to the remainder of the NSW population at 25 per cent of the value of respondents within the Murrumbidgee catchment leads to all options generating a positive NPV, as does extrapolation to the population of Adelaide.

The costs of acquiring sufficient water to implement the 'water management' or combined options exhibit nearly as great an amount of leverage as non-use environmental values but are only sufficient to generate a positive NPV for the 'water management' option. There is a relatively large amount of uncertainty surrounding the opportunity costs of water used to create an artificial flood on the MRF. This uncertainty arises from the incomplete water reform process in NSW and hence uncertain future returns from irrigation enterprises. The degree of this uncertainty leads to a large range in the possible NPVT outcomes (from \$4.6m to –\$22.6m for the 'water management' option). The impact of potential income from future water sales on opportunity costs (both during years when a flood is not released and from water sales downstream of the MRF) is also sufficient to generate a positive NPV for the 'water management' option.

The benefits to recreational users of the MRF are also potentially large enough to alter the outcome of the NPVT for the 'combined strategies' option. Their degree of leverage is large enough to suggest that gathering additional data on recreational visits in the region to facilitate a more accurate estimate would be cost effective.

The sensitivity of the aggregate values to multiple variations in the costs or benefits was not assessed in this study. With the exception of the environmental values, costs of water acquisition, future sales of water and the impact of recreational values it is unlikely that a combination of changes would be large enough to alter the NPVT result for the strategies. This is because all other values are relatively small and would require large changes in combination to be sufficient to alter the NPVT outcomes.

The validity of the initial assumptions and the relaxation of these assumptions in the sensitivity tests will need to be judged by policy makers. In particular, policy makers will need to judge the extent to which environmental values generated by MRF wetlands extend beyond the Murrumbidgee Catchment and whether interstate values, particularly in the ACT, can be drawn upon for policy purposes. Policy makers will also need to assess the likelihood that a combination of impacts would occur that would alter the outcomes of the sensitivity tests.

Hypothesis One – stronger MRF test
A stronger test of Hypothesis One requires that all sensitivity tests generate a positive aggregate NPV, while a weak test would only require the 'best estimate' aggregate total to be positive. Positive NPVT results in Table 8.8 are in bold type. The stronger test of Hypothesis One is accepted for the MRF region because the 'grazing management' option generates a positive NPV under all sensitivity tests. Hence, it is highly unlikely that a combination of incorrect assumptions would lead to a negative 'grazing management' NPV. That is, adoption of the 'grazing management' strategy is low risk and it is very unlikely that a combination of risk and uncertainty about the assumptions in the bio-economic model would lead to a negative NPV.

8.4   CONCLUSIONS

The bio-economic integration undertaken in this chapter indicates that changing wetland management in both the USE and MRF is likely to increase overall community well being. This is confirmed by a weak test of Hypothesis One in the USE and a stronger test in the MRF. However, under the current distribution of property rights there is no effective mechanism for achieving a change to wetland management in either case study region. Furthermore, as indicated by the distributional analysis, significant costs are imposed on wetland owners in both case study areas that could compromise the bio-economic analysis if uncompensated. These policy issues are the focus in the following chapter.

Table 8.7 Schedule of MRF sensitivity tests conducted

Parameter	Sensitivity test values
Discount rate	Base level (7%), 4%, and 10%.
Time period of management changes	Base level (10 years except water acquisition over 5 years), 5 years (5 years water acquisition), and 15 years (10 years water acquisition)
Grazing production losses – wetlands that are no longer grazed	Base level, 50% of rotational rate, and 25% of rotational rate.
Grazing production losses – ratio of buffer strip	Base level, 50% higher, and 50% lower.
Grazing production losses – dse yield from grazing wetlands	Base level, 25% higher, and 25% lower.
Grazing enterprise returns	Base level, 50% higher, and 50% lower.
Timber production losses	Base level, 20% higher, and 20% lower.
Timber enterprise returns	Base level, 50% higher, and 50% lower.
Cost of alternative stock water supplies	Base level, 30% higher, and 30% lower.
Capital costs – opportunity cost of water	Base level, 50% lower, 50% higher, and 100% higher.
Capital costs – engineering works	Base level, 30% higher, and 30% lower.
Capital costs – revegetation	Basel level, 15% of wetlands require revegetation, 10% of wetlands require revegetation, and no wetlands require revegetation.
Capital costs – fencing	Base level, 30% higher, and 30% lower.
Ongoing costs – maintenance and management	Base level, 20% higher, and 40% lower.
Ongoing costs – engineering works	Base level, 20% higher, and 40% lower.
Ongoing – holding and using water licences	Base level, no charges for environmental users, and higher ongoing costs of water use.
Ongoing – reduced opportunity costs of water	Base level, water sales 50% higher, water sales 100% higher, 15% of flood resold @ $17/ML, and 30% of flood resold @ $17/ML.

Table 8.7 Continued

Parameter	Sensitivity test values
Non-use environmental values – confidence intervals (CI)	Base level, Upper 95% CI, and lower 95% CI.
Non-use environmental values – extrapolation of willingness to pay (WTP) estimates.	Base level, include future population growth in catchment, include 30% of non-respondents, include Adelaide population, include rest of NSW population at 25% of mean WTP, and, use protest free WTP estimates.
Non-use environmental values – tests of environmental outcomes	Base level, 20% more healthy wetlands, 30% less healthy wetlands, 20% more native birds, 30% less native birds, 20% more native fish, and 50% less native fish.
Non-use environmental values – tests of social outcomes	Base level, adoption causes 5 fewer farmers, adoption causes 10 fewer farmers.
Recreation consumers' surplus – alternative consumers' surplus	Base level, 50% higher, and 50% lower.
Recreation consumers' surplus – extra visitors	Base level, no additional visitors, 100% more visitors.
Recreation consumers' surplus – additional surplus to visitors	Base level, $5 extra benefits, and $2 extra benefits.

Table 8.8 Summary of MRF Sensitivity tests

Sensitivity test	Water management	Grazing management	Timber management	Combined strategies
Totals per Table 8.2	−$4,432,000	$5,061,000	−$1,661,000	−$9,711,000
Discount rate				
Highest NPV	−$4,050,000	$6,019,000	−$241,000	−$7,004,000
Lowest NPV	−$4,432,000	$3,536,000	−$4,074,000	−$13,533,000
Time period of adoption				
Highest NPV	−$579,000	$5,695,000	−$899,000	−$4,491,000
Lowest NPV	−$4,589,000	$4,277,000	−$2,604,000	−$11,558,000
Grazing production losses				
Highest NPV	−$4,432,000	$6,885,000	−$1,661,000	−$7,887,000
Lowest NPV	−$4,432,000	$3,965,000	−$1,661,000	−$10,807,000
Grazing enterprise returns				
Highest NPV	−$4,432,000	$6,629,000	−$1,661,000	−$8,142,000
Lowest NPV	−$4,432,000	$3,493,000	−$1,661,000	−$11,279,000
Costs of alternative stock water supply				
Highest NPV	−$4,432,000	$8,059,000	−$1,661,000	−$6,713,000
Lowest NPV	−$4,432,000	$5,061,0000	−$1,661,000	−$9,711,000
Timber production losses				
Highest NPV	−$4,432,000	$5,061,000	−$726,000	−$8,775,000
Lowest NPV	−$4,432,000	$5,061,000	−$4,000,000	−$12,050,000

Table 8.8 Continued

Sensitivity test	Water management	Grazing management	Timber management	Combined strategies
Capital costs of water acquisition				
Highest NPV	**$4,648,000**	**$5,061,000**	–$1,661,000	–$630,000
Lowest NPV	–$22,593,000	**$5,061,000**	–$1,661,000	–$27,872,000
Capital costs of wetland rehabilitation				
Highest NPV	–$4,087,000	**$5,439,000**	–$1,661,000	–$9,333,000
Lowest NPV	–$4,777,000	**$4,226,000**	–$1,661,000	–$10,546,000
Costs of ongoing wetland and remnant management (including water income)				
Highest NPV	**$1,814,000**	**$5,536,000**	–$1,661,000	–$3,465,000
Lowest NPV	–$7,555,000	**$4,824,000**	–$1,661,000	–$12,834,000
Benefits from recreation				
Highest NPV	–$693,000	**$14,340,000**	–$1,661,000	**$5,800,000**
Lowest NPV	–$5,174,000	**$3,219,000**	–$1,661,000	–$12,789,000
Non-use environmental values – relaxation of assumptions				
Highest NPV	**$14,458,000**	**$25,749,000**	**$4,238,477**	**$17,233,000**
Lowest NPV	–$5,553,000	**$3,813,000**	–$3,378,476	–$11,248,000
Non-use environmental values – size of environmental attributes				
Highest NPV	–$4,059,000	**$5,337,000**	–$1,538,000	–$9,509,000
Lowest NPV	–$6,143,000	**$3,350,000**	–$3,372,000	–$11,422,000

Notes   A single change of assumptions may affect alternative strategies differently hence the maximum and minimum
variations may not correspond with the same test.
Positive NPVs are bold type.

NOTES

1. Non-use environmental values are considered conservative because they are only extrapolated from the sampled respondents across the proportion of the population that responded to the questionnaire, exclude other populations that may hold values for the wetlands, and do not include future population growth.
2. The inclusion of the 'timber management' option within the 'combined strategies' option leads to synergistic effects. Hence, it should not be concluded that the 'water management' and 'grazing management' options should be applied together in preference to the 'combined strategies' option.

9.   Designing and Evaluating Wetland Management Policies

The conclusions from the bio-economic modelling indicate that changing wetland benefits could yield a net benefit to the community. Achieving these potential benefits requires a policy mechanism that would deliver the required change in wetland outputs. However, wetland policy mechanisms are not cost free. Rather resources are used as transaction costs in policy development and implementation as well as the resultant resource reallocation process detailed in Chapter 2. Hence, many policy options may not deliver a net benefit to the community once transaction costs are taken into account. In this chapter threshold policy analysis is applied to the evaluation of potential wetland management policy in the presence of uncertainty about transaction costs. This framework facilitates an evaluation of Hypothesis Two and allows conclusions to be drawn about the potential to increase community welfare through increased production of wetland protection outputs.

As with any policy evaluation, a basis for comparing alternative options must be established. In this case the point of comparison is the BAU property right and policy framework. Hence, the BAU distribution of property rights and range of policy instruments must be defined, including their ongoing costs. The alternative policy options must then be systematically identified, including their relative transaction costs and wetland protection effectiveness. These comparisons provide a means of evaluating the alternatives against the BAU policy framework. A formal assessment of the likely cost-effectiveness of these options using policy threshold analysis is the vehicle for evaluating Hypothesis Two.

The chapter comprises four parts. In the first part, the methodology used to identify, develop and compare policy instruments is reviewed and extended. A brief review of the constraints to wetland management change as perceived by wetland owners in the case study regions is also included in this section to ensure the methodology covers all potential policy development aspects. The BAU property right framework is defined in the second part of the chapter for the USE and MRF case studies. In the third part of the chapter the methodology is applied, firstly to identify policy opportunities, then to develop, select and adapt policy instruments to fit these opportunities, and finally, to assess the transaction costs of these policies. The chapter concludes with an assessment of the relative cost-effectiveness of the potential new policy instruments for wetland protection against each other and against the menu of current policies. This assessment allows qualitative evaluation of Hypothesis Two.

9.1   HOW TO IDENTIFY AND COMPARE WETLAND POLICIES

9.1.1 Identifying Potential Wetland Management Policies

Policy development is the generic term for the design and implementation of institutions and organisations (by government) to achieve a desired change to outcomes. Policy is directed towards influencing the behaviour of wetland managers (public, private or both) through altering their wetland management incentives. Ongoing readjustment of policies may be necessary due to uncertainty about future preferences and incomplete information about the transaction costs of wetland owners and government.

Accepting Hypothesis One for at least some changes to wetland management in the MRF and USE case study areas in Chapter 8 indicates the presence of market or government failure in the production of wetland protection outputs. The question then arises as to how these failures may be systematically identified and addressed in line with the sources of market and government failure discussed in Chapter 2. Our approach is to combine a search procedure developed by Weimer and Vining (1992) with the theory about market and government failures and the distributional analysis reported in Chapter 8.

The Weimer and Vining (1992) search procedure for identifying the source of market or government failures is shown in Figure 9.1. Weimer and Vining's process has two key features:

1. identification of market or government failures (the focus in this part of Chapter 9); and,
2. comparing the government failure costs of any intervention against the benefits of reducing any market failures that may be present (the focus in the following parts of Chapter 9).

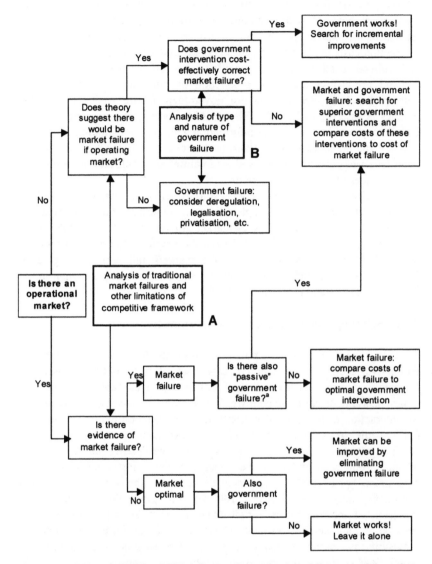

Figure 9.1 Systematic assessment of market and government failure

The potential for market failures such as those discussed in Chapter 2 are assessed at box 'A' within Weimer and Vining's process. These include unclear or incomplete specification of property rights, the impacts of market transaction costs in identifying consumers or producers, negotiating contracts and collecting payment, and specific issues arising from lumpiness in wetland production and joint production of multiple wetland protection outputs. Similarly, the potential for government failure arising from BAU policies is assessed at box 'B'. The possible sources of government failure include cost and imprecision in information gathering, principal-agent issues, political and bureaucratic incentives, lack of coordination or duplication with other levels of government, derived externalities and spillovers or unintended consequences of government actions.

The distribution of the costs and benefits of changing wetland management (identified in Chapter 8) is an important source of evidence about the likely scale and scope of market failures. The relative scale of the costs and benefits can be identified from the output of the economic model thus indicating the products for which markets fail and the degree of influence wetland policies would need to employ to achieve a change in the production of wetland protection outputs.

9.1.2 Selecting and Adapting Policy Instruments

A wide range of potential policy instruments is available within the facilitative, inducive and coercive categories of instruments discussed in Chapter 3. A range of these instruments is shown in Table 9.1. Potential policy instruments are directed towards changing the incentives generated by the interaction of the current property right base, co-ordinating institutions (such as rules of exchange) and facilitative organisations.

The instruments in Table 9.1 should not necessarily be regarded as distinct from each other. Rather many of these instruments lie on a continuum. For example, government production, either directly or through contracting out, is essentially a 100 per cent production subsidy while provision of information is a non-financial input subsidy. Similarly, the creation and allocation of property rights may take the form of liability law provisions, performance standards, specified management technologies or prohibitions (when they are non-tradable or compensable). As such, application of each of these instruments may take a wide variety of forms. For example, taxes and charges may be applied as development fees, taxes on damaging inputs, licence fees or other mechanisms.

Differing jurisdictional responsibilities will influence the level and form that policy options can take. For example, state rather than national governments hold most property right powers in Australia. Similarly, the delivery mechanism for a policy instrument will differ significantly dependingon the level of jurisdiction at which it is applied. For example, management subsidies via tax systems differ significantly depending on whether the tax base is local, regional or national.

Table 9.1 Range of potential wetland policy instruments

Category	Instrument
Coerce	Government production
	Prohibition of wetland resource uses
	Specified management actions or specified best management practices
	Duty of care performance standard
Induce	Output taxes and charges (applied to damaging outputs)
	Input taxes and charges (applied to damaging inputs)
	Input subsidies (lump sums and on-going)
	Liability law provisions
Facilitate	Create, clarify or allocate property rights (where linked to a fee these become inducive)
	Provision of information (including technical advice, measurement advice or requirements, and certification schemes)
	Voluntary agreements

Source Primarily adapted from Russell and Powell (1999). Additional input from Weimer and Vining (1992) and National Center for Environmental Economics (2001).

The trade-offs between policy transaction cost components and the resultant incentive are also important. For example, Russell and Powell (1999) divide policy instruments between those that specify to producers '*what* outcome is to be achieved' and instruments that specify '*how* the outcome is to be achieved' as shown in Table 9.2. Policies that specify '*what* is to be achieved' will require effective detection and potentially prosecution. Policies that specify '*how* it is to be achieved' will require detailed information about production processes and thus may have high information, enactment and implementation costs. Similarly, policies that specify '*how*' an outcome is to be achieved provide little stimulus to technical change and innovation.

Table 9.2 Nature of potential policy instruments

	Specifying what is to be achieved	Not specifying what is to be achieved
Specifying how to achieve whatever is to be achieved	• Government production • Prohibitions • Combined technology and performance standards	• Lump-sum subsidies • Liability law provisions (with minimum standards) • Technology based information assistance • Most certification schemes
Not specifying how to achieve whatever is to be achieved	• Technology standards or BMP • Duty of care requirements • Voluntary agreements	• Create, clarify or allocate property rights • Output taxes • Input taxes • Liability provisions (with no minimum standards) • General technical assistance • Information reporting

Source Adapted from Russell and Powell (1999). Note that on-going input subsidies are not mentioned as they come in a variety of forms with different levels of specification.

Another way of examining this issue is to ask whether policy instruments treat all wetland owners the same or each differently, as shown in Figure 9.2. Falconer, Dupraz and Whitby (2001) conclude that homogeneous instruments are likely to be more appropriate where wetland owners' net costs and wetland protection outputs are homogeneous, while instruments that facilitate site specific arrangements are more appropriate where wetland owners' costs or wetland protection outputs are heterogeneous. These conclusions result from the cost tradeoffs in fine-tuning instruments at the individual scale compared to the resultant benefit.

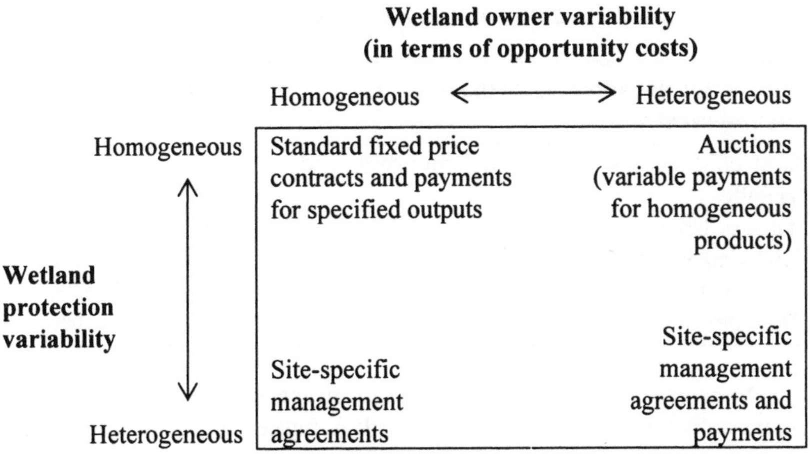

**Wetland owner variability
(in terms of opportunity costs)**

Homogeneous $\longleftrightarrow$ Heterogeneous

	Homogeneous		Heterogeneous
Homogeneous	Standard fixed price contracts and payments for specified outputs		Auctions (variable payments for homogeneous products)
Wetland protection variability			
Heterogeneous	Site-specific management agreements		Site-specific management agreements and payments

Source Adapted from Falconer, Dupraz and Whitby (2001).

Figure 9.2 Instrument appropriateness and producer/production type

9.1.3   Perceived Constraints to Wetland Management

Wetland owner perceptions provide important guidance as to the transaction costs they bear in engaging with alternative wetland policy options. Wetland owners may favour some policy options. In these cases, landholders perceive higher net benefits from adoption. For others, inaccurate perceptions may require additional communications and thus adoption costs. Addressing wetland owner concerns also provides a safety check to policy development by ensuring it encompasses actual constraints to changing wetland management that may not be identified elsewhere.

In each case study area, wetland owner perceptions were assessed via a survey. Wetland owners were asked the reasons why they had not adopted a range of wetland management strategies that were identified as important to maintaining healthy wetlands in their region. Options included the cost or profit impact of the action; time or labour constraints; knowledge constraints; considering the strategy not applicable to their wetlands; or no interest. The results are shown in Table 9.3 for those who had not already adopted wetland management strategies.

Table 9.3 Perceived constraints to adoption of management actions

Reason for not adopting wetland management strategy	Case study area	
	USE	**MRF**
Cost of strategy or impact on farm profits and viability	23%	21%
Time or labour constraints	10%	8%
Knowledge constraints	7%	8%
Not considered applicable to my wetlands	48%	53%
Not interest in adoption	12%	10%

On average about half of all wetland owners considered each wetland strategy 'not applicable' to their wetland. A further 20 per cent of wetland owners considered the cost of the management action or the impact of the action on farm profits and viability prohibitive. The high proportion of 'not applicable' or 'not interested' responses suggests that many wetland owners do not perceive a linkage between wetland management and the private monetary and non-monetary values generated. Hence, an extension program may be necessary before other facilitative or inducive programs proceed.

Wetland owners were also asked to suggest what additional incentives would be most useful. The most desired incentives are reported for each case study region in Table 9.4. Financial assistance was the most desired but material management inputs were also important, particularly to facilitate fencing to change stock management in and around wetlands.

Table 9.4 Desired wetland management incentives

Desired incentive	Case study area	
	USE	**MRF**
Financial assistance	30%	14%
Federal or local tax breaks	28%	6%
Wetland or property management training/assistance	16%	12%
Fencing assistance	25%	10%
Revegetation assistance	12%	7%
Feral/nuisance animal control assistance	0%	7%
Water for wetlands (and more coordinated management)	26%	14%

9.1.4 Comparing Alternative Policies

A number of alternative policies are likely to be identified, each of which would achieve an increase in wetland protection outputs. The most cost-effective policy instrument or instrument mix should then be selected provided net benefits remain after taking into account the policy transaction costs (PTC) and direct costs of changing wetland management. The range of potential PTC identified in Chapter 3 is defined in more detail in Table 9.5. The emphasis in this book is on economic efficiency but other considerations such as equity, ethical and fairness concerns are all likely to be of importance to the policy maker. PTC are a combination of fixed and variable costs. Hence, some economies of scale can be anticipated from a single policy instrument over a mix of policies. However, these economies must be traded off against the higher marginal costs of achieving outcomes using a single policy instrument with a heterogeneous target population.

Comparing across PTCs requires a scale of their relative costs. Such a scale of costs is shown in Table 9.6 for each PTC. The likely change to wetland protection outputs that would result from each policy instrument when appropriately implemented must also be assessed. For some incentives, structural restrictions are imposed by the level at which the incentive is applied and the possible scale of the incentive. For example, most local government incentives are limited to the geographic area of the jurisdiction. Note that many of the measures in Table 9.6 are largely subjective due to the lack of objective data available, however this approach is consistent with the qualitative nature of the threshold policy analysis process.

Table 9.5 Formal definition of policy transaction cost criteria

Cost criterion	Definition
Government policy transaction costs	
Design information	Defining the scale and scope of the problem to be addressed and gathering and analysing information about a potential policy instrument.
Enactment	Costs of legislation including deadweight costs of lobbying.
Implementation	Regulatory design and development of agency structures and protocols required for administering the policy instrument.
Administration	Ongoing costs including negotiation, contracting and government transfer costs.
Detection	Monitoring compliance and effectiveness together with evaluation of the policy instrument.
Prosecution	Enforcement of compliance through legal systems.
Risk	Includes risk of adverse outcomes due to failure in the policy instrument implementation process or due to unintended consequences.
Market policy transaction costs	
Direct costs	Direct fees or charges that are netted off government transaction costs.
Additional information	Cost of additional information beyond that required for direct compliance with the policy instrument.
Contracting	Costs of negotiation and contracting.
Detection and protection	Monitoring and enforcement costs of claiming, codifying or defending property rights or prosecution.
Other	
Dynamic attributes	Incentives for innovation in management to improve environmental outcomes, reduce costs, and increase flexibility in the face of exogenous change.

Table 9.6 Definition of measures for policy transaction cost criteria

Policy criterion	Measure of criterion		
	Low	**Medium**	**High**
Government policy transaction costs			
Design information	Already exists	Existing information can be adapted / little new information.	Significant new information must be collected
Enactment	No new legislation required, little or no new regulations and no significant lobbying	Templates for legislation and regulations available in other jurisdictions or minor lobbying	New legislation and/or regulation required and/or significant lobbying
Implementation	Implementation through existing structures and processes – few new resources required	Some new structures and processes required but within existing organisations.	New organisations required or significant enlargement of existing organisations
Administration	Homogeneous treatment of landholders – no site visits required – or few transfers through government	Heterogeneous treatment of landholders or single site visit Small transfers through government	Multiple site visits or heterogeneous treatment and site visit required or significant transfers through government
Detection	Effective within existing procedures (low marginal cost to these), no onsite monitoring	Site visit required or development of new monitoring procedures	Ongoing site visits required and/or costly measurement strategies
Prosecution	No prosecution option	Existing mechanisms leading to a well defined, rarely contested set of penalties (few legal suits)	Prosecution requires action through law courts or penalties are regularly contested

223

Table 9.6 Continued

Policy criterion	Measure of criterion		
	Low	**Medium**	**High**
Risk	Removes proven threats to healthy existing wetlands using proven policy instrument	Proven policy instrument applied to a new issue/location or threats untested.	Unproven policy instrument or new potential management solutions
Market policy transaction costs			
Direct costs	No direct fees or charges	Nominal fees or charges	Full cost recovery of administration and monitoring
Additional information	No additional information required	Provision of information collected for other uses anyway or cheaply and easily collected	Supply of previously uncollected information requiring new methods
Contracting	No written agreements and no more than one meeting	Non-legally binding written agreement or addition to existing requirements or few meetings	New legally binding agreement (requiring legal input) or multiple meetings
Detection and protection	No change to property rights or requires greater 'duty of care' or similar to retain existing rights	Property rights only retained/obtained by simple application	Property rights require defence or challenge through complicated process requiring new information

Table 9.6 Continued

Policy criterion	Measure of criterion		
	Low	**Medium**	**High**
Other factors			
Dynamic attributes	Mandated actions – no opportunity to innovate	Mandated actions but significant site adjustment or broad specification – some innovation	No mandated action – only outcome is specified
Overall effectiveness in achieving wetland protection			
Effectiveness	Unlikely to significantly impact on aggregate outcomes in isolation but may be important signal in policy instrument mix	Important supporting role to other policies and will achieve some management change in isolation	Significant driver of changing wetland management – key element of policy instrument mix

Notes Sources for the rationale behind most criterion measures are based on literature discussed previously or in Chapter 3 and are not repeated here. Other sources include the National Center for Environmental Economics (2001) and Wiersma (1991) (dynamic attributes), Stavins (1995) (administration, contracting and other areas), and Polinsky and Shavell (1992) and Kaplow (1992) (prosecution costs).

225

In addition to the actual transaction costs of the policy itself, there may also be impacts on the transaction costs associated with continuing current wetland uses. For example, enacting a more restrictive zoning policy may require an application process before wetland owners can graze wetlands. Assessing the scale and scope of changes to these BAU transaction costs follows a similar methodology to that for other policy attributes. The main difference is that these impacts may be positive or negative.

9.2   THE BAU POLICY BASE

The BAU base comprises two elements: the property right framework; and, any policy instruments currently applied to modify the incentives created by this framework. The existing property right framework is described in section 9.2.1. The existing policies and their transaction costs are the focus in section 9.2, including definitions of their transaction costs as a basis for comparing alternative policies.

9.2.1 The BAU Property Right Base

In order to compare alternative wetland policy options a comparative base must be established. The base is akin to the BAU economic base established for each case study area in Chapter 4. The BAU policy base is driven by the underlying property rights structure and any institutional or organisational structures specific to wetlands. Property rights are defined as 'a claim to a benefit (or income) stream that the State will agree to protect through the assignment of duty to others who may covet, or somehow interfere with, the benefit stream' (Bromley 1991, p. 2). Hence, property rights in the USE and MRF are defined with respect to the benefit streams that resource owners are able to enjoy.

Potential benefit streams include the full range of outputs from wetland resources such as passive recreation, food and fibre products or aesthetic benefits. Important attributes of property rights include:

- whether potential consumers can be excluded from the benefit stream;
- whether the benefit stream is divisible (in space and scope); and
- whether they are alienable (or transferable).

The BAU policy base is defined by populating a matrix that encompasses the resources of interest together with the attributes of the property rights held over these resources. An example matrix is shown in Figure 9.3, including sample descriptions for several cells. The state is assumed to hold any residual property rights (or to be the notional beneficiary of restrictions on property right usage).

Resource	Rights held by landowner	Rights held by others (not the state)	Restrictions on rights (state beneficiary)
Land			
Surface water			
Ground water			
Fauna – domesticated		Specify benefit streams	
Fauna – native		in relevant cell	
Native vegetation			
Other resources			

- access and withdrawal rights subject to historic use.
- volumetric specification of rights is currently underway.

- Game species accessible via purchase of a hunting licence (takings limits apply).
- Pests (superabundant species) can be harvested via a licence.

- Permit required to clear native vegetation.
- Permit requires a management plan and approval under relevant legislation.

Figure 9.3 Example property rights and benefit streams matrix

9.2.2 The BAU Policy Instrument Base and Transaction Costs

The information compiled by populating a matrix such as that shown in Figure 9.3 provides a basis for defining the existing BAU policy instruments and comparing these against alternative policy options. The first stage in developing and comparing policy instruments is to define the instruments currently available. For the case study areas these are shown in Table 9.7. These instruments build on, or alter the incentives provided by property rights. The mechanism for comparing alternative policies is threshold policy analysis.

The BAU policy transaction costs comprise sunk and ongoing (or avoidable) costs. Sunk policy transaction costs are defined as policy instrument costs that cannot be avoided if the policy is ended and which cannot be used in other policy instruments. Sunk costs are primarily those incurred by government in designing and implementing the policy instrument. Hence, information and research, enactment and implementation costs are entirely composed of sunk policy transaction costs. Ongoing costs are those that can be avoided if the policy instrument is changed or ended. It is these costs that must be identified for existing USE and MRF policies in order to facilitate comparison between the costs of maintaining BAU policies against alternative policy options.

Ongoing costs are assessed for each of the remaining policy transaction cost criteria through a two-stage process. First, the relevant attributes of the policy are defined including how they relate to the ongoing policy transaction costs. A sample of this process is shown in Table 9.8 for one existing wetland policy instrument, namely Landcare tax rebates and deductions.

Table 9.7 Existing policy instruments in the USE and MRF

Policy instrument	Availability	
	USE	**MRF**
Management advice – government agencies	✓	✓
Landcare tax rebate / deduction	✓	✓
Local council rate rebate	Restricted*	✗
Govt materials grants	✓	✓
Greening Australia materials grants	n.a.	✓
Grants from NHT	✓	✓
Wetlands Waterlink grants / Drainage levy rebate	✓	n.a.

Notes   Some grants have long waiting lists and may no longer be available.
   *   Rate rebates are available on NPWS covenanted lands in SA.

Table 9.8 Landcare tax rebate and deduction sample description matrix

Policy instrument	Landcare tax rebates and deduction
Jurisdiction	Federal government
Incentive type	Induce
Description	Incentives to reduce the cost of Landcare actions are offered under Sections 75B and 75D of the *Income Taxation Assessment Act* and claimed as part of tax reporting. Eligible expenses relate to revegetation and include any property planning specifically for the purposes of the revegetation project, tree planting and maintenance costs, and fencing to exclude livestock.
Eligibility	Only primary producers and businesses on rural land are eligible.
Monitoring, accountability and administration costs	Works must be part of a farm management plan approved by relevant State/Territory department of agriculture. Deductions subject to tax reporting and auditing requirements.
Scale of incentives	The measure can be received as a deduction or a tax rebate of 34 cents in the dollar. Rebates are available where taxable income is $20,700 or less (maximum rebate of $1,700 per annum on $5,000 expenditure). There is no limit on the size of the tax deduction for Landcare works.

The descriptions of ongoing transaction costs are then compared against the criteria in Table 9.6 to develop a matrix of transaction costs for each category such as that shown in Table 9.9. Sunk cost categories are shown as not applicable in Table 9.9 (information, enactment, implementation). Significant variation in the relative transaction costs between the policies exists, reflecting the trade-offs in policy instrument design. For example, applying the measurement criteria in Table 9.6 to Landcare tax rebates or tax deductions yields the following assessments:

- administrative costs are low – homogeneous treatment of landholders through the tax system and no site visits;
- detection costs are low – low marginal costs to existing taxation audits;

Table 9.9 BAU policy instrument transaction costs

Policy instrument	Government policy transaction costs				Market policy transaction costs				Dynamic impacts	Change to BAU transaction costs	Wetland protection
	Administrate	Detection	Prosecution	Risk	Direct costs	More info	Contract	Detect / protect			
Management advice – government agencies	M	L	L	M	L	L	L	L	M	M –	M
Landcare tax rebate / deduction	L	L	M	L	L	M	L	L	M	NC	L
Local council rate rebate	L	L	M	L	L	L	M	L	L	NC	M
Drainage levy rebate	L	L	M	L	L	L	M	L	L	NC	L
Govt materials grants	M	M	H	L	L	L	H	L	L	NC	M
Greening Australia materials grants	M	M	M	L	L	L	M	L	M	NC	H
Grants from NHT	H	M	H	M	L	M	H	L	M	NC	L
Wetlands Waterlink grants	H	M	H	L	L	L	H	L	L	NC	H

Notes H = High, M = Medium, L = Low, NC = no change, + = positive, and – = negative.

- prosecution costs are medium – existing prosecution mechanisms for tax violations lead to a well defined, rarely-contested set of penalties;
- risk is low – tax incentives encourage wetland management that removes known threats using proven techniques;
- direct costs are low – no direct fees or charges to access tax incentives;
- additional information costs are medium – claiming the tax incentive requires retention of invoices and actions consistent with a farm management plan;
- contracting costs are low – no new agreements are required to claim tax incentives;
- private detection/protection costs are low – claiming a tax incentive does not change property rights or duty of care responsibilities;
- dynamic impacts are medium – the eligible actions are broadly specified with some opportunity for innovation;
- BAU transaction costs are unchanged; and
- wetland protection effectiveness is low – tax incentives will increase wetland protection by reducing costs but changes are unlikely to be large enough in isolation to significantly impact on wetland protection outputs.

9.3 ALTERNATIVE POLICY INSTRUMENTS

9.3.1 Identifying Effective Policy Opportunities in the MRF and USE

The methodology used to identify opportunities for policy instruments described in Section 9.1 is composed of three elements:

1. the theory developed in Chapter 2 is combined with an assessment of current institutional arrangements (such as property right allocations and wetland policies) to identify policy opportunities;
2. the bio-economic modelling output is used to identify the scale and scope of market or government failures and assist in targeting policies; and
3. wetland owners perceptions are examined to detect other unidentified policy opportunities or to identify where wetland owner perceptions differ from information incorporated in the bio-economic model.

Theory applied to the BAU policy framework
Wetlands are a combination of resource inputs (land, water, flora, fauna and climatic inputs, among others) that produce a bundle of wetland protection outputs when appropriately managed. The existing rights structures of these resources are examined by applying the theoretical rationale identified in

Chapter 2 to identify potential sources of market or government failures. Other considerations of importance (for example, whether a perverse wetland management incentive may be created) should also be considered in this process. In practice, this requires an examination of the existing property rights structures and policy instruments defined in Section 9.2 against the theoretical framework in Chapter 2 across four areas:

- property rights over wetland resource inputs;
- property rights over wetland protection outputs;
- reducing market transaction costs in producing wetland outputs; and,
- reducing government transaction costs within BAU policy.

The property rights held by individuals in the MRF and USE do not always meet the full set of desirable attributes discussed in Chapter 2 (specifically in Figure 2.1) in practise. Specifically, property rights to both wetland inputs and outputs are not always fully excludable, divisible and transferable.

Consider for example policy opportunities relating to splitting wetlands primarily managed for conservation from other lands held under the same title but managed for other uses such as primary production. Current transaction costs are high because potential conservation oriented wetland owners must acquire and manage other resource combinations as well as wetlands (for example agricultural lands). Streamlining the divisibility and transferability attributes of property rights could potentially reduce transaction costs. However, a potential problem is that absentee wetland owners may not manage fire, pest and weeds as effectively as on-site primary production managers.

Similarly improved incentives for wetland management may arise from improving the ability of wetland owners to capture the benefits from duck hunting, for example by directly selling performance oriented hunting permits on their land. However, there are ethical concerns about directly pricing native game species and an emphasis on successful hunting outcomes rather than healthy wetlands and species management. A range of perverse output incentives also exists creating further opportunities for property right reforms. For example, wetland owners hold the right to native vegetation outputs that are consumed by domestic livestock but do not hold rights to native fauna unless accessed via a licence thus creating an incentive to graze native vegetation with domestic livestock and minimise populations of native animals. The property right policy opportunities that were identified for the two case study areas are presented in Table 9.10.

Table 9.10 Property right policy opportunities in MRF or USE

Property right	Case study		Policy opportunity
	MRF	**USE**	
Input resources			
Land	✓	✓	Wetlands cannot easily be split from larger properties.
Land	✓	✓	Only government can hold and enforce partial property rights over wetlands through conservation covenants.
Surface water	✓		Irrigation management of water resource does not consider wetlands.
Surface water	✓		Potential to create special water property rights for wetlands.
Capital and labour	✓	✓	Approval process for rehabilitation works in wetlands.
Full bundle	✓	✓	Uncertainty about the future separability of property rights following recreation or rehabilitation of wetlands.
Wetland outputs			
Native fauna (game only)		✓	Wetland owners game species rights limited to access – additional rights may increase wetland protection incentives.
Native fauna (game only)		✓	Administratively complex or prohibited for owners to 'ranch' game species.
Native fauna (non-game)	✓	✓	Administratively complex or prohibited for owners to 'ranch' non-game species.
Fish	✓		Wetland owners have no rights to fish in their wetlands.
Native flora (timber)	✓	✓	Access to timber resources unclear or restricted
Biodiversity conservation	✓	✓	Rights to biodiversity values of wetlands are unclear.
Existence and bequest values	✓	✓	Wetland owner's rights to these values are unclear.

The transaction costs incurred in assembling the requisite mix of inputs to wetland production or selling wetland outputs using either the private or government sectors may provide further policy opportunities. USE and MRF wetland owners do not own all the resource inputs into wetlands, nor do they consume all the wetland protection outputs that are produced. Hence, in many cases, wetland owners may need to negotiate agreements with other resource owners or consumers of wetland protection outputs in order to receive a net benefit from conserving their wetlands. Government provision of wetland outputs faces similar problems due to the lack of information and incentive frameworks and resultant derived externalities and other distortions.

The transaction cost policy opportunities that were identified in the USE and MRF are shown in Table 9.11. For example, developing more effective mechanisms to link potential recreation consumers with the owners of suitable wetlands will reduce transaction costs and may increase the production of wetland protection outputs. Similar opportunities can be identified for reducing government failure such as devolved grant programs to improve targeting and reduce program management costs.

Targeting policy opportunities using bio-economic modelling

The bio-economic model constructed in Chapters 4 through 8 provides information about the relative values of alternative combinations of outputs produced using wetland resources. The distributional analysis of the bio-economic models shows that the monetary costs incurred by wetland owners in changing management outweigh the monetary benefits they receive in every strategy (see Tables 8.3 and 8.4). Policies that successfully target the relevant input or output mixes are likely to be more cost-effective. Specifically, policy must generate a transfer from the non-monetary beneficiaries of wetland management changes to wetland owners if voluntary changes to management are to be anticipated. The scale of transfer that must be achieved in order to encourage changes in wetland management may not be the full difference between monetary costs and benefits to wetland owners. This is because the non-monetary values of farmers were not included in the aggregate value estimates. While these values were not estimated in Chapter 8, surveys of USE and MRF wetland owners indicated that most wetland owners regard their wetlands as an asset (Whitten and Bennett 2000a,c).

The USE bio-economic model indicates that the net monetary benefits to wetland owners of adopting the 'wetland retention' strategy are negative $3.4m (see Table 8.3) but that a transaction cost free change to management would generate \$5.2m in net benefits to society. The net monetary costs to wetland owners are driven by wetland management costs including:[1]

- loss of current income sources (\$1.2m);
- wetland repair or capital investment costs (\$1.4m); and
- ongoing wetland management costs (\$1.6m).

These costs are offset by non-monetary benefits to the wider community (\$8.6m), that wetland owners are not currently able to draw on, and gains to income from changing wetland management (\$0.8m).

In the MRF a transfer from the non-monetary beneficiaries to wetland owners could potentially generate net benefits to the community (\$5.1m) as a whole under the 'grazing management' strategy. The net cost to MRF wetland owners is driven by loss of existing income (\$3.1m), wetland repair/investment costs (\$1.7m) and ongoing wetland management costs (\$1.2m). However, the estimated benefits from changing wetland management accrue to the wider community (\$11.0m).

The resultant policy opportunities therefore lie in:

1. developing mechanisms that allow wetland owners to draw sufficient benefits from the potential \$8.6m non-monetary benefits to generate a net benefit (including their own wetland non-monetary values);
2. reducing wetland management costs sufficiently to generate a net benefit (once their own non-use values are taken into account); or
3. a combination of options 1 and 2 generates a net benefit to wetland owners (again including wetland owner's non-monetary values).

Incorporating wetland owner perceptions

Analysis of the perceptions of USE and MRF wetland owners showed that the main constraint to the adoption of many wetland management strategies was wetland owners' perceptions that the strategy was not applicable, or lack of interest in applying the strategy. The high proportion of wetland owners in these categories suggests that a targeted information campaign to inform wetland owners about the relative costs and benefits of wetland management strategies would be an important policy opportunity in both the USE and MRF.

Table 9.11 Policy opportunities to reduce transaction costs

Policy target	Case study		Description
	MRF	**USE**	
Improving market provision			
Recreation	✓	✓	Defining recreation outputs may facilitate market or increase private benefits.
Non-use outputs (eg biodiversity)	✓	✓	Mechanisms helping to define these products may facilitate market or increase private benefits.
Recreation in and around wetlands		✓	Mechanisms to link wetland owners with recreation consumers.
Innovative wetland products	✓	✓	Mechanisms facilitating innovative new enterprises.
Subsidised wetland management	✓	✓	Private net costs of changing wetland management but net public benefits.
Efficient wetland management		✓	Information to target wetland management may generate public benefits.
Joint products from wetlands		✓	Non-traditional ownership/management structures may be more cost effective.

Table 9.11 Continued

Policy target	Case study		Description
	MRF	**USE**	
Reducing government failure			
Scope of Landcare tax incentives	✓	✓	Many wetland protection activities are not included – including these would reduce management costs.
Inter-jurisdictional spillovers	✓	✓	Improve alignment of geographic distribution of benefits and costs – potentially via offering incentives beyond geographic boundaries or through boundary realignment.
Grants and advice	✓	✓	Devolved grant programs may have lower operating costs and better targeting thus improving cost effectiveness.
Reduce duplication	✓	✓	Targeting expenditure to avoid duplication and cost shifting could improve efficiency.
Perverse incentives	✓	✓	Identify where current government provision strategies introduce counter productive incentives to damage wetlands.

The next most important constraint is the impact on farm costs or profits. Impacts on farm costs and profits are identified as a significant driver of wetland management change within the bio-economic model. The distributional analysis undertaken in Chapter 8 indicates that changing wetland management will impose significant costs on wetland owners. The resultant policy opportunities were identified previously.

Policy Instruments and Policy Transaction Costs

The policy opportunities identified in Section 9.3.1 translate into a set of alternative policy instruments, each of which targets one or more of the opportunities. The emphasis in this section is on the transaction costs of alternative policy instruments and their impact on the net benefits of changing wetland policy rather than the instruments themselves. However, description of the transaction costs is reliant on describing each policy instrument in a format such as that shown in Table 9.8, including the nature of the design, enactment, and implementation policy transaction costs. A summary of the policy instruments is shown in Table 9.12. Note that the list of policy instruments in Table 9.12 is not complete (there may be others we did not find), and that all may not necessarily be viable. That is, the costs of implementation may outweigh the benefits. Identifying the relativities of costs and benefits is the focus in this section.

As discussed in Chapter 3, the ideal assessment of relative policy cost-effectiveness would involve estimation of the net benefits of policy instrument adoption taking into account the transaction costs induced by the instrument (both government and market) and impacts on existing transaction costs. However, methodological constraints prevent such an application. Hence, the use of threshold policy analysis as an alternative qualitative evaluation process was developed in Section 3.4. Threshold policy analysis requires that the PTC of each instrument is qualitatively measured, condensed into an aggregate measure and compared against the range of policy alternatives in order to identify the most cost-effective set.

The initial measurement of individual PTCs for each policy instrument in Table 9.12 is undertaken by applying the criteria developed in Table 9.6 to each instrument. The results generate the matrix of relative transaction costs against each alternative policy option that is presented in Table 9.13. For example, applying the measurement criteria in Table 9.6 to a new policy instrument introducing stewardship payments to wetland owners yields the following assessments:

- design and information costs are medium – some new information about individual wetland management will be required to target stewardship payment
- enactment costs are medium – templates are available for similar programs and could be adapted (for example, the Bushtender program in Victoria). There may be some lobbying relating to payment amounts and targets;
- implementation costs are medium – some new structures will be needed within an existing organisation to deliver the instrument;
- administrative costs are high – generated by heterogeneous treatment of landholders through differential stewardship payments that require more detailed evaluation and a site visit to assess eligibility;
- detection costs are high – ongoing site visits are required or the development of new monitoring strategies;
- prosecution costs are medium – prosecutions are considered unlikely due to the costs of prosecution but could be costly if undertaken;
- risk is medium – stewardship payment mechanisms are proven overseas but have not been applied to wetlands in Australia;
- direct costs are low – no direct fees or charges apply;
- additional information costs are high – collection or assembly of new information is required to apply for stewardship payments and possibly to show ongoing compliance;
- contracting costs are high – stewardship payments are likely to require a legally binding agreement with consequent negotiation and private administration costs;
- private detection/protection costs are low – a stewardship payment changes property rights or duty of care responsibilities by agreement;
- dynamic impacts are medium – eligible management actions are broadly specified with some opportunity for innovation;
- BAU transaction costs are unchanged; and
- wetland protection effectiveness is high – stewardship payments are defined to be greater than monetary losses less non-monetary benefits to wetland owners. Hence, significant changes to wetland management and consequent increases in wetland protection outputs are anticipated.

Table 9.13 reports measures against each individual PTC and shows considerable variation in these costs. Threshold policy analysis involves comparing the aggregate PTCs of each option to identify whether the benefits are likely to outweigh the costs. That is whether the wetland protection effectiveness of each policy option is outweighed by the sum of PTCs and wetland production costs.

Table 9.12 Potential new policy instruments in the USE and MRF

Policy instrument	Description	Case study	
		MRF	USE
Accreditation or licensing schemes	License potentially damaging activities subject to preventative management strategies or activities being employed..	✓	✓
Assistance in legal cases	Assistance in using legal system to prevent or control external impacts on wetlands.	✓	✓
Broaden tax incentives – management	Options include: 1. tighten eligibility for deduction of damaging capital works; 2. broaden deductions to non-business lands, interest payments and potentially labour; 3. grant primary producer status to conservation land managers (extends option 2 to GST input refunds and diesel fuel rebate); and 4. extend heritage structures 20% tax rebate to conservation.	✓	✓
Broaden tax incentives – NPOs	NPO options include: 1. tax deductibility of the bargain sale gap prices for NPOs; 2. capital gains tax exemptions for sales to NPOs; and 3. higher tax incentives for high conservation value assets.	✓	✓
Conservation covenants	Voluntarily entered, but permanently legally binding restriction on landholder property rights managed by non-government organisations.	✓	✓
Conservation wetland sales	Relaxation of local government restrictions on land parcel size sales (and related) could reduce the transaction costs of wetland protection and lead to improved management.	✓	✓
Devolved management of environmental water	An independent trust could improve management efficiency and reduce potential for capture or political influence.	✓	

Table 9.12 Continued

Policy instrument	Description	Case study	
		MRF	USE
Education/ extension	Targets 'not interested' or 'not applicable' wetland owners. May motivate self-interest in maintaining private wetland values in response to improved understanding (Young, Gunningham, Elix, Lambert, Howard and McCrone 1996).	✓	✓
Extend rate rebates / concessions	Rate rebates are restricted to NPWS covenants. Extension to land meeting minimum requirements would reduce costs. Could also extend to other levies (e.g. PP boards in NSW).	✓	✓
Farm management planning	Farm management planning (including wetlands): 1. encourages landowners to consider wetlands as an integrated aspect of whole farm management; and 2. reduces transaction costs of other incentives.	✓	✓
Flexible environmental water allocation	Manage environmental water allocations to include floodplain flows.	✓	
GIS database access	Access to government information to assist in program targeting and management. May reduce costs of private sector.	✓	✓
Land for wildlife (wetlands)	Targets already interested wetland owners by recognising their management via a voluntary, non-binding agreement, and providing information to improve wetland management.	✓	✓
Markets for wetland preservation	Competitive bidding for harvest and non-harvest rights (including harvest deferral) in State Forests NSW wetlands.	✓	
New enterprise training	Access to local government business development programs may help develop innovative wetland enterprises or products.	✓	✓

241

Table 9.12 *Continued*

Policy instrument	Description	Case study	
		MRF	USE
NPO fee waivers	Reduce stamp duty and other fees levied on NGOs for property transfers and conservation management applications.	✓	✓
Non-profit organisation support	NPOs may offer efficient wetland management structures. Government could provide or subsidise capacity building in Australia. (In the US some large NPOs undertake this role, see Cestero 1999).		✓
Operationalise duty of care	Specify minimum wetland management performance standard.	✓	✓
Ranching for wildlife	Managing native fauna in their natural environment in order to harvest a proportion of the fauna for sale.	✓	✓
Real estate tools for NPOs (training)	• Option to purchase within a specified time and price; • Rights of first refusal at the offer price. • Options on conservation covenant purchase prior to sale.	✓	✓
Removal of perverse tax incentives	Remove tax deduction or rebates for construction of any drought water storage in a wetland (often the easiest site for such storages).		✓
Remove perverse water subsidies	Fully include all costs of water supply (see Fisher 2000; Marsden and Associates 2001 for more information on current pricing).	✓	
Repair/investment subsidies	Subsidises upfront costs of changing wetland management.	✓	✓
Resource based zoning	Require landholders to maintain wetland resource bundle such as water and land (similar to native vegetation clearance laws).	✓	✓
Revolving funds	Signals the conservation value of wetlands to buyer. Forms include: 1. urgent land purchases on-sold to government or others; 2. short-term bridging funding to allow NPO fundraising; and 3. adding a conservation covenant and on-selling.		✓

242

Table 9.13 Transaction costs of alternative policy instruments

Policy instrument	Government policy transaction costs							Market policy transaction costs				Dynamic impacts	Change to BAU transaction costs	Wetland protection
	Design	Enact	Implement	Administrate	Detection	Prosecution	Risk	Direct costs	More info	Contract	Detect / protect			
Accreditation or licensing schemes	M	M	H	M	H	H	M	M	H	H	M	M	M –	L
Assistance in legal cases	M	H	L	L	n.a.	n.a.	M	L	H	H	L	H	L +	L
Broaden tax incentives – management	M	H	L	M	L	M	L	L	M	M	L	M	NC	H
Broaden tax incentives – NPOs	M	M	L	M	L	M	L	L	M	M	L	M	NC	M
Conservation covenants	L	H	L	L	M	M	L	L	H	H	L	M	H +	H
Conservation wetland sales	L	L	L	L	L	M	M	L	M	M	L	M	L +	L
Devolved management of environmental water	H	H	H	M	M	L	H	L	L	L	L	H	NC	H
Education / extension	M	L	M	M	L	L	L	L	L	L	L	H	H +	H
Extend rate rebates / concessions	L	L	L	M	M	M	L	L	M	M	L	L	NC	M
Farm management planning	L	L	L	L	L	L	L	L	M	M	L	M	M +	M
Flexible environmental water allocation	M	H	M	L	n.a.	n.a.	M	L	L	L	L	M	NC	M
GIS database access	L	L	M	L	L	L	M	L	L	M	L	H	M +	M

243

Table 9.13 Continued

Policy instrument	Government policy transaction costs							Market policy transaction costs				Dynamic impacts	Change to BAU transaction costs	Wetland protection
	Design	Enact	Implement	Administrate	Detection	Prosecution	Risk	Direct costs	More info	Contract	Detect / protect			
Land for wildlife (wetlands)	L	L	M	M	M	L	L	L	L	M	L	H	H+	H
Markets for wetland preservation	M	H	L	L	L	M	M	L	L	H	L	L	M+	L
New enterprise training	L	L	L	L	L	L	H	L	L	L	L	H	L+	L
NPO fee waivers	L	M	L	L	L	M	L	L	M	H	L	L	L+	L
Non-profit organisation support	H	L	M	L	M	L	M	M	L	L	L	H	M+	M
Operationalise duty of care	H	H	L	H	M	H	M	L	H	L	H	H	L–	M
Ranching for wildlife	L	M	M	L	L	H	H	L	H	H	L	M	H+	M
Real estate tools for NPOs (training)	M	L	L	L	L	L	H	L	L	H	L	H	L+	L
Remove perverse tax incentives	M	M	M	L	M	M	L	L	L	L	L	L	NC	M
Remove perverse water subsidies	M	M	M	H	M	M	M	L	M	M	L	L	NC	L
Repair / investment subsidies – MRF	M	M	M	M	M	H	L	L	H	H	L	L	NC	H
Repair/ investment subsidies – USE	L	L	L	M	M	M	L	L	H	H	H	L	NC	H
Resource based zoning	M	H	L	M	M	H	H	L	L	L	H	L	M–	L
Revolving funds	L	M	H	M	M	H	L	L	M	H	L	M	H+	H

Table 9.13 Continued

Policy instrument	Government policy transaction costs							Market policy transaction costs				Dynamic impacts	Change to BAU transaction costs	Wetland protection
	Design	Enact	Implement	Administrate	Detection	Prosecution	Risk	Direct costs	More info	Contract	Detect / protect			
'Safe harbour' scheme	M	H	M	M	M	H	M	L	H	H	L	M	M+	M
Signalling measures	L	M	M	M	M	L	H	L	L	L	L	H	NC	L
Simplify wetland rehabilitation / re-creation	L	M	L	M	M	H	M	L	M	M	L	M	M+	M
Stewardship payments	M	M	M	H	H	M	M	L	H	H	L	M	NC	H
Water covenants	M	M	L	L	L	M	M	M	M	H	L	M	H+	M
Wetlands tourism infrastructure	H	L	L	H	n.a.	n.a.	H	L	M	L	L	H	H+	M
Wetlands tourism promotion	M	L	L	L	n.a.	n.a.	H	L	L	L	L	H	H+	M
Zoning regulations	H	H	L	M	M	H	M	L	L	L	H	L	H−	M

Notes   H = High, M = Medium, L = Low, NC = no change, + = positive, and − = negative.

245

9.4   POLICY THRESHOLD ANALYSIS AND WETLAND POLICY INSTRUMENTS

9.4.1   Policy Threshold Analysis of Instruments

Assessment of the cost-effectiveness (or economic efficiency) of alternative wetland policy instruments is undertaken using *policy threshold analysis*. Policy threshold analysis involves a comparison of the likely range of the uncertain net policy transaction costs against the benefit of the additional environmental outputs so produced. Threshold policy analysis asks how large the net policy transaction costs would need to be to eliminate the net benefits from additional wetland protection.2 A cost effective policy instrument will generate a net benefit to the community via increased wetland protection outputs or reduced market or government failure costs according to the threshold policy analysis. In this case the sum of the PTCs in Table 9.13 and wetland production costs will be less than the benefits from wetland protection. That is, threshold policy analysis asks whether the policy option is likely to be cost-effective for wetland protection.

In order to compare the cost-effectiveness of alternative policies, even at a qualitatively-based policy threshold analysis level, a comparison mechanism that is systematic in its approach must be designed. The mechanism applied is to assign a weighting to each transaction cost criterion specifying its relative contribution to total transaction costs. Ideally these weightings would be available from a meta-analysis of the relative importance of different transaction costs across a wide range of policy instrument alternatives. In the absence of such information the weightings are derived from a combination of relative transaction cost estimates in the papers cited in Table 3.3 and the authors' judgements.3 The use of transaction cost estimates from other papers is analogous to the use of benefit transfer within the bio-economic model and may become increasingly powerful as more policy transaction cost studies are undertaken. This approach is a pragmatic response to a lack of quantitative information.

The weightings allow policies to be grouped to provide information for policy making in a less than perfect information environment. The weightings assigned to transaction cost criteria are varied to conduct a sensitivity analysis of their impact on the cost-effectiveness conclusions. The weightings assigned to each transaction cost criterion are shown in Table 9.14 along with alternative weightings used for sensitivity analysis. Administrative transaction costs are weighted most heavily (four times design or enactment costs) because they are judged to be larger than other costs (based in part on the references discussed in Table 3.3) and involve ongoing financial commitment by governments. The impact of wetland policies on BAU transaction costs may be either positive or negative and is weighted at 75 per cent of administrative costs. Policies that are more dynamic are judged to reduce future wetland protection costs – hence this category is negatively weighted.

The results of the weighting exercise are shown in Table 9.16 as 'overall transaction costs' and are grouped into high, medium and low. In order to assess their likely cost effectiveness they are compared against their relative outcome in terms of biophysical wetland protection using the policy instrument cost-effectiveness rating table shown in Table 9.15. Hence, a policy instrument that would incur high net transaction costs, but has high wetland protection effectiveness, is classified 'unclear', while a policy instrument with medium wetland effectiveness but low wetland transaction costs is classified 'likely'. Cost effectiveness of alternative policy options using this methodology is shown in the final column in Table 9.16 (according to which policies are grouped). Sensitivity tests of the transaction cost weightings were undertaken according to the alternative weightings shown in Table 9.14. Sensitivity analysis of the impacts of transaction cost weightings indicated few changes in the overall cost-effectiveness rankings.

Several conclusions can be drawn from the summary data presented in Table 9.16. Policies that are evaluated as 'likely' to meet the threshold policy analysis test have been judged to have total costs (including transaction costs) lower than their benefits. Hence, these policies are considered 'best bets' for adoption in the case study areas. Where concerns about the extent of the transaction costs associated with these policies remain, estimation of these costs should be undertaken. That is, the threshold policy analysis is acting as a 'filter' to identify policies worthy of further investigation. Similarly, policies evaluated as 'unlikely' to be cost-effective should not be considered for adoption with respect to the case study areas because they are considered highly unlikely to generate a net benefit. Finally, the analysis shows that only two of the current USE and MRF policies are regarded as likely to be cost-effective and one is regarded as not cost-effective in its current form.

The conclusions regarding policies ranked as 'unclear' are more complex. In these cases, the relatively coarse, judgement-based information is insufficient to identify whether these policies are likely to generate a net benefit when all transaction and production costs and benefits are considered. Additional information is required to assist in judgements about their likely cost effectiveness. In some cases, part of this information may be available from the bio-economic model together with estimates of transaction costs from other sources.

Table 9.14 Transaction cost weights – aggregation and sensitivity analysis

Transaction cost type			Base Case	Equal group weights*	Equal cost weights	Admin weight halved	BAU TC weight halved	BAU TC weight doubled
Government policy transaction costs		Design	1	1	1	1	1	1
		Enact	1	1	1	1	1	1
		Implement	1.5	1.5	1	1.5	1.5	1.5
		Administrate	4	4	1	2	4	4
		Detection	1	1	1	1	1	1
		Prosecution	0.5	0.5	1	0.5	0.5	0.5
		Risk	0.5	0.5	1	0.5	0.5	0.5
Market policy transaction costs		Direct costs	1	2.7	1	1	1	1
		More information	1.5	4.1	1	1.5	1.5	1.5
		Contract	1.5	4.1	1	1.5	1.5	1.5
		Detect / protect	1	2.7	1	1	1	1
Dynamic			–1.5	–4.	–1	–1.5	–1.5	–1.5
Change to BAU transaction costs			3	9.5	1	3	1.5	6

Notes *   Equal group weights: equal weighting to government, market (including dynamic) and current transaction costs as bundles.
       TC   transaction costs

As an example, consider the case of repair/investment subsidies in the USE and MRF. The capital costs associated with wetland management changes to achieve the desired strategies amount to $1.4m in the USE and $1.7m in the MRF. Evidence from existing schemes can be used to anchor transaction cost estimates in a similar fashion to where benefit transfer is used in the bio-economic modelling when other estimates are not available. USE program evidence suggests that a team of two individuals could

Table 9.15 Policy instrument cost-effectiveness rating table

| | | Policy instrument wetland protection effectiveness | | |
		Low	*Medium*	*High*
Policy transaction costs	*Low*	Unclear	Likely	Likely
	Medium	Unlikely	Unclear	Likely
	High	Unlikely	Unlikely	Unclear

implement, administer and monitor a $1m to $2m program over approximately two years (costing at least $400,000) (USEDSFMPSC 1999). Approximately, an additional 20 per cent of transfer values ($360,000 in the USE and $420,000 in the MRF) will be incurred in tax collection and redistribution according to Campbell and Bond (1997).4 Finally, landowners will also incur transaction costs in applying for and receiving subsidies. If these are also in the order of ten to twenty per cent of the subsidy, total program transaction costs will be approximately eighty per cent of the value of the subsidy. That is, total costs (including transaction costs) amount to 1.8 times capital costs. This generates a benefit-cost ratio of about 1.4:1 in the USE and 1.1:1 in the MRF. Recalling that the benefit estimates in Chapter 8 are conservative due to the restrictive assumptions about extrapolation of environmental values (see for example the impact of sensitivity tests) and because wetland owner non-monetary benefits are not included, repair/subsidy programs are likely to be cost effective in the USE and MRF regions. Similar analyses could be performed for other policy instruments classified as 'unclear' in Table 9.16.

The transaction costs of some alternative policy instruments in Table 9.16 exhibit a degree of specificity to one or both of the case study areas and to their application in isolation. As an example consider the removal of perverse water price subsidies in the MRF. Economic theory suggests that their removal would be relatively simple. However, their removal requires additional monitoring because of the complex incentive impacts this would induce in the policy environment. These impacts include increasing the price of water to irrigators, inducing more efficient water allocation and management but also increasing the cost of acquiring water to flood wetlands and increasing the incentives to wetland owners to modify wetlands for water harvesting and storage. The degree of these impacts may well differ significantly between regions. Hence, caution must be exercised in application within policy instrument packages and in extrapolating the results of the threshold policy analysis undertaken in this section to wetlands outside the case study areas.

Finally, adoption of some policy instruments may generate net benefits (or costs) beyond wetland protection in the case study areas or where it is likely that they would apply to a broad range of resource packages within the case study areas. For example, rate rebates and related tools would likely be applied to wetlands and remnant vegetation meeting specified criteria. The benefits or costs that would arise beyond wetlands are not considered in Table 9.16 but should be considered as part of a holistic policy analysis. Thus policies such as rate rebates or farm management planning may generate sufficient net benefits beyond wetlands to be considered highly cost-effective. The mix of fixed and variable costs in policy instrument application should also be considered in this context (see for example Falconer, Dupraz and Whitby 2001). For example, there may be economies of scale associated with the application of policies with relatively high fixed costs across wider areas than the case study regions.5

9.4.2 Evaluation of Hypothesis Two

Policies that were concluded to be 'likely' to be cost effective are differentiated by mode of operation and jurisdiction in Table 9.17 (excluding BAU policies). The criterion for accepting Hypothesis Two is the evaluation of non-adopted, cost-effective policy instruments (according to the policy threshold analysis criteria) for a majority of the cells in the array in Table 3.1. This conservative test of Hypothesis Two is considered appropriate because it is based on the qualitative information included in the threshold policy analysis and is dependent on the author's judgements about the relative net policy transaction costs of alternative policies. Basing the test on a single cell is not considered desirable given the paucity of estimates of the costs of market and government failure of alternative policy instruments. Table 9.17 shows that cost-effective policies have been identified for five of a potential nine categories. Hence, the test of Hypothesis Two is accepted and it is concluded that alternative policies can reduce the extent of government or market failures in the production of wetland protection outputs in the case study areas.

Table 9.16 Wetland policy instrument cost-effectiveness

Policy instrument	Type	Jurisdiction	Transaction costs	Wetland protection	Cost-effectiveness*
Broaden tax incentives – management	Induce	Federal	Medium	High	Likely
Conservation covenants	Facilitate	State	Low	High	Likely
Education/ extension	Facilitate	State	Low	High	Likely
Flexible environmental water allocation	Facilitate	State	Medium	High	Likely
Land for wildlife (wetlands)	Facilitate	State	Low	High	Likely
Non-profit organisation support	Facilitate	Federal	Low	Medium	Likely
Revolving funds	Facilitate	State	Medium	High	Likely
Water covenants	Facilitate	State	Low	High	Likely
Wetlands tourism infrastructure	Facilitate	Local	Low	Medium	Likely
Wetlands tourism promotion	Facilitate	Local	Low	Medium	Likely
Broaden tax incentives – NPOs	Induce	Federal	Medium	Medium	Unclear
Conservation wetland sales	Facilitate	Local/State	Low	Low	Unclear
Devolved management of environmental water	Facilitate	State	High	High	Unclear
Extend rate rebates / concessions	Induce	Local	Medium	Medium	Unclear

Table 9.16 Continued

Policy instrument	Type	Jurisdiction	Transaction costs	Wetland protection	Cost-effectiveness*
Farm management planning	Facilitate	State	Medium	Medium	Unclear
GIS database access	Facilitate	State	Low	Low	Unclear
Markets for wetland preservation	Facilitate	State	Low	Low	Unclear
New enterprise development training	Facilitate	Local	Low	Low	Unclear
Real estate tools for NPOs	Facilitate	Non-specific	Low	Low	Unclear
Removal of perverse tax incentives	Induce	Federal	Medium	Medium	Unclear
Remove perverse water subsidies	Induce	State	Medium	Medium	Unclear
Repair/investment subsidies – MRF	Induce	State	High	High	Unclear
Repair/investment subsidies – USE	Induce	State	High	High	Unclear
Signalling measures	Facilitate	State	Low	Low	Unclear
Simplify wetland rehabilitation/ re-creation	Facilitate	Local/State	Medium	Medium	Unclear
Stewardship payments	Induce	State	High	High	Unclear
Accreditation or licensing schemes	Compel	State	High	Low	Unlikely
Assistance in legal cases	Facilitate	State	Medium	Low	Unlikely
'Safe harbour' scheme	Compel	State	High	Medium	Unlikely

Table 9.16 Continued

Policy instrument	Type	Jurisdiction	Transaction costs	Wetland protection	Cost-effectiveness*
NPO fee waivers	Induce	State	Medium	Low	Unlikely
Operationalise 'duty of care'	Compel	State	High	Medium	Unlikely
Ranching for wildlife	Facilitate	State	High	Medium	Unlikely
Resource based zoning	Compel	State	High	Low	Unlikely
Zoning regulations	Compel	Local	High	Medium	Unlikely
BAU policies					
Drainage levy rebate	Induce	Regional	Low	Medium	Likely
Greening Australia materials grants	Induce	Regional	Medium	High	Likely
Management advice – government agencies	Facilitate	State	Medium	Medium	Unclear
Landcare tax rebate / deduction	Induce	Federal	Low	Low	Unclear
Local council rate rebate	Induce	Local	Low	Low	Unclear
Grants from NHT	Induce	Federal	High	Low	Unlikely

Notes * Cost effectiveness is evaluation using the ratings developed in Table 9.15.

253

Table 9.17 Mode and jurisdiction of cost-effective wetland policy instrument

		Type of policy instrument		
		Facilitative	*Inducive*	*Coercive*
Level of government involved	*Local*	• Wetlands tourism promotion (USE) • Wetlands tourism infrastructure (USE)	Nil	Nil
	State	• Conservation covenants • Land for wildlife (wetlands) • Education/ extension • Revolving funds • Flexible management of environmental water allocation (MRF) • Water covenants (MRF)	Repair/ investment subsidies*	Nil
	Federal	• Non-profit organisation support	Broaden tax incentives – management	Nil

Notes * Repair/investment subsidies were classified as 'unclear' in Table 9.16, however a more detailed discussion in the associated text indicates that they are likely to be cost-effective.

9.5   CONCLUSIONS

The policy threshold analysis of potential policy instruments to achieve wetland management changes indicates adoption of specific policies is 'likely' to generate a net benefit to the community. These policies can be regarded as 'best bets' in terms of achieving a cost effective increase in the production of wetland protection outputs. This conclusion builds on that in Chapter 8 that the benefits from additional wetland protection outputs exceeded their production costs. These conclusions are based on a weak test of Hypothesis Two. While the test is regarded as weak, the conservative nature of the decision criterion used strengthens confidence in the conclusion.

There are a number of strengths in the approach undertaken in this chapter despite the potential weaknesses attached to the evaluation of Hypothesis

Two. First, the policy instrument development and assessment process incorporates recognition of the importance of transaction costs in identifying the scale of net benefits generated by alternative policy instruments. Furthermore, it is recognised that transaction costs differ between alternative policies, as does policy instrument biophysical effectiveness in achieving wetland protection, and that these may be traded off in comparing relative policy instrument cost-effectiveness. Finally, use of the threshold policy analysis process to generate 'best bet' policies is a useful tool in focusing additional policy instrument development effort in a policy making environment subject to uncertain and incomplete information about transaction costs.

NOTES

1. The bio-economic model can be used to provide more detailed information about the specific nature of these costs for further targeting.
2. The converse is also assessed where policy reduces transaction costs. That is, how much lower would transaction costs need to be in order to generate a net benefit to the wider community.
3. The impact of discounting transaction costs over a relevant time horizon (30 years) is implicitly incorporated in the weights.
4. Alston and Hurd (1990) and Findlay and Jones (1982) provide similar estimates.
5. Specifically this would mean that the fixed costs have a lower weighting in the policy threshold analysis process.

10. Conclusions

The goal of this book has been to advance the design of policy relating to the production of environmental outputs and specifically wetland policy design. This goal has been addressed across two dimensions: methodological and applied. Hence, this concluding chapter will bring together the elements of these two dimensions that have been developed here. It is not the role of this chapter to provide a summary of the chapters that precede it. However, in drawing out the major methodological and application messages, a broad overview of the results presented in the other chapters is provided. The opportunity to look at the wider implications of the research reported in the book is also taken. Finally, some possible ways forward to address shortcomings remaining in the methodology used and its application are also advanced.

10.1 METHODOLOGICAL ASPECTS

The divergence between the social and private values provided by environmental resources has long been recognised, but what has frequently been absent is a rigorous and systematic methodology for the development of institutions to ensure that society moves toward a socially efficient outcome. The approach developed in this book fills that gap.

The approach is built around a theoretical appreciation of differences between alternative mechanisms though which society makes choices regarding the use of resources. Recognition that both the market and the planned mechanisms and even a mixture of elements of both are likely to be flawed in various ways leads to a conclusion that opportunities to secure resource use efficiency improvements are likely to be available. This conclusion comes with a key caveat: there is no guarantee that because an element of 'failure' can be detected in an existing mechanism for resource use choice, an improvement in social well-being will be possible. The implication of this caveat is that an empirical analysis of the likely impact on social well-being resulting from alternative resource use configurations will be necessary to test if the 'failure' can be satisfactorily countered.

Hence, the second pillar of the framework involves the development of an empirical process to assess social well-being implications of change where there are biophysical impacts. This process is called bio-economic modelling. In essence, a bio-economic model invokes the welfare economic principles of benefit-cost analysis but embeds that economic technique into a biophysical context which itself is modelled. Thus bio-economic modelling requires the merging of the biophysical modelling required to predict the effects of specified changes in resource management with the economic modelling required to introduce society's values into the choice process.

Bio-economic modelling is therefore a construct that integrates various economic and biophysical tools of data collection and analysis. Particularly challenging in this array of tools are the non-market valuation techniques. These are required so that the value changes society enjoys or endures because of non-marketed biophysical impacts can be integrated into the overall calculus of net social well-being.

What the bio-economic modelling provides is an understanding of whether or not it is worthwhile considering changes in resource use. It shows by how much social well-being is changed by the adoption of specific changes but it also gives an indication of who are the likely beneficiaries of change and who are likely to bear the costs. Hence, bio-economic modelling results help to provide direction to those in a position to change the ways in which society chooses between resources uses. The results of biophysical modelling therefore help to establish where, as a society, we should be going. The next step is to know the best way to get there. That is the final pillar of the approach developed in this book.

The selection of the mix of market and planned system elements that will drive the allocation of resources toward that which is indicated by the biophysical modelling is the process of policy development. The policy development process used in this book feeds off the results of the bio-economic modelling, in so far as that modelling shows the distribution of benefits and costs amongst various groups within society. However, it also embraces the new institutional economics by recognising the different levels of transaction costs associated with different policy alternatives. What results is called 'threshold policy' analysis. Under this approach, policy alternatives to achieve the goals indicated by the bio-economic modelling results are assessed by the policy maker weighing up the likely cost effectiveness of their application against the likely extent of the transaction costs they will invoke. It is acknowledged that this approach is a 'second-best' approach to policy selection. The 'first-best' approach would be to integrate estimates of all transaction costs into the bio-economic modelling analysis. However, the threshold approach deals with the reality of a paucity of transaction cost estimation studies. What results is not a definitive statement of which policy strategy is best but rather a series of 'best-bet' policies that are likely to involve transaction costs that are less than the net social well-being improvement indicated by the bio-economic model. The policy maker is therefore offered a selection of policy alternatives. Indeed, a mix of policies is likely required to achieve the policy goals given the heterogeneity amongst wetland owners and in the management changes desired.

The three pillars of the analytical framework developed in this book and summarised above present an approach to decision-making where private and social values diverge across a range of natural resources. Its strengths are its capacity to integrate a diverse range of information types – including environmental, social and economic – into a cohesive decision making process, its transparency in performing this task and its generality. Weaknesses arise from missing data – particularly those associated with transaction costs, poorly understood biophysical relationships and inaccurate estimates of values. Most of the latter problems can be at least partially accounted for using sensitivity analysis to determine if potential inaccuracies are likely to cause critical changes to the policy conclusions drawn from an analysis.

10.2 APPLICATION ASPECTS

The specific target for applying the methodological framework in the research reported in this book was wetlands. Two Australian Case studies were investigated using the framework, and some key findings relevant to the management of those wetland systems were established. For both cases, the application of the bio-economic modelling showed that there was potential for improvements in social well-being from a change in wetland management practices. It is worth noting, however, that not all the alternative management options considered in the bio-economic modelling phase proved beneficial. This provides a cautionary tale for those who advocate change simply because aspects of market and government failure can be shown to be present. That is, the amount of change is also important.

Furthermore, the transaction costs of some policy measures were considered to outweigh the net benefits shown to be available from change in the bio-economic modelling. In other words, the selection of the policy vehicle was shown to be critical in the process of achieving change because of differential transaction costs. Hence, even where system failure is evident and the bio-economic model demonstrates a potential net gain to society, decision makers who select policy instruments without due regard for their transaction costs could leave society worse off through effecting a change.

These results provide policy makers with concrete information on which to base their choices. The findings show that the outputs produced by wetland protection actions generate values to both wetland owners and the wider community. In the case of the wider community the benefits generated by additional wetland protection outweigh the direct costs of producing these outputs. However, under the current policy framework, of which the current property right distribution is an element, the costs to wetland owners of producing additional wetland protection outputs outweighs the benefits they receive. That is, the private benefits of additional wetland protection are often outweighed by the private costs incurred.

The implications of the nature and distribution of the values generated by USE and MRF wetland protection outputs are two-fold and relate to the extension of wetland protection values beyond wetland owners and across political jurisdictions. The extension of values for wetland protection outputs beyond the landowner is not in itself a problem. Rather it is the source of the potential gains from trade from private ownership of property rights over resources. However, in the instance of the case study wetlands, wetland owners are unable to capture these values. Hence, the first implication is that the wider community is justified in considering ways in which individual wetland owners' decisions can be influenced in order to increase the returns to the community as a whole. That is, the uncaptured extension of values for wetland protection outputs beyond the landowner justifies the consideration of, but not necessarily implementation of, alternative policy options.

The analysis of the values generated by wetlands shows that uncaptured wetland protection values extend beyond the landowner and the immediate geographical region of the case study and State in which they are located. For example, ACT residents were shown to hold non-use values for USE wetlands and Adelaide residents for MRF wetlands. However, some values (such as recreation surpluses) are more closely centred on wetlands. Hence, the second implication is that the distribution of the values generated by wetland protection outputs is not aligned with political boundaries. Consideration of alternative policy options should therefore proceed at multiple policy levels, thus complicating the decision process – particularly when considering optimal policy mixes.

The policy process is further complicated by the alternative decision modes used by society (market, government and mixed) and alternative policy levels available (facilitative, inducive and coercive). Therefore, a wide array of policy options for enhancing production of wetland protection outputs are generated for each case study region. Each policy option will also incur a range of transaction costs including design, implementation and administration costs. Hence, the second area of implications for wetland management in the case study regions results from the development of threshold policy analysis as a structured and rigorous methodology for simplifying selection amongst these alternative policy options. The 'best bet' policy options that result are likely to generate wetland protection benefits to the wider community that outweigh the additional transaction costs incurred in their implementation and ongoing management. Hence, further consideration should be given to their adoption in the relevant jurisdiction(s).

Other application aspects of the work reported here relate to the use of various techniques. The bio-economic modelling approach involved the development of ecosystem models that related wetland management strategies with outcomes that are of specific interest to the people who make up society. Put simply, the ecological relationships were human centred in that people are the agents of change and the outcomes of the changes were predicted in terms of value relevant factors to humans.

The case study work also demonstrated the capacity of non-market valuation techniques to inform bio-economic models in a reliable and policy consistent fashion. The use of choice modelling to estimate the non-use values arising from alternative wetland management strategies was shown to be particularly relevant to the integration of ecological models into the overall bio-economic models because of its focus on the environmental attributes of change. These attributes can be both the outputs of the ecological modelling and the inputs of the economic modelling, so establishing a key linkage.

10.3 WIDER IMPLICATIONS

The tools and techniques developed and applied in this book have wide application potential. The application potential can be divided into three layers:

1. production of wetland protection outputs beyond the case study areas;
2. design of policy relating to the production of environmental outputs more generally; and
3. broader policy design in Australia and internationally.

At the first level, the main findings have established that there is scope for policy development and implementation to increase the production of wetland protection outputs in the USE of SA and MRF in NSW. Wetlands in these case study regions are located in agricultural landscapes. The primary threats to wetland protection outputs arise from competition for wetland resources for production of food and fibre products. These findings can be extrapolated with a high level of confidence to wetland systems that have similar biophysical characteristics, in which wetland protection outputs are threatened by a similar array of processes and in which the costs of restoration and management are similar. A simplified adaptation of the bio-economic models constructed for the USE and MRF case study areas that incorporate any region specific differences could support extrapolation where differences are minimal.

Extrapolation to wetlands that differ significantly from the case study systems is more complex. For example, other important wetlands in Australia and internationally are located in coastal regions and tropical regions with different social and demographic characteristics. Other processes may threaten these wetlands, such as urban or industrial development. The costs of restoration and management may also differ significantly if, for example, water is diverted to urban/industrial uses or more resource inputs are required. The bio-economic modelling approach undertaken in this dissertation would be directly applicable in such cases. However, the data inputs would need to specify the costs and benefits of wetland protection in the new location. Similar criteria would apply to application of threshold policy analysis in new and significantly different locations. That is, policies that specifically address the costs and benefits in such systems would need to be developed and assessed for their relative transaction costs and the likelihood that the benefits generated outweigh the production and transaction costs incurred.

The second level of wider implications addresses the primary goal in this dissertation, namely, advancing the design of policy relating to the production of environmental outputs. The bio-economic modelling process linked to policy development and assessment undertaken in this dissertation has a number of strengths. The primary strength of the bio-economic model is the integration of biophysical and economic information directly into the process of comparing alternative outcomes. The bio-economic modelling process is directly applicable wherever private and social values are hypothesised to differ and these values are dependent on outcomes defined by alternative future biophysical states that are, at least in part, determined by human management. Other strengths are a rigorous methodology for estimating and combining economic values and a systematic assessment of sources of risk and uncertainty through sensitivity analysis. Finally, information within the bio-economic model relating to the distribution and nature of the costs and benefits of alternative strategies provides a valuable input to policy development. This approach offers potential in considering sustainability issues because it integrates economic, environmental and social criteria into a single, rigorous framework for analysis.

Additional important implications for advancing environmental and broader policy development flow from the policy development and assessment methodology applied in this book. The first stage of this process is the development of a systematic approach to policy design by identifying the alternative policy options relative to the BAU policy framework. Policy opportunities are identified using theory to isolate policy opportunities, bio-economic modelling to identify whether these policies will impact on the impact or distribution of key costs and benefits, and resource owner perceptions as a check to ensure all opportunities are covered including addressing information gaps between perceived and actual outcomes. Potential policy options can be developed for each jurisdiction and which influence wetland owners in different ways (facilitate, induce, coerce). This systematic approach is useful for identifying policy options for production of environmental outputs and for policy generation more generally.

In most cases a wide range of policy options will be generated between which a decision must then be made as to the policy or policy mix that is selected (including continuation of BAU). Decision criteria should be based on consideration of the relative transaction costs of alternative policy options – ideally via a cost-benefit analysis of the transaction costs associated with alternative policies and the net benefits generated when they are taken into account. Threshold policy analysis was developed as a rigorous methodology for advancing policy evaluation in the absence of quantitative information and in the presence of uncertainty. By evaluating policy options against a broad range of policy transaction costs, each of which is assigned a weighting, it is possible to systematically evaluate and rank policies in order to identify where additional policy evaluation efforts should be focused. Using this approach it was shown that the policies that address wetland protection incur a range of transaction costs and deliver differing levels of wetland protection effectiveness. Sensitivity analysis can also be undertaken within this process to identify the relative importance of different categories of information. This approach is applicable to evaluating policy within the environmental sector and the broader economy where incomplete information is available for policy development.

10.4 OPPORTUNITIES TO MOVE FORWARD

There are numerous avenues for further research that arise from the findings of the research reported here. First, the bio-economic modelling undertaken in this dissertation is based, in part, on predictions of future biophysical conditions in case study wetlands given a specified management regime. The future biophysical conditions in wetlands determine the nature and scale of wetland protection outputs, and hence the values generated under alternative wetland management strategies. These biophysical outcomes are uncertain and the potential distribution of possible outcomes is unknown. This uncertainty can have significant impact on the conclusions from the bio-economic model as shown by the sensitivity analysis. There is considerable scope for research directed towards improving the accuracy of the information input to the biophysical model in terms of the range and probability distribution of potential outcomes and more clearly focusing ecological research on human activities and values.

A related opportunity is the potential to incorporate the impacts of uncertainty about biophysical outcomes within the bio-economic model through inclusion in non-market valuation techniques. In particular, there has been little exploration of the possibility and consequences of including measures of biophysical uncertainty as a descriptive attribute within the choice modelling non-market valuation technique.

A second avenue for further research relates to the extrapolation of the consumers' surpluses estimated from choice modelling and other stated preference questionnaires. Non-use values generated by wetland protection outputs comprise the largest single value within the bio-economic model. There are two aspects to extrapolation of these values within the bio-economic model, each of which follows a very conservative approach in the absence of better information. The first aspect is extrapolation to the non-respondent proportion of the population who are assumed to hold no values within the bio-economic model. The second aspect relates to extrapolation beyond the survey population but within the geographic region in which the wetlands are located. The non-respondent proportion of this population is also assumed to hold no values within the core bio-economic model. That is, the issue of framing effects in stated preference questionnaires is critical in regard to extrapolation. Sensitivity analysis of these extrapolation assumptions shows the significance of the non-use values to the conclusions drawn from the bio-economic model. Detailed assessment of the nature and variation in non-use values held by the community, and the framing effects of alternative questionnaire designs, would improve the accuracy of the bio-economic model.

The intersection of bio-economic modelling and policy provides other research opportunities. In most cases, the generation of wetland protection can proceed via a number of alternative paths and management changes. One research opportunity is to identify whether the value generated by an increase in wetland protection outputs incorporates an element of path dependency. That is, are values only attributed to scale of changes at the endpoint (to wetland protection outputs, inputs and opportunity costs), or are they also dependent on the path taken to achieve these changes?

A broad range of potential policies for increasing wetland protection outputs were identified in this research. Three further broad areas of research relate to these policy options. The first of these is to reduce the significant uncertainty surrounding the individual behavioural responses to alternative policy options. This uncertainty results from two key components. First, while wetland owners in the USE and MRF regard their wetlands as an asset overall, the specific distribution of values attached to wetland outcomes is unknown. Second, the individual transaction costs faced by wetland owners in accessing benefits from policies are also uncertain and are also likely to be heterogeneous. Hence, the relative net benefits generated to wetland owners from alternative policy options and their likely uptake and effectiveness, individually and as a component within a policy mix, is uncertain.

The lack of information available for delineating and estimating policy transaction costs is the second opportunity for future policy option research. Alternative policy options are poorly defined in terms of their policy design, implementation and management costs and how they impact on individuals' transaction costs. This opportunity for further research can be applied at two scales. At the case study specific scale, policy transaction costs incurred by government in policy development, implementation and administration, remain unquantified but their importance in identifying 'best bets' for policy adoption has been demonstrated. Quantifying the government incurred transaction costs associated with alternative policy options would reduce the uncertainty associated with policy selection. Further research in this case should be restricted to the 'best bet' options and the more favoured 'unclear' options. A caveat applies in that the costs of reducing this uncertainty should also be taken into account in allocating resources to such research (as should also be applied to the previous opportunities for further research).

At a broader scale, appropriate methodologies for quantitatively estimating transaction costs are not well developed for many categories of transaction costs. More specific definitions of the range of policy transaction costs and agreed methodologies for their estimation would provide an important contribution to decisions between alternative policy options. A related area for research is in identifying or developing potential policy designs that minimise transaction costs. These policies may be alternative policy structures or approaches that incur lower policy transaction costs.

The third area of policy research relates to quantifying the uncertain benefits generated by alternative policy options. In particular, estimation of the benefits generated by multiple output policies (such as input tax concessions) and the synergistic benefits generated by alternative policy mixes are poorly understood. Improved understanding and methods for quantification would assist in assessing the full benefits from policy adoption and in identifying appropriate policy mixes for implementation. Similarly, integrated development and implementation of an optimal mix of policies may incur different transaction costs than their development and implementation as stand-alone strategies.

So whilst the framework developed here has been demonstrated to be a rigorous and systematic way of integrating various elements of information for the policy choice process, there remain components of its methodology that will require further development. It is only with such development that the costs of implementing this type of decision support framework can be brought down to the point where it will be feasible to implement on a broad scale.

References

Adamowicz, W. L., P. Boxall, M. Williams, and J. Louviere (1998), 'Stated Preference Approaches for Measuring Passive Use Values: Choice Experiments and Contingent Valuation', *American Journal of Agricultural Economics,* **80**, 64–75.

Adamowicz, W. L., J. Louviere and J. Swait (1998), *Introduction to Attribute-Based Stated Choice Methods: Final Report to Resource Valuation Branch, NOAA, US Department of Commerce*, Edmonton, Alberta, Advanis Inc.

Agriculture New South Wales (2001), *Farm Enterprise Budgets,* www.agric.nsw.gov.au.

Alston, J. M. and R. H. Hurd (1990), 'Some Neglected Social Costs of Government Spending in Farm Programs', *American Journal of Agricultural Economics,* February, 149–56.

Amacher, G. S., R. J. Brazee, J. W. Bulkley and R. A. Moll (1989), *Application of Wetland Valuation Techniques: Examples from Great Lakes Coastal Wetlands*, School of Natural Resources, University of Michigan, Ann Arbor.

Anderson, N. H. (1982), *Methods of Information Integration Theory*, New York, Academic Press.

Anderson, T. L. and D. R. Leal (1991), *Free Market Environmentalism*, San Francisco, Pacific Research Institute for Public Policy.

Arrow, K.J. (1951), *Social Choice and Individual Values*, New York, John Wiley and Sons.

Atkins, B. (1988), *Wetlands of the Bakers Range and Marcollat Watercourses, Environmental Characteristics*, Adelaide, Ecologic and Associates.

Australian Bureau of Statistics (2001), www.abs.gov.au.

Barber, A. (1993), *Benefit:Cost Analyses of on-Farm Pasture Renovation Strategies and Catchment Drainage Options*, Keith, Department of Primary Industries South Australia.

Barbier, E. B., M. Acreman and D.Knowler (1997), *Economic Valuation of Wetlands: A Guide for Policy Makers and Planners*, Gland, Switzerland, Ramsar Convention Bureau.

Barzel, Y. (1997), *Economic Analysis of Property Rights (2nd edn.)*, Cambridge, Cambridge University Press.

Bateman, I. (1993), 'Valuation of the Environment, Methods and Techniques: Revealed Preference Methods', in R. K. Turner, *Sustainable Environmental Economics and Management: Principles and Practice*, London, Belhaven Press.

Ben-Akiva, M. and S. R. Lerman (1993), *Discrete Choice Analysis: Theory and Application to Travel Demand*, Cambridge, Massachusetts, The MIT Press.

Bennett, J. W. (1995), *The Travel Cost Method of Estimating the Value of Recreational Use of Natural Areas*, Environmental and Resource Economics.

Bennett, J. and W. L. Adamowicz (2001), 'Some Fundamentals of Environmental Choice Modelling', in J. Bennett and R. Blamey, *The Choice Modelling Approach to Environmental Valuation*, Cheltenham, Edward Elgar.

Bennett, J., R. Blamey and M. Morrison (1997), *Valuing Damage to South Australian Wetlands Using the Contingent Valuation Method*, Canberra, LWRRDC Occasional Paper 13/97.

Bennett, J. and S. Whitten (2000), *The Economic Value of Conserving/Enhancing Gol Gol Lake and Gol Gol Swamp: a Consultancy Report to the Gol Gol Community Reference Group*, Gundaroo, Environmental and Resource Economics.

Bennison, G. and P. Suter (1990), 'Macroinvertebrates', in N. Mackay and D. Eastburn, *The Murray*, Canberra, MDBC.

Blackburn, G. (1983), 'Soils', in M. J. Tyler, C. R. T. Twidale, J. K. Ling and J. W. Holmes, *Natural History of the South East*, Adelaide, Royal Society of South Australia.

Blamey, R. K., J. C. Rolfe, J. W. Bennett and M. D. Morrison (1997), *Environmental Choice Modelling: Issues and Qualitative Insights*, Canberra, The University of New South Wales.

Bowes, M. D. and J. B. Loomis (1980), 'A Note on the Use of Travel Cost Models with Unequal Zonal Populations', *Land Economics*, **56**, 465–70.

Briggs, S. V., S. A. Thornton and W. G. Lawler (1997), 'Relationships between Hydrological Control of River Red Gum Wetlands and Waterbird Breeding', *Emu*, **97**, 31–42.

Brock, M. A. and M. T. Casanova (1997), 'Plant Life at the Edge of Wetlands: Ecological Responses to Wetting and Patterns', in N. Klomp and I. Lunt, *Frontiers in ecology: Building the Links*, Elsevier Science Ltd.

Brock, M. A. and M. T. Casanova (2000), *Are There Plants in Your Wetland? Revegetating Wetlands*, Armidale, LWRRDC, UNE, DLWC and EA.

Bromley, D. W. (1989), 'Entitlements, Missing Markets and Environmental Uncertainty', *Journal of Environmental Economics and Management,* 17, 181–194.

Bromley, D. W. (1991), *Environment and Economy,* Oxford, Blackwell.

Brouwer, R. (2000), 'Environmental Value Transfer: State of the Art and Future Prospects', *Ecological Economics,* 32, 137–152.

Brubaker, E. (1995), *Property Rights in the Defence of Nature,* London, Earthscan.

Buchan, A. (1995a), *State of the Rivers Report Murrumbidgee Catchment 1994–1995 Volume 1,* Wagga Wagga, DLWC – Murrumbidgee Region.

Buchan, A. (1995b), *State of the Rivers Report Murrumbidgee Catchment 1994–1995 Volume 2,* Wagga Wagga, DLWC – Murrumbidgee Region.

Buchanan, J. M. (1965), 'An Economic Theory of Clubs', *Economica,* 32, 1–14.

Buchanan, J.M. and G. Tullock (1965), *The Calculus of Consent: Logical Foundations of Constitutional Democracy,* Ann Arbor, University of Michigan Press.

Buxton, G. L. (1967), *The Riverina 1861–1891, an Australian Regional Study,* Melbourne, Melbourne University Press.

Cacho, O., R. Greiner and L. Fullon (2001), 'An Economic Analysis of Farm Forestry as a Means of Controlling Dryland Salinity', *Australian Journal of Agricultural and Resource Economics,* 45 (2), 233–256.

Cadwallader, P. and B. Lawrence (1990), 'Fish', in N. Mackay and D. Eastburn, *The Murray,* Canberra, MDBC.

Cairns, J. J. and J. R. Heckman (1996), 'Restoration Ecology: The State of an Emerging Field', *Annual Review of Energy and Environment,* 21, 167–189.

Campbell, H. F. and K. A. Bond (1997), 'The Cost of Public Funds in Australia', *The Economic Record,* 73 (220), 22–34.

CARE (1998), *Input-Output Table for the Central West Division NSW for 1995/96,* Armidale, CARE.

Caughley, G. and A. Gunn (1996), *Conservation Biology in Theory and Practice,* Cambridge MA, Blackwell Science.

Cestero, B. (1999), *Beyond the Hundredth Meeting: A Field Guide to Collaborative Conservation on the Wests Public Lands,* Tucson, Arizona, Sonoran Institute.

Christensen, J. B. and C. Price (1982), 'A Note on the Use of Travel Cost Models with Unequal Zonal Populations: Comment', *Land Economics,* 58 (3), 395–99.

Cicchetti, C.J. and V.K. Smith (1973), 'Congestion, Quality Deterioration, and Optimal Use: Wilderness Protection in the Spanish Peaks Primitive Area', *Social Science Research,* 2, 15–30.

Close, A. (1990), 'The Impact of Man on the Natural Flow Regime', in N. Mackay and D. Eastburn, *The Murray*, Canberra, MDBC.

Coase, R. (1937), 'The Nature of the Firm', *Economica*, **4**, 386–405.

Coase, R. (1960), 'The Problem of Social Cost', *The Journal of Law and Economics*, **3**, 1–44.

Colby, B. G. (1990), 'Transactions Costs and Efficiency in Western Water Allocation', *American Journal of Agricultural Economics*, **72** (5), 1184–1192.

Commonwealth Government of Australia (1997), *Wetlands Policy of the Commonwealth Government of Australia*, Canberra, Environment Australia.

Cooper, J. and J. Loomis (1993), 'Testing Whether Waterfowl Hunting Benefits Increase with Greater Water Deliveries to Wetlands', *Environmental and Resource Economics*, **3**, 545–561.

Cornes, R. and T. Sandler (1996), *The Theory of Externalities, Public Goods and Club Goods (2nd edn.)*, Cambridge, Cambridge University Press.

Cox, C. B. and P. D. Moore (2000), *Biogeography: An Ecological and Evolutionary Approach*, Oxford, Blackwell Science.

Croft, T. and G. A. Carpenter (1996), *The Biological Resources of the South East of South Australia (Draft)*, Adelaide, Native Vegetation Conservation Section DENR SA.

Demsetz, H. (1970), 'The Private Production of Public Goods', *Journal of Law and Economics*, **13**, 293–307.

Department of Finance (1991), *Handbook of Cost-Benefit Analysis*, Canberra, Australian Government Publishing Service.

Department of Land and Water Conservation NSW (1996), *Murrumbidgee Valley Strategic Water Management Plan (Draft)*, DLWC Technical Report No. 95/22, Leeton, DLWC.

Desvousges, W. H., M. C. Naughton, and G. R. Parsons (1992), 'Benefit Transfer: Conceptual Problems in Estimating Water Quality Benefits Using Existing Studies', *Water Resources Research*, **28** (3), 675–683.

Diamond, J. M. (1975), 'The Island Dilemma: Lessons of Modern Biogeographic Studies for the Design of Nature Reserves', *Biological Conservation*, **7**, 129–146.

Ducks Unlimited (2001), *Frequently Asked Questions – What Are Wetlands?*, http://www.ducks.org/about/faq/faq_conservation.asp#Wetlands.

Environment Australia (2001), *A Directory of Important Wetlands in Australia (3rd edn)*, Canberra, Environment Australia.

Environmental Defense (2000), *Progress on the Back Forty: An Analysis of Three Incentive-Based Approaches to Endangered Species Conservation on Private Land*, Washington D.C., Environmental Defense.

Environmental Impacts Assessments Branch (1995), The Upper South East Dryland Salinity and Flood Management Plan Assessment Report, Adelaide, Department of Housing and Urban Development SA.

Falconer, K., P. Dupraz, and M. Whitby (2001), 'An Investigation of Policy Administrative Costs Using Panel Data for the English Environmentally Sensitive Areas', *Journal of Agricultural Economics,* **52** (1), 83–103.

Farber, S. (1987), 'The Value of Coastal Wetlands for Protection of Property against Hurricane Wind Damage', *Journal of Environmental Economics and Management,* **14** (3), 143–151.

Farber, S. (1996), 'Welfare Loss of Wetlands Disintegration: A Louisiana Study', *Contemporary Economic Policy,* **14** (2), 92–106.

Findlay, C. C. and R. L. Jones (1982), 'The Marginal Cost of Australian Income Taxation', *The Economic Record,* Sept, 253–262.

Fisher, T. (2000), *Lessons from Australia's First Practical Experiment in Integrated Microeconomic and Environmental Reform,* Microeconomic Reform and the Environment, Workshop Proceedings, Melbourne, 8 September 2000, Ausinfo, Canberra.

Folke, C. (1991), 'The Societal Value of Wetland Life-Support', in C. Folke and T. Kaberger, *Linking the Natural Environment and the Economy: Essays from the Eco-Eco Group,* Kluwer Academic Publishers.

Fordham, A. E. (1998), *Ecological Study of Wetlands in the Marcollat Watercourse,* Adelaide, Department of Botany and Zoology University of Adelaide.

Forest Creek Management Plan Committee (Unpublished Proposal), *Proposal for Lower Forest Creek Stock Watering,* Forest Creek Management Plan Committee.

Forestry Commission of NSW (1986), *Management Plan for the Murrumbidgee Management Area,* Forestry Commission of NSW.

Forman, R. T. T. (1995), *Land Mosaics: The Ecology of Landscapes and Regions,* Cambridge, Cambridge University Press.

Freebairn, J. (1995), 'Reconsidering the Marginal Welfare Cost of Taxation', *Economic Record,* **71**, 121–31.

Gangadharan, L. (2000), 'Transaction Costs in Pollution Markets: An Empirical Study', *Land Economics,* **76** (4), 601–614.

Gerrans, P. (1994), *An Economics Valuation of the Jandakot Wetlands,* Perth, Edith Cowan University.

Glaeser, E. L. and A. Shleifer (2001), 'Not-for-Profit Entrepreneurs', *Journal of Public Economics,* **81**, 99–115.

Gren, I. (1995), 'Costs and Benefits of Restoring Wetlands: Two Swedish Case Studies', *Ecological Engineering,* **4**, 153–62.

Grose, J. and M. Holics (1994), *Natural Resources of the Murrumbidgee Irrigation Area, Tabita and Benerembah Irrigation Districts,* Sydney, NSW DLWC Technical Services.

Grose, J. and W. Makewita (1997), *Natural Resources of the Wah Wah Irrigation District, Stock and Domestic District*, Sydney, NSW DLWC Centre for Natural Resources.

Gwartney, J. (1985), 'Private Property, Freedom and the West', *The Intercollegiate Review,* Spring, 39–49.

Hanley, N. and C. L. Spash (1993), *Cost-Benefit Analysis and the Environment*, Aldershot, Edward Elgar.

Harris, J. H. (1995), 'Carp: The Prospects for Control?' *Water,* May-June, 25–28.

Hausman, J. and D. McFadden (1984), 'Specification Tests for the Multinomial Logit Model', *Econometrica,* **52**, 1219–1240.

Hayek, F. A. (1945), 'The Use of Knowledge in Society', *American Economic Review,* **35** (4), 519–30.

Heaney, A., S. Beare and R. Bell (2001), 'Evaluating Improvements in Irrigation Efficiency as a Salinity Mitigation Option on the South Australian Riverland', *Australian Journal of Agricultural and Resource Economics,* **45** (3), 477–493.

Heimlich, R. E., K. D. Wiebe, R. Claassen, D. Gadsby, and R. M. House (1998), *Wetlands and Agriculture: Private Interests and Public Benefits*, Washington, DC, Resource Economics Division, Economic Research Service, United States Department of Agriculture.

Henscher, D. A. and L. W. Johnson (1981), *Applied Discrete Choice Modelling*, London, Croom Helm.

Hicks, J. R. (1940), 'The Valuation of the Social Income', *Economica,* 7, 105–124.

Hodge, I. (1995), *Environmental Economics: Individual Incentives and Public Choices*, London, Macmillan Press Ltd.

Hyman, D. N. (1990), *Public Finance: A Contemporary Application of Theory to Policy*, Chicago, The Dryden Press.

Jackson, E. A. and W. H. Litchfield (1954), *The Soils and Potential Land Use in Part of County Cardwell (Hundreds of Coombe and Richards) in the Coonalpyn Downs, South Australia*, Melbourne, CSIRO.

Johansson, P. (1993), *Cost-Benefit Analysis of Environmental Change*, Cambridge, Cambridge University Press.

Junk, W. J., P. B. Bayley, and R. E. Sparks (1989), 'The Flood Pulse Concept in River-Floodplain Systems', *Canadian Special Publication of Fish and Aquatic Sciences,* **106**, 110–127.

Kaldor, N. (1939), 'Welfare Propositions of Economics and Interpersonal Comparisons of Utility', *Economic Journal,* **49,** 549–551.

Kaplow, L. (1992), 'Rules Versus Standards: An Economic Analysis', *Duke Law Journal,* **42**, 557.

Kasper, W. (1998), *Property Rights and Competition: An Essay on the Constitution of Capitalism*, Sydney, Policy Monograph No. 41, The Centre for Independent Studies.

Kasper, W. and M.E. Streit (1998), *Institutional Economics – Social Order and Public Policy,* Edward Elgar, Northampton, Mass.

Kemp, A. and A. Hafi, (2001), *Benefits of Increased Irrigation Efficiency in the Murrumbidgee Irrigation Area*, Canberra, ABARE Conference Paper 2001.10, ABARE.

Kingsford, R. T. (2000), 'Ecological Impacts of Dams, Water Diversions and River Management on Floodplain Wetlands in Australia', *Austral Ecology,* **25**, 109–127.

Kling, C. L. (1987), 'A Simulation Approach to Comparing Multiple Site Recreation Demand Models Using Chesapeake Bay Survey Data', *Marine Resource Economics,* **4**, 95–109.

Kling, C. L. (1988), 'Comparing Welfare Estimates of Environmental Quality Changes from Recreation Demand Models', *Journal of Environmental Economics and Management,* **15**, 331–341.

Knight, F. H. (1924), 'Some Fallacies in the Interpretation of Social Cost', *Quarterly Journal of Economics,* **38,** 582–606,

Krinsky, I. and A. L.Robb (1986), 'On Approximating the Statistical Properties of Elasticities', *Review of Economics and Statistics,* **72**, 189–190.

Krutilla, K. (1999), 'Environmental Policy Transactions Costs', *Handbook of Environmental and Resource Economics*, in J. C. J. M. van den Bergh, Cheltenham, Edward Elgar.

Lancaster, K. J. (1966), 'A New Approach to Consumer Theory', *Journal of Political Economy,* **74**, 132–57.

Lane, J. E. (1993), *The Public Sector: Concepts, Models and Approaches*, London, Sage Publications.

Lant, C. L. and R. S. Roberts (1990), 'Greenbelts in the Cornbelt: Riparian Wetlands, Intrinsic Values, and Market Failure', *Environment and Planning A,* **22**, 1375–88.

Layard, P. R. G. and A. A. Walters (1978), *Microeconomic Theory*, New York, McGraw-Hill.

Leibenstein, H. (1982), 'Notes on X-Efficiency and Bureaucracy', in R. C. O. Mathews and G. B. Stafford, *The Grants Economy and Collective Consumption: Proceedings of a Conference Held by the International Economics Association at Cambridge U.K.*, Macmillan.

Libecap, G. D. (1989), *Contracting for Property Rights*, Cambridge, Cambridge University Press.

Lindsay, R. and T. Gleeson (1998), *Changing Structure of Farming, ABARE Current Issues*, Canberra, ABARE.

Lockwood, M. and D. Carberry (1998), *Stated Preference Surveys of Remnant Native Vegetation Conservation*, Albury, Johnstone Centre.

Louviere, J. (2001), 'Choice Experiments: An Overview of Concepts and Issues', in J. Bennett and R. Blamey, *The Choice Modelling Approach to Environmental Valuation*, Cheltenham, Edward Elgar.

Louviere, J. J., D. A. Henscher and J. D. Swait (2000), *Stated Choice Methods: Analysis and Application*, Cambridge, Cambridge University Press.

Lueck, D. (2000), 'The Law and Politics of Federal Wildlife Preservation', in T. L. Anderson, *Political Environmentalism: Going Behind the Green Curtain*, Stanford, California, Hoover Institution Press.

MacArthur, R. H. and E. O. Wilson (1967), *The Theory of Island Biogeography*, Princeton NJ, Princeton University Press.

MacKenzie, G. A. and F. Stadter (1992), *Groundwater Occurence and the Impacts of Various Land Management Practices in the Upper South East of South Australia*, Adelaide, Groundwater Branch SA Department of Mines and Energy.

MacNally, R. (1998), *Ecological Significance of Coarse Woody Debris on Floodplains*, Proceedings of 1998 Riverine Environment Forum, Canberra, MDBC.

MacNally, R. (1999), *Ecological Significance of Coarse Woody Debris (CWD) on Floodplains*, Proceedings of 1999 Riverine Environment Research Forum, Canberra, MDBC.

Maher, P. (1988), 'Threatened Avifauna of Western New South Wales', *National Parks Journal*, **32** (4), 11–16.

Mallawaarachchi, T. and J. Quiggin (2001), 'Modelling Socially Optimal Land Allocations for Sugar Cane Growing in North Queensland: A Linked Mathematical Programming and Choice Modelling Study', *Australian Journal of Agricultural and Resource Economics*, **45** (3), 383–409.

Marsden and Associates (2001), *Forestry and National Competition Policy*, Camberwell, Victoria.

McCann, L. (1999), *Agency Perceptions of Alternative Salinity Policies: are they Measuring Transactions Costs?*, Paper Presented at the 43rd Annual Conference of the Australian Agricultural and Resource Economics Society, Christchurch, New Zealand.

McCann, L. and K. W. Easter (1999), 'Transaction Costs of Policies to Reduce Agricultural Phosphorous Pollution in the Minnesota River', *Land Economics*, **75** (3), 402–414.

McCann, L. and K. W. Easter (2000), 'Estimates of Public Sector Transaction Costs in NRCS Programs', *Journal of Agricultural and Applied Economics*, **32** (3), 555–563.

McFadden, D. (1974), 'Conditional Logit Analysis of Qualitative Choice Behaviour', in P. Zarembka, *Frontiers in Econometrics*, New York, Academic Press.

MIA & Districts Community Land and Water Management Plan Taskforce (1998), *MIA & Districts Community Land and Water Management Plan*, MCMC.

Montgomery, M. R. and Bean, R. (1999), 'Market Failure, Government Failure, and the Private Supply of Public Goods: The Case of Climate-Controlled Walkway Networks', *Public Choice*, **99**, 403–437.

Morrison, M. (2000), 'Aggregation Biases in Stated Preference Studies', *Australian Economic Papers*, **39** (2), 215–230.

Morrison, M. (2001), 'Non-Market Valuation Databases: How Useful Are They?' *Economic Analysis and Policy*, **31** (1), 33–55.

Morrison, M. D., J. W. Bennett and R. K. Blamey (1997), *Designing Choice Modelling Surveys Using Focus Groups: Results from the Macquarie Marshes and Gwydir Wetlands Case Studies*, Canberra, The University of New South Wales.

Morrison, M. D., J. W. Bennett and R. K. Blamey (1998), *Valuing Improved Wetland Quality Using Choice Modelling*, Canberra, The University of New South Wales.

Morrison, M. D., J. W. Bennett and R. K. Blamey (1999), 'Valuing Improved Wetland Quality Using Choice Modelling', *Water Resources Research*, **35**, 2805–2814.

Morrison, M. D., R. K. Blamey, J. W. Bennett and J. J. Louviere (1996), *A Comparison of Stated Preference Techniques for Estimating Environmental Values*, Canberra, The University of New South Wales.

Mueller, D. C. (1989), *Public Choice II: A Revised Edition of Public Choice*, Cambridge, Cambridge University Press.

Murray-Darling Basin Ministerial Council (1995), *An Audit of Water Use in the Murray-Darling Basin*, Canberra, Murray-Darling Basin Ministerial Council.

Murrumbidgee Catchment Management Committee (1998), *Murrumbidgee Catchment Action Plan for Integrated Natural Resources Management*, Wagga Wagga, MCMC.

National Center for Environmental Economics (2001), *The United States Experience with Economic Incentives for Protecting the Environment*, Washington DC, National Center for Environmental Economics, U.S. Environmental Protection Agency.

National Parks and Wildlife Service South Australia and Department of Environment and Planning South Australia (1992), *Watervalley Wetlands Management Plan*, Adelaide, National Parks and Wildlife Service South Australia and Department of Environment and Planning South Australia.

New, T. R. (2000), *Conservation Biology: An Introduction for Southern Australia*, South Melbourne, Oxford University Press.

OECD (1999), *Handbook of Incentive Measures for Biodiversity: Design and Implementation*, Paris, OECD.

OECD (2001), *Multifunctionality: Towards an Analytical Framework*, Paris, OECD.

Offenbach, L. A. and B. K. Goodwin (1994), 'A Travel-Cost Analysis of the Demand for Hunting Trips in Kansas', *Review of Agricultural Economics,* **16**, 55–61.

Olson, M. (1965), *The Logic of Collective Action*, Amsterdam, Holland University Press.

Olson, M. and M. Bailey (1981), 'Positive Time Preference', *Journal of Political Economy,* **89** (1), 1–25.

Ostrom, E. (1990), *Governing the Commons: The Evolution of Institutions for Collective Action*, Cambridge, Cambridge University Press.

Ostrom, E. and E. Schlager (1996), *The Formation of Property Rights*, Washington D.C., Island Press.

Pigou, A.C. (1920) *The Economics of Welfare*, Macmillan, London.

Polasky, S., H. Doremus and B. Rettig (1997), 'Endangered Species Conservation on Private Land', *Contemporary Economic Policy,* **15**, 66–76.

Polinsky, A. M. and S. Shavell (1992), 'Enforcement Costs and the Optimal Magnitude and Probability of Fines', *Journal of Law and Economics,* **35**, 133–48.

Power, M. E., W. E. Dietrich and J. C.Finlay (1996), 'Dams and Downstream Aquatic Biodiversity: Potential Food Web Consequences of Hydrologic and Geomorphic Change', *Environmental Management,* **20** (6), 887-895.

Ramsar Convention Bureau (1998), *What Are Wetlands?*, http://www.ramsar.org/about_infopack_1e.htm.

Randall, A. (1993), 'The Problem of Market Failure', in R. Dorfman and N. Dorfman, *Economics of the Environment: Selected Readings (3rd edn.)*, New York, Norton and Company.

Rao, P. and R. L. Miller (1971), *Applied Econometrics*, Belmont, California, Wadsworth Publishing Company.

Read Sturgess and Associates (2000), *Economic Assessment of Recreational Values of Victorian Parks*, Melbourne, consultancy undertaken for the Department of Natural Resources and Environment, Victoria.

Ricketts, M. (1994), *The Economics of Business Enterprise: An Introduction to Economic Organisation and the Theory of the Firm (2nd edn.)*, Hemel Hempstead, Harvester Wheatsheaf.

Robertson, A. I. (1997), *Land-Water Linkages in Floodplain River Systems: The Influence of Domestic Stock*, Elsevier Science Ltd.

Rolfe, J. C. and J. W. Bennett (2000), *Testing for Framing Effects in Environmental Choice Modelling*, Canberra, The University of New South Wales.

Ruijgrok, E. C. M. (2001), 'Transferring Economic Values on the Basis of an Ecological Classification of Nature', *Ecological Economics,* **39**, 399–408.

Russell, C. S. and P. T. Powell (1999), 'Practical Considerations and Comparison of Instruments of Environmental Policy', in C. J. M. van den Bergh, *Handbook of Environmental and Resource Economics*, Cheltenham, Edward Elgar.

Samuelson, P. A. (1954), 'The Pure Theory of Public Expenditure', *Review of Economics and Statistics,* **36**, 387–89.

Sandler, T. and J. T. Tschirhart (1980), 'The Economic Theory of Clubs: An Evaluative Survey', *Journal of Economic Literature* **18**, 1481–1521.

Sappidean, B. (1992), 'Valuing the Recreation Benefits of Sale Wetlands Using Contingent Valuation', in M. Lockwood and T. DeLacy, *Valuing Natural Areas: Applications and Problems of the Contingent Valuation Method*, Charles Sturt University, Albury, Johnstone Centre of Parks, Recreation and Heritage.

Schmid, A. A. (1989), *Benefit-Cost Analysis, a Political Economy Approach*, Boulder, Westview Press.

Scodari, P. F. (1990), *Wetlands Protection: The Role of Economics*, Washington D.C., The Environmental Law Institute.

Sidgwick, H. (1887), 'Principles of Political Economy', *Handbook of Public Economics (Vol. 2)*, as quoted in A. J. Auerbach and M. Feldstein, Amsterdam, North Holland.

Sierra Club (2001), *Sierra Club Conservation Policies, Wetlands*, http://www.sierraclub.org/policy/conservation/wetlands.asp.

Sinden, J. A. (1989), *Valuation of Unpriced Benefits and Costs of River Management: A Case Study of the Recreation Benefits in the Ovens and King Basin*, Melbourne, Department of Conservation and Environment.

Sinden, J. A. and D. J. Thampapillai (1995), *Introduction to Benefit-Cost Analysis*, Melbourne, Longman.

Smith, B. J. (1999), 'Western Wetlands: The Backwater of Wetlands Regulation', *Natural Resources Journal,* **39**, 357–413.

Smith, V. K. (1988), 'Selection and Recreation Demand', *American Journal of Agricultural Economics,* **70**, 29–36.

Smith, V. K. and W. H. Desvouges (1986), *Measuring Water Quality Benefits*, Boston, Kluwer-Nijhoff.

Sparks, R. E. (1995), 'Need for Ecosystem Management of Large Rivers and Their Floodplains', *BioScience,* **45** (3), 168–182.

Stavins, R. N. (1995), 'Transaction Costs and Markets for Pollution Control', *Resources,* Spring, 9–20.

Stiglitz, J. E. (2000), *Economics of the Public Sector (3rd edn)*, New York, W.W. Norton and Company.

Stone, A. (1992), 'Contingent Valuation of the Barmah Wetlands, Victoria', in M. Lockwood and T. DeLacy, *Valuing Natural Areas: Applications and Problems of the Contingent Valuation Method*, Charles Sturt University, Albury, Johnstone Centre of Parks, Recreation and Heritage.

Stroup, R. L. (1997), 'The Economics of Compensating Property Owners', *Contemporary Economic Policy*, **15**, 55–65.

Taylor, J. K. (1933), *A Soil Survey of the Hundreds of Laffer and Willalooka, South Australia*, Adelaide, CSIRO.

Thibodeau, F. R. and B. D. Ostro (1981), 'An Economic Analysis of Wetland Protection', *Journal of Environmental Management*, **12** (1), 19–30.

Thompson, D. B. (1999), 'Beyond Benefit-Cost Analysis: Institutional Transaction Costs and Regulation of Water Quality', *The Natural Resources Journal*, **39**, 517–41.

Thompson, M. B. and M. J.Tyler (1983), 'Reptiles and Amphibians', in M. J. Tyler, C. R. T. Twidale, J. K. Ling and J. W. Holmes, *Natural History of the South East*, Adelaide, Royal Society of South Australia.

Thornton, S. (1994), *Register of Wetlands on the Floodplain of the Murrumbidgee between Wagga and Hay Weir*, Canberra, National Parks and Wildlife Service (NSW),

Thornton, S. A. and S. V. Briggs (1994), 'A Survey of Hydrological Changes to Wetlands of the Murrumbidgee', *Wetlands (Australia)*, **13**.

Thurstone, L. L. (1927), 'A Law of Comparative Judgement', *Psychological Review*, **4**, 273–286.

Turner, R. K., D. Pearce and I. Bateman (1994), *Environmental Economics, an Elementary Introduction*, Hemel Hempstead, Hertfordshire, Harvester Wheatsheaf.

United States Environment Protection Agency (2001), *Wetlands Definitions*, http://www.epa.gov/owow/wetlands/what/definitions.html.

Upper South East Dryland Salinity and Flood Management Plan Steering Committee (1993), *Upper South East Dryland Salinity and Flood Management Plan Draft Environmental Impact Statement – for Public Comment*, Adelaide, Natural Resources Council of South Australia.

Upper South East Dryland Salinity and Flood Management Plan Steering Committee (1999), *Upper South East Dryland Salinity and Flood Management Plan: Progress Report – October 1999*, Adelaide, Natural Resources Council of South Australia.

Vining, A. R. and D. L. Weimer (1990), 'Government Supply and Government Production Failure: A Framework Based on Contestability', *Journal of Public Policy*, **10** (1), 1–22.

Walker, K. F., F. Sheldon and J. T. Puckridge (1995), 'A Perspective on Dryland River Ecosystems', *Regulated Rivers*, **11**, 85–104.

Ward, J. V. (1998), 'Riverine Landscapes: Biodiversity Patterns, Disturbance Regimes, and Aquatic Conservation', *Biological Conservation,* **83** (3), 269–278.

Ward, J. V. and J. A. Stanford (1995), 'The Serial Discontinuity Concept: Extending the Model to Large Floodplain Rivers', *Regulated Rivers,* **10,** 159–168.

Warren, P. and M. Wurst (1999), *Crop and Livestock Gross Margin Estimates,* Adelaide, PIRSA.

Weimer, D. L. and A. R. Vining (1992), *Policy Analysis: Concepts and Practice (2nd edn.),* Englewood Cliffs, New Jersey, Prentice Hall.

Whitby, M. and C. Saunders (1996), 'Estimating the Supply of Conservation Goods in Britain: A Comparison of the Financial Efficiency of Two Policy Instruments', *Land Economics,* **72** (3), 313–25.

White, J. (1997), *The Ramsar Convention and Wetlands and Wildlife,* Adelaide, Wetlands and Wildlife.

Whitten, S. M. and J. W. Bennett (1999), *Wetland Ecosystems and Landuse in the Murrumbidgee Catchment – Wagga Wagga to Hay and Including Mirrool Creek,* Canberra, The University of New South Wales.

Whitten, S. M. and J. W. Bennett (2000a), *Farmer Perceptions of Wetlands and Wetland Management on the Murrumbidgee River between Wagga Wagga and Hay Including Mirrool Creek,* Canberra, The University of New South Wales.

Whitten, S. M. and J. W. Bennett (2000b), *Potential Wetland Management Strategies - Murrumbidgee Floodplain Wagga Wagga to Hay,* Canberra, The University of New South Wales.

Whitten, S. M. and J. W. Bennett (2000c), 'Wetland Management Trade-Offs in the Upper South-East of South Australia', *Rural Society,* **10** (3), 341–360.

Whitten, S. M. and J. W. Bennett (2002), 'A Travel Cost Study of Duck Hunting in the Upper South East of South Australia', *Australian Geographer,* **33** (2), 192–207.

Wiersma, D. (1991), 'Static and Dynamic Efficiency of Pollution Control Strategies', *Environmental and Resource Economics,* **1,** 63–82.

Williamson, O. E. (1986), *Economic Organisation: Firms, Markets and Policy Control,* Brighton, Wheatsheaf Books Ltd.

Williamson, O. E. (1999), *The New Institutional Economics: Taking Stock Looking Ahead,* Business and Policy Working Paper BPP-76, University of California, Berkeley.

Williamson, O. E. and S. G. E. Winter (1991), *The Nature of the Firm: Origins, Evolution and Development,* New York, Oxford University Press.

Willis, K. G. and G. Garrod (1991), 'An Individual Travel-Cost Method of Evaluating Forest Recreation', *Journal of Agricultural Economics,* **42,** 33–42.

Wills, I. (1997), *Economics and the Environment, a Signalling and Incentives Approach*, St Leonards, Sydney, Allen and Unwin.

Wolf, C. (1988), *Markets or Governments: Choosing between Imperfect Alternatives*, Cambridge, Massachusetts, MIT Press.

Woodward, R. T. and Y. S. Wui (2001), 'The Economic Value of Wetland Services: A Meta Analysis', *Ecological Economics,* **37,** 257–270.

Young, M. D., N. Gunningham, J. Elix, J. Lambert, B. P. Howard and E. McCrone (1996), *Reimbursing the Future, Biodiversity Series Paper No. 9*, Canberra, Department of Environment Sport and Territories.

Index